Entrepreneurship and Multinationals

Entrepreneurship and Multinationals

Global Business and the Making of the Modern World

Geoffrey Jones

Isidor Straus Professor of Business History, Harvard Business School, USA

Edward Elgar
Cheltenham, UK • Northampton, MA, USA

Published by
Edward Elgar Publishing Limited
The Lypiatts
15 Lansdown Road
Cheltenham
Glos GL50 2JA
UK

Edward Elgar Publishing, Inc.
William Pratt House
9 Dewey Court
Northampton
Massachusetts 01060
USA

A catalogue record for this book
is available from the British Library

Library of Congress Control Number: 2013933494

This book is available electronically in the ElgarOnline.com Business Subject Collection, E-ISBN 978 1 78254 818 8

ISBN 978 1 78195 194 1

Typeset by Cambrian Typesetters, Camberley, Surrey

Contents

Figures and tables

FIGURES

TABLES

Preface

This book is about the history of entrepreneurship and multinationals in the making of the modern world. Although it is, to some extent, a compilation of separate essays, there is an underlying unity in the argument about business enterprises as actors in the story of globalization.

The first two chapters have never been published. The others are based on articles originally published in conference volumes and journals which are not widely accessible. They have been substantially revised to incorporate new research, achieve coherence, and deliver continuity of argument. Business historians, like other academic disciplines, spend increasing amounts of time talking to each other rather than broader audiences, even when addressing topics which concern us all, such as globalization. They publish in specialized journals and other outlets which few beyond the discipline read. The motivation behind gathering the essays in this book together was to make them more accessible to a wider range of people, and to develop a wider framework in the spirit of believing that the whole is greater than the sum of the parts.

Boston, Massachusetts
January 2013

Acknowledgments

Chapter 2 is a revised version of an unpublished paper which originated as the annual Heckscher Lecture at the Stockholm School of Economics in 2006. I am grateful to Håkan Lindgren for the invitation to this lecture series. Chapter 3 is a revised version of an article which originally appeared in *EurAmerica*, volume 41, in 2011. Chapter 4 is a revised version of an article co-authored with the late Frances Bostock and originally published in *Business History Review*, volume 70, in 1996. Chapter 5 is a revised version of a conference paper originally published in *Business and Economic History,* volume 16, in 1987. Chapter 6 is a revised version of an essay originally published in Waseda University's *Institute of Asia-Pacific Studies,* number 39, in 1997. Chapter 7 is a revised version of an article co-authored with Christina Lubinski and originally published in *Enterprise & Society,* volume 13, in 2012. Chapter 8 is a revised version of an article originally published in *Entreprises et Histoire,* volume 49, in 2007. Chapter 9 is a revised version of an article originally published in *Zeitschrift für Unternehmensgeschichte*, volume 51, in 2006. I am grateful to the editors of these journals for permission to republish revised versions of these articles.

During the years many colleagues have contributed to the arguments in the essays. I owe special debts to my co-authors of Chapters 4 and 7, the late Frankie Bostock and Christina Lubinski respectively. Mark Casson, the late Alfred D. Chandler Jr., Walter Friedman, Patrick Fridenson, Pankaj Ghemawat, Tarun Khanna, the late Tom McCraw, David Merrett, Tom Nicholas, Kenny Yasumuro and Mira Wilkins have been sources of intellectual inspiration over the years. I have been employed at the Harvard Business School since 2000, and the faculty and MBA students have been major influences on my research. The research for most of the essays in this volume has been generously funded by the Division of Research and Faculty Development at the Harvard Business School, to whom I am most grateful. As usual, I should thank the awesome Dylan for keeping everything in proportion.

1. Business enterprises and the making of the modern world

FIRMS AS ACTORS

Entrepreneurs and firms have been important actors in the making of our modern global world. Forty years ago this would not have needed to be said. As the pace of globalization speeded up from the 1960s, the term "multinational enterprise" (hereafter MNE) was coined, and there was an outpouring of discussion, much of it critical, about the political, social, and economic role of large global firms. MNEs were perceived to be so powerful that they posed a threat to the nation state.[1]

Yet as historians, economists and other scholars have discovered that globalization has a long history, so the role of business enterprises has tended to be written out of the script. The neglect of firms is apparent across disciplines. For several decades academic historians devoted almost no attention to business as such, as they focused on the role of culture, race, gender, and religion in historical developments. Mainstream historians, Beckert recently observed, "largely ceded interpretative hegemony when it comes to matters of economic change to economists, political scientists, sociologists, and a host of popular writers."[2] A renewal of interest in the "history of capitalism" is finally beginning to correct this peculiar omission.[3]

Economic historians, often in recent decades trained in economics and employed in economics departments, have remained focused on economic change, but have often paid little attention to firms. In exploring globalization, they have done pioneering work in quantifying historical trends in the integration of world markets. They have shown that the second half of the nineteenth century witnessed a deeper globalization than ever seen previously using that criterion. By 1914 world capital, commodity and labor markets were closely integrated, and more integrated than they were to be for several decades thereafter. Yet this literature has had much more to say about international trade and institutional structures than about entrepreneurship and MNEs. Indeed, the story of the creation of the nineteenth-century global economy has been written without mentioning a single business enterprise.[4] Political scientists, although more interested in firms, have focused primarily on the politics and policy decisions which impacted and drove globalization.[5] Sociologists, who have approached the subject of globalization from the perspective of organizations, have primarily focused on states and intergovernmental organizations.[6]

This book makes the case that the role of business needs to be more centrally incorporated into narratives explaining the making of the modern world. Broadly, it explores a number of key questions. Were entrepreneurs and firms architects, co-architects, or consumers of the modern world? How important were they compared with governments and other institutional actors in building global capitalism? Were they followers of fashions and trends, or creators of them? Could they dictate to consumers and governments? Or were they dictated to? MNEs have been described by Alfred D. Chandler and Bruce Mazlish, two prominent historians, as a "new kind of Leviathan," which had "an impact on almost every sphere of modern life from policymaking on the environment to international security, from issues of personal identity to issues of community, and from the future of work to the future of the nation-state."[7] How powerful were these so-called Leviathans, and how did their power change over time? If business was a shaper of global capitalism, was it a force for good, or otherwise?

These questions remain as relevant today as in the past, and perhaps even more so, given both the pace of globalization in today's world, and the re-appearance of multiple critics. This book is motivated by the belief that it is important to provide robust historical evidence on which to inform opinions and judgments about both the present and the future.

A (VERY) SHORT HISTORY OF GLOBALIZATION

Globalization has deep historical roots. Our globalized modern world is the outcome of many past globalizations. In the deepest sense, the process of globalization began some 80 000 years ago when *Homo sapiens* began migrating from Africa to colonize the world. Over time, they subjugated all other forms of life, including alternative hominids such as Neathanderals.

As civilizations emerged long afterwards, stronger political structures expanded to cover large geographical areas. Empires such Ancient Assyria and Egypt, Greece and Roman, Maya and Mongol, Byzantine and Arab, Khmer and Mughal, were not only political systems, but provided structures for religions, ideologies, technologies and trade to spread geographically.[8] If globalization is considered, in the words of the management scholar Bruce Kogut, as a "process of increasing integration in world civilization," then it has a long lineage.[9]

This lineage was never linear. Empires rose and fell, for reasons which historians still debate, but none of them persisted for "ever." They faced the challenge of physical distance in a world where people, as well as their ideas and trade, could travel only as fast as a horse or sailing ship could carry them. These constraints did not prevent major waves of globalization. The voyages of discovery of Spanish and Portuguese explorers to the New World and Asia in the fifteenth and sixteenth centuries saw a substantial transfer of technology – and disease – across continents. Entire civilizations in the Americas were decimated in the process. The New World also provided large supplies of the silver required by China, in exchange for which European merchants purchased manufactured and other exotic goods from the sophisticated Chinese economy.[10] Subsequently, global trading links between the Americas, Europe, and Africa had major economic, social, and cultural consequences, including the forced transfer of at least 10 million Africans to the Americas as slaves between the sixteenth and nineteenth centuries.

There was, then, a long history of integrating once-isolated geographies through trade and conquest. However, until the nineteenth century the cost and difficulty of travelling persistently served as a brake on the process of integration. Periodic wars further disrupted international commerce. World trade may only have grown a little over 1 percent per year between 1500 and 1800.[11]

The advent of modern economic growth, which began with the Industrial Revolution in eighteenth-century Britain, was a genuinely game-changing event, even if we know now its origins and timing were more evolutionary than sudden. At the heart of the change was energy. Before the eighteenth century, animals were the primary source of energy, assisted by limited use of wind and waterpower. The use of coal to generate steam gave human society far more energy than it had ever possessed in the past. In 1700 animals provided two-thirds of Britain's energy source, with watermills a further tenth. By 1850 steampower provided 30 percent of Britain's power.[12] As the age of fossil fuels – coal, and later oil – took hold, the transport and communication constraints on globalization were relaxed.

As steamdriven railroads began to spread from Britain to around the world from the 1830s, accompanied by faster sailing ships and then steamships, the impact of geographical distance shrank. For commerce, this meant the opening of new markets and the possibility of exploiting natural resources in distant lands. The impact of the nineteenth-century discovery of the principles of electricity, the invention of the battery and the generator as sources of power, and the creation of devices to transmit and distribute electricity resulted in a further relaxation in the constraints imposed by distance. The first, and most radical, outcome was a revolution in communications caused by the electric telegraph. The first successful transatlantic cable connection was in 1866. Information could now cross continents in minutes, even if it was initially very expensive to send messages. This enabled the European empires spreading over Asia and Africa to manage and control local populations better than ever before, just as it better enabled the European settlers in the United States and Canada to move westwards into the lands inhabited by indigenous peoples. For business, it was now feasible, if still challenging, for business enterprises to manage assets across large geographical distances and over political borders. The telegraph made becoming an MNE a feasible proposition.

The international political economy was important also. Western imperialism involved the forcible removal of political barriers to globalization. The British and other European empires represented another round of globalization by coercion.[13] Even in nominally independent Latin America and elsewhere, the British, and later the Americans, imposed their view of international law which guaranteed property rights.[14]

It was in this era that firms became really important also. Certainly they were not entirely insignificant earlier. The European chartered trading companies of the seventeenth and eighteenth centuries built large global trading networks on the basis of support and privileges conferred by their home governments. However during the late nineteenth century thousands of businesses crossed borders. They engaged in extensive foreign direct investment (hereafter FDI).[15] They took diverse organizational forms, like "free-standing" companies which operated exclusively internationally without prior domestic businesses.[16] They were often joined in networks or business groups.[17]

Business historians have been exploring how these firms were an important component of nineteenth-century globalization since the pioneering studies of Mira Wilkins.[18] They were the facilitators of globalization. Firms from the industrialized Western countries scoured the globe in search of markets and natural resources. They were the orchestrators of the rapid increase in trade flows seen during this era, and they built most of the infrastructure of the global economy, including telegraph and railroad lines, and ports. Firms began building factories in foreign countries. By 1914 Singer had taken the sewing machine around the world, and accounted for upwards of 90 percent of the machines in use worldwide. By 1914 world FDI was equivalent to 9 percent of world output, a ratio which was not to be reached again until the 1990s.

There were evident winners and losers from the first global economy. By 1914 there was a major gap in wealth between the industrialized West and the Rest of the world. China and India were the great centers of global handicraft manufacturing in the pre-industrial world. China accounted for roughly one-third of total world manufacturing as late as 1800. Both countries were transformed into exporters of primary commodities such as tea and silk over the course of the nineteenth century.[19] The historian Pomeranz famously, and controversially, described the income gap between the West and China and India as the "Great Divergence."[20]

At least in part because of the reaction to the Great Divergence, the first global economy, at least as defined above, proved transitory. As the following chapters will discuss, World War I and the Great Depression in 1929 ushered in an era of constrained globalization. The sequestration of enemy-owned affiliates by US, British and other Allied governments during World War I signaled the end of the era when foreign companies could operate in most countries on more or less the same terms as domestic ones. The spread of Communism after the Russian Revolution in 1917, and the decolonization after the end of World War II, resulted in further restrictions on foreign owner- ship. Tariffs and exchange controls proliferated. Immigration flows collapsed as governments introduced quotas and work visas. The integration of capital, commodity, and labor markets collapsed. The gold standard, the monetary system which was the key institution in financial globalization, fell apart.[21]

These developments were paradoxical given that technology continued to shrink geographical distances. The advent of cinema and radio provided during the interwar years unprecedented opportunities to see lifestyles real or imagined elsewhere. Telephones and automobiles became items of mass consumption. Commercial air travel was expensive, but quite widespread by the postwar decades. Any argument that globalization is an inevitable outcome of technological progress is severely challenged by this evidence. Politics, it seemed, trumped technology in reversing globalization.

The nature of this reversal requires careful definition. The widely used concept of "de-globalization" works best when applied to the disintegration of capital, financial, and labor markets. This was a striking reversal of the trends which had got underway during the nineteenth century. Yet there were also continuities with the past. De Grazia has explored how the global consumer culture which had emerged during the late nineteenth century continued to expand and deepen during the interwar years.[22] Miller's study of the maritime world of shipping, trading and ports identified continuities throughout the era of so-called de-globalization. "Globalization entails primarily global interchange and connectedness," Miller observed, "for which integrated markets can be fundamentally constructive but not indis- pensable."[23] Link has posited the emergence of an "alternative illiberal inter- nationalism" which was characterized by a flow of ideas and technologies between the liberal states of the West and the totalitarian regimes of Nazi Germany and the Soviet Union.[24]

It is evident that the interwar era also saw the creation of new mini-global worlds based on the alternative currency areas which appeared in the wake of collapse of the gold standard in the early 1930s. The sterling area, the franc area, and the dollar area influenced flows of capital and of trade during the 1930s, and were significant influences on international business and trade for several decades thereafter.[25]

There were also new mutant globalizations based on ideology and coercion. As the Japanese army invaded China and then the rest of East and Southeast Asia in the 1930s and 1940s, it established the Greater East-Asia Co-Prosperity Sphere. Japanese companies followed their soldiers to capture resources and find markets. In the same period, the Nazi regime in Germany, whose malign impact on the beauty and pharmaceutical company Beiersdorf is the subject of Chapter 7, launched its own globalization wave through conquest. As the German armies conquered neighboring countries, German firms, both private and state-owned, followed in their wake, seeking to acquire local firms to create their own multinationals. The regime itself sought to utilize the economic resources of conquered countries. As the Reichswehr attacked Russia in 1942, its soldiers included nationals from virtually every European country except Britain.[26] Appropriately for a criminal regime in which the mass murder of Jews, Roma, gays, and political opponents was accompanied by looting for personal gain, this warped globalization ended with the defeat of the Nazi regime in 1945, as did the Greater East-Asia Co-Prosperity Sphere.

A more persistent globalization was pursued in the Communist world. Unlike the Nazi and Japanese globalizations, this was a strictly non-capitalist endeavor by a regime committed to state planning and ownership of the means of production. Communism closed Russia, and then Eastern Europe, China, and elsewhere to global capitalism. Behind these closed barriers, the Communist rulers after 1945 encouraged countries to specialize in particular sectors, and trade with one another. An institutional framework, through an organization called Comecon, was put in place to oversee financial and trading relationships within this group.[27] Until political relations between Communist China and the Soviet Union deteriorated in the late 1950s, this Communist world covered a significant percentage of the global world.[28] The Communist model also attracted developing countries such as India, which engaged in large-scale state planning in order to achieve industrial catch-up, and developed close trading and technological relationships with the Soviet Union. The opening of China to global capitalism, beginning in the 1980s, and the disintegration of the Soviet Union in 1989, spelled the end of this era of Communist globalization.

Finally, and most relevantly for this book, while global markets disintegrated, global firms did not. During the first global economy MNEs were facilitators of globalization. During the subsequent decades they functioned as preservers of globalization. As the following chapters demonstrate, capital and trade flows across borders may have stumbled, but firms continued to straddle borders, and indeed to make new investments. The challenge of managing distance was certainly now joined, and often exceeded, by the challenge of managing governments.[29] However, entrepreneurs were creative in devising new strategies to overcome such political and other risks. During the postwar decades, capitalist enterprises were excluded from Communist countries and restricted in much of the rest of the world, but global firms remained active and there were vibrant transfers of brands and ideas across borders. The globalization of business was constrained, not ended. A new generation of businesses enterprises also perceived government restrictions and regulations as entrepreneurial opportunities rather than obstacles to globalization. The creation of the Eurodollar and Eurobond markets in London during the 1960s was in essence an entrepreneurial reaction to the welter of government restrictions, especially in the United States, on banking. These new global financial markets, in turn, undermined the capacities of national governments to control their financial markets.[30]

From the late 1940s a new global world began to be constructed in the Western world and Japan. Between 1950 and 1973 the annual real GDP growth of developed market economies averaged around 5 percent. So-called economic miracles in Western Europe and Japan enabled income levels and innovation to catch up rapidly with the United States. International agreements such as GATT and the formation of the European Union stimulated the reduction of barriers to trade and capital flows, though government intervention even in Western economies remained far more widespread than in the first global economy. Many European countries, for example, restricted or banned foreign companies in some or all industries. By 1980, the integration of worldwide capital, commodity, and labor markets was still limited compared with the early twentieth century.[31]

During the 1980s the scale and scope of globalization widened dramatically. Both politics and technology were important drivers of the second global economy. In the West, a new generation of political leaders such as Reagan in the United States and Thatcher in Britain deregulated and privatized their economies. Even more important were the reentries of China and Russia into global capitalism, along with the liberalization of Indian government policies from the 1990s.[32] Finally, the emergence of the World Wide Web and the internet in the 1990s enabled a new level of interconnectedness. The integration of capital, commodity, and trade markets again reached high levels, although strong boundaries remained on labor mobility. Firms again served as powerful facilitators of globalization. As government-imposed barriers fell in former Communist countries, so Western, Japanese and other firms entered markets with their products and brands, becoming powerful agents of economic reintegration of closed economies into the global world.

It is again not a straightforward matter to define the nature of the globalization of this period. The revolution in the speed of communicating information across borders associated with the Web generated many claims that the world had become borderless or "flat."[33] This, in turn, provoked a stream of literature asserting how regional and "spiky" the global world remained. Innovation appeared in hubs and cities where knowledge workers clustered. The flattening of income differentials also seemed muted. Although some regions of India, China, and other countries grew at fast rates in these decades, many countries in sub-Saharan Africa and elsewhere remained desperately poor.[34] Within India, China, and elsewhere, major income differentials opened up between the rich and the rest. Brazil, which implemented minimum wages and a social welfare program named Bolsa Familia from the 1990s, was a rare exception to this trend.[35] Several of the following chapters directly address these debates concerning the nature of the second global economy, and the role of firms within them.

OUTLINE OF THE BOOK

The remaining chapters provide different perspectives on the role of entrepreneurs and firms in building the modern world. They explore their role as facilitators and preservers of globalization, their status as Leviathans, and the nature of their overall impact.

Chapter 2 begins by exploring the role of entrepreneurs and firms in the story of the Great Divergence, or the gap in wealth between the West and the Rest. This chapter argues that there is currently a "missing gap" between the currently fashionable institutional and human capital explanations of global wealth and poverty and the actual creators of wealth and innovation. The gap is entrepreneurs and firms. This chapter employs this lens to examine why the response to modern economic growth from entrepreneurs in most of the Rest was stunted during the first global economy, and how this changed during the subsequent eras of constrained globalization and the second global economy. While the focus is on domestic entrepreneurship, the chapter also asks why, although the MNE appeared like a well-designed vehicle to transfer entrepreneurial skills to developing countries, its success in such knowledge diffusion has often been patchy.

Chapter 3 explores the tension between MNEs as shapers and as creators of the modern world through a case study of the global beauty industry. During the first global economy Western MNEs diffused Western beauty norms and brands around the world. Yet to the surprise of many pioneering entrepreneurs in the industry, while corporate advertising could shape consumer preferences, it turned out that inherited cultural and social norms were very resilient, even within the context of an international consumer culture. The chapter ends by exploring the paradoxical nature of the second global economy. On the one hand, global brands have been rolled out to such once closed economies as China and Russia. On the other hand, there has been a strong trend towards the localization of these brands. Moreover, globalization has now emerged as a powerful diffuser of non-Western beauty norms.

In Chapter 4, the growth of US-based MNE manufacturing investment in Britain during the first six decades of the twentieth century is examined using a specially built database. The continuity of global business even in the era of constrained globalization is very evident in this study which shows almost as many new US entrants to Britain during the 1930s as during the 1920s. Equally striking is the evidence on the impact of the US firms on the British economy. In 1962, US-owned firms were responsible for 7 percent of British manufacturing output, but more importantly they were clustered in dynamic high-technology and branded consumer products sectors. They also undertook substantial R&D in Britain, and were active in exporting. While the case study supports the positive case for the impact of MNEs on host economies, it also highlights the heterogeneity of the population of firms, as it shows the wide dispersion in size of affiliates, as well as how MNE strategies, including entry and exit, evolved over time.

In Chapter 5, the unit of analysis shifts to a single MNE, and its impact on a single host developing country. The Imperial Bank of Iran was a form of business organization quite different from the US manufacturing firms seen in the previous chapter, and it provides further evidence of the heterogeneity of business enterprises involved in global business. The impact of the Bank on Iran is shown to have been decidedly mixed. By providing modern financial services, it was an agent of development. Yet it was also, like the Anglo-Persian Oil Company, the other large foreign company in Iran, an agent of British imperial influence in the late nineteenth and early twentieth centuries. The resentment of Iranians towards these quasi-imperial institutions formed an important component of the events which led ultimately to the Islamic Revolution in the country in 1978.

Chapter 6 also explores the impact of MNEs by looking more broadly at the Asia region. The economic experience of Asia over the last two centuries provides dramatic evidence of discontinuities in world history. China and India began the nineteenth century as the global centers of handicraft manufacturing. They ended the century as primary commodity producers. Over the course of the twentieth century both countries underwent huge shifts in their political systems. By the early twenty-first century they were on their way to becoming global economic giants again. The chapter explores the role of MNEs in this evolving story, and looks especially at their economic and social impact, which is shown to have been heavily influenced by local institutional, societal and cultural circumstances.

The following chapters explore the extent to which the ability of MNEs to shape the modern world was constrained, especially by governments, from World War I onwards.

As Chapter 7's case study of Beiersdorf explores, this was no easy task. This German pharmaceutical and personal care manufacturer was a precocious MNE investor before World War I, but suffered the loss of all its foreign assets as a result of Germany's defeat in the war. The firm showed great resilience as it rebuilt its international business, seeking to "cloak" its businesses through their ownership in neutral countries. It also showed resilience in the face of the advent of the Nazi regime in 1933, when as a firm with a strong Jewish presence, both in ownership and in management, it faced great perils even in its home economy. While the company successfully navigated the Nazi era in Germany, with its senior management leaving the country and handing the business to their non-Jewish colleagues, the "cloaking" strategy proved unable to save Beiersdorf's foreign affiliates. The chapter shows that it took another 40 years for the firm to fully buy back its ownership of the iconic Nivea brand in several important markets.

Political risk and its management is also a major focus of Chapter 8. In Asia and Africa, decolonization after World War II was often followed by hostility to foreign firms, reinforced by growing proclivities towards state planning which left little role for private capitalism, foreign or local. Many MNEs divested, or were expropriated. The chapter explores these issues with the case of the consumer products company Unilever in India and Turkey. Unilever stayed in both countries. It pioneered the employment of local nationals, and sought to align its strategies with host governments. Even then the firm struggled to survive the difficult political and economic terrain of the 1970s. If Unilever was a Leviathan, it was a decidedly toothless one in the face of such assertive governments.

Finally, Chapter 9 looks at the vexed issue of the nationality of firms. Despite much rhetoric about the "stateless firms" of today, this chapter suggests that if there was ever an era when the nationality of firms was not important it was during the first global economy. During the era of constrained globalization the nationality of firms rose up political agendas, and it has never really gone away. During the second global economy, nationality mattered, and its importance seems to be intensifying.

NOTES

1. Raymond Vernon, *Sovereignty at Bay: The Multinational Spread of US Enterprises*, New York: Basic Books, 1971.
2. Sven Beckert, "The history of American capitalism," in Eric Foner and Lisa McGirr (eds), *American History Now*, Philadelphia, PA: Temple University Press, 2011, p. 315.
3. Idem; Michael Zakim and Gary J. Kornblith (eds), *Capitalism Takes Command: The Social Transformation of Nineteenth Century America*, Chicago, IL: University of Chicago Press, 2012.
4. Michael D. Bordo, Alan M. Taylor, and Jeffrey G. Williamson (eds), *Globalization in Historical Perspective*, Chicago, IL: University of Chicago Press, 2003.

5. Jeffry A. Frieden, *Global Capitalism: Its Fall and Rise in the Twentieth Century*, New York: W.W. Norton, 2006, does feature firms, although not as the primary focus. See also Alfred D. Chandler and Bruce Mazlish (eds), *Leviathans, Multinational Corporations and the New Global History*, Cambridge: Cambridge University Press, 2005, pp. 9–10.
6. Mauro F. Guillen, "Is globalization civilizing, destructive or feeble? A critique of five key debates in the social science literature," *Annual Review of Sociology*, **27** (2001), pp. 235–60.
7. Chandler and Mazlish, *Leviathans*, p. 2.
8. Karl Moore and David Lewis, *Birth of the Multinational*, Copenhagen: Copenhagen Business School Press, 1999.
9. Bruce Kogut, "Globalization," in M. Warner (ed.), *Concise International Encyclopedia of Business and Management*, London: International Thomson Business Press, 1997.
10. D. O. Flynn and A. Giráldez, "Cycles of silver: global economic unity through the mid-eighteenth century," *Journal of World History*, **13** (2) (2002), pp. 391–427.
11. Ronald Findlay and Kevin H. O'Rourke, "Commodity market integration 1500–2000," in Bordo et al., *Globalization*.
12. Roger Fouquet, *Heat, Power and Light*, Cheltenham, UK and Northampton, MA, USA: Edward Elgar, 2008, p. 125.
13. Gary B. Magee and Andrew S. Thompson, *Empire and Globalization: Networks of People, Gods and Capital in the British World, c.1850–1914*, Cambridge: Cambridge University Press, 2010; P. J. Cain, and A. G. Hopkins, *British Imperialism: 1688–2000*, London: Longman, 2002; Christopher A. Bayley, *The Birth of the Modern World 1780–1914*, Oxford: Blackwell, 2004.
14. Geoffrey Jones, *Multinationals and Global Capitalism*, Oxford: Oxford University Press, 2005, pp. 24–5.
15. For surveys of the literature on the history of multinationals, see Jones, *Multinationals*, and idem, "Globalization," in Geoffrey Jones and Jonathan Zeitlin (eds), *Oxford Handbook of Business History*, Oxford: Oxford University Press, 2008.
16. Mira Wilkins, "The free-standing company, 1870–1914: an important type of British foreign direct investment", *Economic History Review*, **41** (2) (1988), pp. 259–85; Mira Wilkins and H. Schröter (eds), *The Free Standing Company in the World Economy, 1836–1996*, Oxford: Oxford University Press, 1998.
17. Geoffrey Jones, *Merchants to Multinationals*, Oxford: Oxford University Press, 2000; Geoffrey Jones and Asli M. Coplan, "Business groups in historical perspectives," in Asli M. Coplan, Takashi Hikino and James R. Lincoln (eds), *The Oxford Handbook of Business Groups*, Oxford: Oxford University Press, 2010.
18. Mira Wilkins and Frank E. Hill, *American Business Abroad: Ford on Six Continents*, Detroit, MI: Wayne State University Press, 1964; reprinted Cambridge: Cambridge University Press, 2011; Mira Wilkins, *The Emergence of Multinational Enterprise*, Cambridge, MA: Harvard University Press, 1970.
19. Paul Bairoch, "International industrialization levels from 1750 to 1980", *Journal of European Economic History*, **11** (2) (1982), pp. 269–333.
20. Kenneth Pomeranz, *The Great Divergence*, Princeton, NJ: Princeton University Press, 2000.
21. Bordo et al., *Globalization*.
22. Victoria de Grazia, *Irresistible Empire: America's Advance through 20th-Century Europe*, Cambridge, MA: Harvard University Press, 2005.
23. Michael Miller, *Europe and the Maritime World*, Cambridge: Cambridge University Press, 2011, p. 10.
24. Stefan Link, "Transnational Fordism: Ford Motor Company, Nazi Germany, and the Soviet Union in the interwar years," unpublished PhD, Harvard University, 2011.
25. The currency blocs probably reinforced some existing pressures towards regionalization rather than served as exclusive drivers of them. See Barry Eichengreen and Douglas A. Irwin, "Trade blocs, currency blocs and the reorientation of world trade in the 1930s," *Journal of International Economics*, **38** (1–2) (1995), pp. 1–24.
26. See, for example, Richard J. Overy, "Goring's multi-national empire," in Alice Teichova and Philipp L. Cottrell (eds), *International Business and Central Europe 1918–1939*, New York: St Martin's Press, 1983, pp. 269–8.

27. A still-useful contemporary study of Comecon is Michael Kaser, *Comecon: Integration Problems of the Planned Economies*, London: Oxford University Press, 1965.
28. William Kirby, "China's internationalization in the early People's Republic: dreams of a socialist world," *China Quarterly*, (December) 2006, pp. 870–90.
29. Christopher Kobrak and Per H. Hansen (eds), *European Business, Dictatorship, and Political Risk*, Oxford: Berghahn Books, 2004.
30. Jones, *Multinationals*, pp. 135–7.
31. Bordo et al., *Globalization*.
32. Arvind Panagariya, *India: The Emerging Giant*, Oxford: Oxford University Press, 2008, pp. 78–109.
33. Kenichi Ohmae, *The Borderless World*, New York: Harper Business, 1990; Thomas L. Friedman, *The World Is Flat: A Brief History of the Twenty-First Century*, New York: Farrar, Straus and Giroux, 2005.
34. Benjamin R. Barber, *Jihad vs. McWorld*, New York: Times Books, 1995; Richard Florida, "The world is spiky," *The Atlantic Monthly*, October, 2005; Joseph F. Stiglitz, *Making Globalization Work*, New York: W.W. Norton, 2006; Pankaj Ghemawat, *Redefining Global Strategy: Crossing Borders in a World Where Differences Still Matter*, Boston, MA: Harvard Business School Press, 2007.
35. Zanny Minton Beddoes, "For richer, for poorer,"*The Economist*, 13 October, 2012.

2. Entrepreneurs, firms, and global wealth since 1850[1]

OVERVIEW

We live today in a world where most people are poor and some are very rich, and the category in which you find yourself is largely determined not by your job, your age, or your gender, but by your location. Despite the fast economic growth of China and India over the past two decades, most people in the world today are very poor. Nearly 3 billion people live on less than $2 a day; almost 1 billion are illiterate. These numbers reflect the continuing wealth gaps between the West and the Rest of the world, as well as the burgeoning wealth gaps inside countries such as China and India, as well as in the developed world.

Although the data are contested, most economic historians would subscribe to the view that the large inequality between regions is relatively "new," at least in historical terms. The timing, however, remains contentious. A broad consensus that incomes had diverged between Europe and China in the early modern period was disrupted around 2000 when Pomeranz put the term "the Great Divergence" into scholarly usage by suggesting that certain regions of China, India, and Western Europe were at broadly similar levels of agricultural productivity, commercial development and the ability of some firms to raise capital in the middle of the eighteenth century. The Great Divergence in wealth between the West and the Rest, then, began with the Industrial Revolution and the advent of modern economic growth in Britain.[2]

The Pomeranz hypothesis provoked a surge of quantitative research on comparative income levels. Much of this research has suggested that differences in income levels between Europe and Asia were already wide in the eighteenth century, and that this reflected trends which began at least 300 years earlier. However it has also become clear that the real income gap was between the most advanced countries in Europe – Britain, the Netherlands, and Belgium – and the other regions, whether China, India, or central and southern Europe. What happened during the nineteenth century was that much more of the West caught up with the advanced North Sea countries, but the Rest did not.[3]

The large income gaps between the developed West and the Rest in 1914 does not mean that there was no convergence. As Bénétrix, O'Rourke, and Williamson have shown, from the late nineteenth century the "periphery" began to follow the path of industrialization set in the West.[4] A number of Latin American countries began such "convergence" from the 1870s, followed by some Asian countries after 1890, followed by parts of sub-Saharan Africa and the Middle East during the interwar years. However the emergence and growth of modern industrial sectors was not sufficient to close the substantial income gaps which had opened. Today the differentials between the West and most of the Rest remain substantial, even if recent decades have seen some convergence between China and other non-Western countries and the West.

Business historians have not been central to the debates about the Great Divergence. As an academic discipline, business history has been primarily concerned to establish why Western countries, and subsequently Japan, grew wealthy. The most important contribution of this literature has been to identify the modern business enterprise as central to the economic performance of economies. Chandler documented the growth in nineteenth-century America of large-scale corporations with professional managers, who he and others saw as driving industrial innovation.[5] Much subsequent business history research has gone into testing this hypothesis, including exploring how, why, and with what consequences, firms and business systems in other Western countries looked different from those in the United States.[6] There has been much less research on the converse of this situation: why, and with what consequences, the entrepreneurs and firms in Latin America, Africa, and most of Asia were so delayed in producing powerhouses of corporate innovation.

In contrast economists, as well as other social scientists, have made major advances in understanding what kept countries poor as well as what made them rich, even if the conclusions remain contested. During the 1970s North identified the role of institutions in providing the incentive structure of economies. He defined institutions quite broadly. He believed that they "consist of both informal constraints (sanctions, taboos, customs, traditions, and codes of conduct), and formal rules (constitutions, laws, property rights).[7] Greif, another prominent institutionalist, defined them as "a system of rules, beliefs, norms and organizations that together generate a regularity of (social) behavior."[8] In his more recent work, North himself has widened his own definitions of institutions even further, and argued that responses to institutions are heavily influenced by culturally conditioned mental models and religious beliefs.[9]

In practice, the primary focus of attention has been systems of property rights. It has been asserted that societies that provide incentives and opportunities for investment will be richer than those that fail to do so, and that the protection of property rights was an essential incentive behind such investment. By reducing transactions costs and facilitating potential gains from

exchange, institutions fuel productivity and growth. The literature has particularly favored the use of three proxies in particular for "institutions": risk of
expropriation; government effectiveness; and constraints on the executive.
North famously identified the Glorious Revolution in England in 1688 as
providing the institutional arrangements which explain why that country had
the Industrial Revolution.[10]

Although most economists now agree that inherited institutions matter for
growth, however, they have disagreed on the nature of this institutional foundation. There has been a considerable emphasis in recent literature on the
impact of colonialism. Engerman and Sokoloff highlighted the impact of colonization in altering the composition of the populations. In Latin America and
the Caribbean, soils and climates gave them a comparative advantage in growing crops for which they used imported slaves or natives. The resulting
extreme inequality in distribution of wealth, they suggest, gave them institutions which contributed to the persistence of substantial inequality. North
America, where there were comparatively few Native Americans and climates
and soils favored mixed and livestock farming, with limited economies of
scale in production, got the right kind of institutions.[11]

Acemoglu, Johnson, and Robinson distinguished between institutions of
"private property" and "extractive institutions". The former provide secure
property rights and are embedded in a broad cross-section of societies.
Extractive institutions concentrate power in the hands of a small elite and
create a high risk of expropriation. These authors use this model to explain
what they describe as the reversal of fortune between apparently affluent (as
proxied by urbanization) Aztecs and Incas in the Americas and Mughals in
India, and little-developed North America and Australia. They argue that this
was caused by European colonialism. In prosperous and densely settled areas,
Europeans introduced or maintained extractive institutions to force people to
work in mines and plantations. In sparsely settled areas, Europeans settled and
created institutions of private property. The spread of industrial technology in
the nineteenth century required a broad mass of society to participate, so the
societies with these institutions were the ones that experienced rapid modern
economic growth.[12]

A different institutional perspective has come from the law and finance
literature. Broadly these authors have argued that the legal tradition each country inherited or adopted in the distant past has had a long-term effect on financial development. Countries that had a common-law system had on average
better investor protections than most civil-law countries, and French civil-law
countries were worse than those with German or Scandinavian civil-law traditions. These authors suggest this had a major effect on financial development,
which in turn can be assumed to have impacted the nature and speed of
economic development.[13]

A second explanation for wealth and poverty has focused on human capital. Thirty years ago Easterlin argued that the answer to why some societies underwent modern economic growth and others did not could be found in the amount of formal schooling provided by societies. Within Europe, the most advanced nations educationally, in northern and Western Europe, were the ones that developed first. Easterlin also speculated that the content of education matters, believing that secular and rationalistic was best.[14] Subsequently, Goldin has made a strong case for attributing American industrial leadership to the unique egalitarian mass provision of post-elementary schooling achieved in the United States during the early twentieth century.[15] Scholars in the law and finance literature have accepted that human capital may be a more basic source of growth than institutions, and that growth and human capital accumulation lead to institutional improvement.[16]

This economics literature has made great progress in developing new ways to measure and identify the causal effects of key variables, but it also has limitations. The literature remains split on methods, data, and interpretation. Much of the work can be criticized for its willingness not to overly engage with historical specifics. The focus on the impact of colonialism skirts around an unusually big elephant in the room often called the "Needham Puzzle" after one of the most prominent historians of technology in China: why did China not have an Industrial Revolution? Although poor institutions – "Oriental Despotism" – are often blamed for this, there is as much evidence that the Chinese state was benign or weak as that it was predatory. The widespread existence of market activities and the importance of private property in China would support such a view. At the very least, there were such considerable fluctuations over time in the effectiveness of governments in China, and in their relationship to market activities, that a monolithic "Oriental Despotism" explanation is not convincing.[17]

On a more conceptual level, the economics literature is heavily oriented towards measurement and causality. Knowing that political and legal institutions or human capital matter is important – but a further set of critical questions relate to how firms and entrepreneurs interact with these aspects of an economy. It is firms and entrepreneurs which create wealth and innovation, rather than governmental institutions or schools. Here the economics literature is less well developed. Institutions and human capital are treated as the first-order causes of economic growth. The assumption is that if a society evolves or adopts the right institutions, or else has good human capital investment, firms and entrepreneurs will more or less appear spontaneously and create economic growth. The business history literature suggests that this is a considerable oversimplification.

This chapter seeks to incorporate the missing gap of firms and entrepreneurs into debates about the causes of global wealth and poverty. It is not intended here to revisit the extensive literature, why the Industrial Revolution occurred first in Britain. Instead, the focus is more on why much of the Rest struggled to catch up.

ARE SOME COUNTRIES JUST MORE ENTREPRENEURIAL THAN OTHERS?

One reason why economists may not have spent much time thinking about the role of business enterprises in the Great Divergence is that there is no interesting story to tell. Are some countries simply more entrepreneurial than others because of cultural factors? If the answer is yes, then there is no need to explore more complex mechanisms which may be at work.

The view that the culture was just wrong has been widely used to explain the Needham Puzzle. By the fourteenth century China had an advanced agriculture with high yields, a considerable knowledge of science and technology, a very large iron and textile industry, and a high level of urbanization.[18] The only thing wrong, as Weber wrote in *The Protestant Ethic and the Spirit of Capitalism*, was the Chinese mindset.[19] Joseph Needham, whose research documented the achievements of pre-modern science and technology in China, came to the same view, as has more recently the economic historian Mokyr.[20]

This issue was also much discussed by earlier generations of business historians before the discipline became primarily focused on organizational issues during the 1960s. Between the late 1940s and the late 1950s the Center for Research in Entrepreneurial History at Harvard assembled an interdisciplinary group of scholars, including economists such as Joseph Schumpeter and North, and younger historians such as Chandler and David Landes, who pursued empirical studies on the rise of entrepreneurship in the transition to capitalism, examining the emergence and social conditioning of entrepreneurship in countries around the world. This stream of research resulted in a body of literature, focused on the historical development of entrepreneurship, which suggested that levels of entrepreneurship did vary significantly between countries.[21] For some, the reason lay in culture. In a classic early study, Landes argued that France's allegedly poor economic performance in the nineteenth century could be attributed to the conservativeness of French entrepreneurs, who saw business as an integral part of family status rather than as an end in itself.[22] Landes continued throughout his career to make the case for the importance of national cultural factors, values, and social attitudes in explaining the development of entrepreneurial activity, and in turn the economic performance of nations.[23] The cultural failure argument appeared in many other debates. Gentrified and complacent British entrepreneurs in the

Victorian era proved a favorite subject for those interested in explaining the "relative decline" of the British economy.[24]

From the start there have been major criticisms of the cultural approach. It is known that in history peoples who shared similar cultures or beliefs had very different paths of development. Often the problem being explained was poorly specified. Landes's search for why French entrepreneurs failed was launched without a clear understanding of what, if anything, had failed. Nineteenth-century French industry is now regarded as a lot more technologically advanced than had been imagined.[25] As the economist Alexander Gerschenkron noted, the notion of "national culture" envisioned in many studies was static and rigidly functionalist, making it difficult for them to truly account for the dynamic nature of entrepreneurial activity or for entrepreneurial change.[26] Schumpeter maintained that entrepreneurs often acted as agents of change rather than being captives of their environment. While national institutions and political boundaries, whether formal or informal, provide the environmental settings for entrepreneurial activity, Schumpeter insisted that they often revealed little about the ways in which new economic opportunities have been created and exploited.[27]

In short, while entrepreneurship is a scarce resource, it is at best insufficient to use inherent cultural differences to explain variations in entrepreneurial and economic performance between countries. This does not mean that variations in cultural and social values at particular points in time might not form part of an explanation why the economic performance of countries diverged. It does mean that such variations demand more complex explanations than inherent cultural differences. The chapter now turns to examining the role of entrepreneurs and firms in creating wealth and poverty in the historical phases of globalization, deglobalization, and re-globalization since the second half of the nineteenth century.

CREATING WEALTH AND POVERTY IN THE FIRST GLOBAL ECONOMY

The global integration of the markets for capital, commodities and people proceeded at a fast pace from the 1820s, and especially from the 1870s as transport and communications costs fell through technological advances, and political barriers to investment fell with the spread of both liberal political ideologies and Western imperialism. Globalization transformed national economies. While Western countries underwent rapid industrialization, countries in the South and Asia were turned into major exporters of commodities and foodstuffs. The scale of transformation was sometimes enormous. India's huge handicraft manufacturing industry lost its markets abroad and increas-

ingly in major cities, and the country became instead a major primary
commodity exporter. While tea had been barely grown in South Asia in the
1830s, India had become the world's largest tea producer by 1900, as British
firms both developed plantations and pursued innovative marketing strategies
which overturned the previous dominance of Chinese tea in the world market.

The domestic entrepreneurial response to these momentous economic shifts
in most of Asia, Latin America, and Africa was not strong. While many
regions of Europe caught up with the home of modern industrialization around
the North Sea, the Rest as a whole lagged over the course of the nineteenth
century. This was surprising in some respects. There were strong commercial
and market traditions in much of Asia and to some extent elsewhere. There
were long-established handicraft industries in China and India, as well as deep
commercial and financial institutions. Expatriate Chinese in Southeast Asia
had good mining skills, and developed and dominated the tin-mining industry
in Malaya after 1848. Much of Latin America descended into decades of political turmoil and strife following independence from Spain in the early nineteenth century, but from mid-century stronger political units formed, and
economic growth resumed, especially in the southern cone. Argentina eventually became one of the world's fastest-growing, and richest, economies.[28] Yet
dynamic and innovative locally owned firms were slow to emerge from these
regions.

So why was it entrepreneurs originating from Western countries which
surged ahead of the Rest during the nineteenth century? The institutionalist
argument, that entrepreneurship was more likely to flourish in a country which
protected property rights, did not expropriate, and functioned effectively than
under the chaotic or rapacious regimes seen in some if not all of the non-
Western world, is a starting point, at least for countries outside colonial
empires. But what was the exact relationship? A major insight is provided by
Baumol's work on the allocation of entrepreneurial activity. Two decades ago,
Baumol argued that the productive contribution of entrepreneurship varied
because of the allocation between productive activities such as innovation and
unproductive activities such as rent-seeking or organized crime. This allocation, Baumol suggested, was in turn influenced by the relative pay-offs offered
by a society to such activities.[29] A subsequent massive collaborative research
project provided much empirical historical support for this hypothesis, including a restatement of the key typologies into productive or redistributive entrepreneurship.[30]

Maurer's study of the Mexican financial system from the late nineteenth
century shows how this mechanism played out in one country by demonstrat-
ing how the existence of an undemocratic political system and the selective
enforcement of property rights shaped the financial and business system.
Limited in its ability to raise taxes to finance infrastructure projects as well as

fend off political opponents, the Mexican government of the dictator Porfirio Diaz relied on banks to provide credit, while the banks relied on the government to enforce property rights. A select few bankers were given extensive privileges producing a highly concentrated banking system. Each bank grew fat in its own protected niche. To overcome the problems associated with information asymmetry, banks lent to their own shareholders and other insiders. In the case of the textile industry, banks lent not to the best firms, but to the best-connected ones. Poorly defined property rights prevented those excluded from the insider networks from pledging collateral and finding another financial route.[31]

There were parallels in the more successful business sector in Argentina. During the late nineteenth century large business groups such as Bemberg and Tornquist grew rapidly. They diversified across commodities, processing, infrastructure, and consumer goods manufacturing. These large and successful businesses were productive in Baumol's terms, opening up new industries, and driving the country's fast development at the time. From another perspective, however, their impact was redistributive. They built businesses on the basis of concessions from the government, and devoted considerable energy to political contacts. They were also heavily engaged in financial transactions and networks. As industries developed, they opted to continue importing heavy machinery, rather than face the cost of investing in making such machines themselves and in training skilled workers. As a result, the technological capabilities of the country remained basic.[32]

As studies of nineteenth-century Mexico, and elsewhere, have shown, as the West pulled away, technological catch-up was a huge entrepreneurial challenge. The new advanced technologies of the West were embedded in institutional, economic, and social contexts quite different from those in the Rest. Entrepreneurs could not simply import them and they would work. Factor endowments fundamentally shaped the commercial viability of different transferred technologies.[33] Relevant technologies needed to be identified, they needed to be adapted, they needed to be financed, and they needed to be used. This was hugely challenging, although not impossible.[34] This explains, in part, why there were such significant regional differences in entrepreneurial performance in many nineteenth-century Latin American countries, despite having the same institutions at the national level.[35]

Conversely, getting the institutions right is often regarded as a key factor behind Japan's unusually successful entry into modern economic growth following the Meiji Restoration in 1868. The resource-poor island nation of Japan seemed an unlikely candidate for economic success. The institutional heritage of the country seemed to make such success even less likely. During the sixteenth century Japan's Shogun military rulers had largely closed the country to foreign trade, expelled foreigners, and imposed a strict feudal regime. This regime had remained in place for centuries before the US ships of Commodore Perry turned up in Tokyo harbor in 1853 demanding that the country open itself up for foreign trade. The Meiji Restoration was effectively a coup by lower samurai, a sub-elite group, based in a few outlying regions of the country, who were determined to resist Western incursion into the country. The new Japanese government moved rapidly, and in the face of rebellions by disaffected former members of the feudal elite, to create a modern institutional infrastructure, including a parliamentary system, a central bank, and a legal system, by explicitly copying institutions in the Western countries.

The institutional reforms of the Meiji era resemble a Baumol-approved strategy for generating a supply of productive rather than redistributive entrepreneurship.[36] Yet the institutional framework constructed in Meiji Japan was surely not one which many of today's institutional theorists would favor. Despite appearances, the reforms were not embedded in a broad cross-section of society – indeed their basic purpose was to extract resources from the mass of the people in order to take the country on a forced march of rapid industrialization, and to wage war on and colonize neighboring countries.

In part, the growth of modern entrepreneurship within this institutional context might be ascribed to the pre-industrial commercial heritage of the country, where a market economy had flourished despite the feudal regime and closed economy. A number of the family-owned *zaibatsu* or business groups which drove modern industrial growth, notably Mitsui, drew on such long-established business traditions. Mitsui had been founded as early as 1673 as a clothing retailer. Yet the firm's subsequent growth as well as new entrants such as Iwasaki Yataro's shipping company Mitsubishi was driven by political patronage. In order to support the government's colonial expansion plans and suppress internal rebellions, Mitsubishi was given ships, credit, and protection against foreign shipping companies by governments during the 1870s. Business–government relations seem to have been closer to nineteenth-century Mexico than to the United States, although there was a great deal more tension between Yataro and the government than between the Mexican business elite and Diaz.[37]

Closer examination of the "institutional arrangements" which promoted growth in many countries in the first global economy raise many questions about the "right" and "wrong" institutions to promote entrepreneurship and firm growth. For example, protection of intellectual property rights and patents would appear important to promote entrepreneurship from an institutional perspective. Yet the evidence that patents in Britain played an important role in the Industrial Revolution and later is weak. The cost of obtaining a patent in eighteenth-century Britain was high, and they were difficult to enforce.[38] Later aspiring nineteenth-century Dutch and other entrepreneurs were able to build businesses in more technologically advanced industries because of the lack of patent protection afforded to foreign companies in those countries.[39] Indeed, Moser's review of the historical evidence strongly suggests that in countries with patent laws the majority of innovations have occurred outside of the patent system, while conversely countries without patent laws produced as many innovations as countries with patent laws during the same time periods, and their innovations were of comparable quality.[40]

There are other important examples where empirical research has challenged the correlation between institutions and entrepreneurship. It was plausible to suggest, for example, that the emergence of larger-scale Chinese business during the nineteenth century was handicapped by the absence of company law and limited liability. Finally, the Company Law passed in 1904 provided the legislative framework for modern business. On closer examination, however, it turns out that the law was a culmination of a trend which had been underway for several decades to facilitate the raising of outside capital. Moreover few Chinese companies registered under the act when it was passed. Most entrepreneurs continued to rely on their own and their family funds.[41] In the case of Brazil in the same period, Musacchio has raised serious doubts concerning the adverse impact of civil law regimes on financial and economic development. Brazil was a French civil law country with apparently inadequate creditor protection and contract enforcement, but he found that Brazilian firms used their own byelaws to offer strong protection for equity investors. The country developed a very strong corporate bond market before 1914, which then shrank in importance despite continued creditor protection.[42]

The role of colonialism poses the most serious challenge to institutional explanations of variations in the allocation of entrepreneurial energy. Colonialism forms an important element of the institutional economics explanation for the lack of growth in developing countries, but much of the treatment is ahistorical. Colonialism changed greatly over time, but most attention is given to the highly exploitative first stages of European colonialism. While colonialism is from today's perspective wholly unacceptable, there was a huge difference between Spanish conquistadores in the sixteenth century looting the Aztec and Inca empires, and pious (if racist) late-Victorian British colonial officials in India and Africa. There was a huge difference also between those Victorian officials and their rapacious eighteenth-century predecessors in the East India Company. The policy regimes of empires changed over time. While traditional Indian handicraft industries suffered from British free trade policies in the nineteenth century, during the interwar decades British India was protectionist, including against British imports. In general, empire was a heterogeneous rather than a homogeneous phenomenon. British colonies got common-law systems, while French colonies got civil-law systems, with all the consequent different alleged effects on corporate governance. In Africa, while the vast Belgian possessions in the Congo in the late nineteenth century

have long been regarded as a prime example of worst-case exploitative imperialism, in the British colonies the relationship between the colonial administration and expatriate business were much more distant and nuanced.[43]

The late nineteenth-century British colonial regime is especially interesting
for its impact on entrepreneurship. The British brought not only political
stability, but their legal system with protection of property rights and contract
enforcement. The empire even offered the prospect of upward social advance-
ment for highly successful business leaders of any ethnicity. Ethnic Indian,
Jewish, Chinese, and other diaspora moved under the imperial umbrella,
frequently being co-opted into the British imperial system. By the late nineteenth century Indian and others were being given knighthoods.[44] In 1892
Dadabhai Naoroji, an Indian, became the first Asian elected to the British
House of Commons.

This raises the puzzle of why the response to modern economic growth by
entrepreneurs in India was muted. The British administrators in India not only
introduced British company laws, they simplified and codified them in ways
which appear to have made them even more enterprise-friendly. The British
Raj also operated a laissez-faire, low-tax-policy regime.[45] Yet when investments began in large-scale industry from the mid-nineteenth century, they
were highly clustered geographically and ethnically. Scotsmen developed the
modern jute industry of Calcutta from the 1860s, while the tiny ethnic minority of Parsees developed the textile industries on the west coast. Modern
indigenous entrepreneurship became, and has remained, highly concentrated
ethnically, with the Marwaris originating from Rajasthan and the Vanias from
Gujerat joining the Parsees as the dominant entrepreneurial groups at least
until the second global economy.[46] It would certainly be possible to construct
an argument that colonialism and the institutional racism that went with it
impacted entrepreneurial cognition. In crude terms, entrepreneurs who were
not white men from Western countries may have felt less qualified to pursue
opportunities, even if they were not. However this does not readily explain
why some ethnic groups became dynamic entrepreneurs in India.

There are some puzzles, therefore, about the historical relationship between
institutions and entrepreneurship, and the same goes if we explore the relationship with human capital. In striking contrast to Goldin's description of
education in early twentieth-century America, many countries in nineteenth-
century Asia, Latin America, and Africa had limited formal education provision, confined largely to the elites. This may have affected the supply of
domestic entrepreneurship in many non-Western countries in the nineteenth
century. There is a large literature on developed countries regarding the importance of professional managerial cadres as firms grew, and of the role of
educational institutions in the background of such managers. Poor educational
levels for the mass of the population also made the management of labor far

more difficult because of poor skill levels and low productivity. The lack of a theory of the supply of entrepreneurship means that the exact impact of low human capital development on the level and allocation of entrepreneurship is less clear-cut. It is probably safe to assume, however, that extreme social inequality, poor literacy levels, and lack of technical education reduced the available pool of productive entrepreneurs in many countries. In the case of colonial India, the high cost of skilled labor has been identified as one important reason, alongside other resource constraints including the high cost of capital, why the country remained inclined to small-scale traditional manufacture.[47]

The quality of Japanese human capital development was plausibly an important driver of the faster development of modern entrepreneurship and management there. Japan had achieved high literacy levels well before Perry arrived in 1853. The Meiji regime enacted compulsory primary education in 1872, before Britain and many other Western countries, and established the first Western-style universities soon afterwards. The *zaibatsu* were recruiting large numbers of university graduates as managers by the 1900s.[48]

Much still remains to be understood about the relationship between education, entrepreneurship, and managerial effectiveness. In nineteenth-century Europe, Sweden's high educational level even when it was very poor, peripheral economy has been widely regarded as important in enabling the country to "catch up" as the century progressed.[49] Yet eighteenth- and nineteenth-century China had widespread literacy which did not translate into modern economic growth.[50] Argentina's fast economic growth during the first global economy can be correlated with the highest literacy rate in Latin America. In 1900 the country's literacy rate of 52 percent was far above Mexico's 22 percent and Brazil's 25 percent, if far lower than the rates of the United States and Canada.[51] Yet such educational attainments could not prevent the country's subsequent poor economic performance for the remainder of the twentieth century.

Nor can human capital be treated as entirely exogenous to firms. Early Japanese industrialization was plagued by skill shortages. Japanese firms responded with in-house training, beginning with shipyards in the 1890s. In turn, a better-trained workforce was able to learn and diffuse techniques from abroad. Centuries of seclusion left Japan with a lack of knowledge of foreign countries and languages. One response was the institutional innovation of using specialist trading companies to engage in importing and exporting. These giant firms, based on the British trading companies in Asia, rationed scarce managerial resources and provided a means to share knowledge about foreign markets and sources of supply.[52]

This brief survey of the historical evidence suggests that neither institutions nor human capital are fully discrete, and that historical case studies provide different answers to the question about what matters most. There are likely to have been other factors at work also. To have entrepreneurship, there must be entrepreneurial opportunities. The growth and size of the American market provides a key component of the Chandlerian explanation for the emergence of large integrated firms in the United States. It seems plausible that both in the case of Britain, the first industrializer, and Japan, the first successful non-Western catch-up, the identification of entrepreneurial opportunities, and the building of managerial structures which permitted their exploitation, were facilitated by geographically compact domestic markets and unusually large capital cities.

The market opportunities for firms and entrepreneurs in most of Asia, Latin America, and Africa were more constrained. They often faced great difficulties if they wanted to sell beyond their local markets because of poor transport and communications infrastructure. In India, market conditions have been identified as one explanation why India's powerful and rich merchants in the seventeenth and eighteenth centuries left manufacturing in the hands of small artisans, pointing to fragmented markets, inadequate transport infrastructure, lawlessness, and disregard for property rights.[53] These constraints were relaxed as the British colonial regime imposed political stability and promoted transport infrastructure, but a well-established argument in the literature on nineteenth-century India has maintained that the small scale of the domestic market retarded the growth of a modern machinery industry.[54]

Yet it was often foreign firms, or ethnic minorities, which took advantage of expanding opportunities. There may well have been an issue of entrepreneurial cognition. Most local entrepreneurs may not have been well informed about the pace of change in advanced economies, and less knowledgeable about their markets, including the market for skilled expertise. Language may have been a factor. A lack of English-speaking ability might have constrained access to advanced knowledge in Latin America. The former imperial powers, Spain and Portugal, were in the backward south of Europe, and were not good role models of modern industrial growth.

Despite the criticism earlier of the overgeneralizations and stereotypes found in the broad cultural explanations of entrepreneurial performance, there has been a renewed interest in the view that cultural values are likely to have framed cognition and exploitation of opportunities. North's search for explanations of the "wide and still widening gap between rich and poor countries" has led him to consider the importance of immensely varied cultures with different combinations of supernatural beliefs and institutions."[55] The problem remains how to really test such a hypothesis against historical evidence. Cross-cultural management theory offers one avenue, by showing how cultures both differ in core values, and how this affects (if not determines) business organization and firm strategies. Hofstede's classic study identified four dimensions of culture which differed between countries: readiness to tolerate inequality (Power Distance); tolerance for uncertainty (Uncertainty Avoidance); relationships between the individual and the collective (Individualism); and attitudes towards gender roles (Masculinity). Hofstede added a new dimension of "Long-Term Orientation" during the late 1980s, followed by a sixth dimension called "Indulgence versus Restraint" in 2010.[56]

It is not implausible to believe, if challenging to demonstrate robustly, that the northern European and Anglo-Saxon combination of individualism and tolerance for uncertainty yielded advantages to their firms in entrepreneurial endeavors over those in many developing countries, especially at the time when starting new industries was quite risky. It is believed, for example, that Chinese mining firms lost out to Western firms in early twentieth-century Malaya because they did not want to risk making large capital investments in new technologies.[57] Of course it is debatable if the cultural characteristics identified by Hofstede, which are based on a study of a large number of IBM employees in 1980, bear much relationship to the cultural values in the nineteenth century. It is known that cultural characteristics change slowly because they are passed on through child-rearing practices, but it is also known that exogenous shocks and in some cases government policies can shift cultural values.

The economist Casson has gone furthest in identifying the features of societies which may cause them to differ in their receptiveness of entrepreneurship. He defines an "entrepreneurial culture" using theories of entrepreneurship that emphasize the functions of innovation, risk-bearing, and arbitrage. Entrepreneurial cultures, he proposes, can thus be defined in terms of attributes – such as scientific and systems thinking – that promote or retard these functions in a society. Cultural differences towards information and "trust" levels may have been especially important in explaining variations in the quality of entrepreneurial judgments.[58]

It is evident that business enterprises in many non-Western societies were often challenged to grow beyond a certain size because their societies found it hard to "trust" non-family members as either managers or equity-holders. Japan was an unusual society where "blood ties" were not decisive in determining trust levels. Arguably, the rapid Japanese move to employing professional managers may have reflected cultural traditions of adopting sons. In science-based industries, in which the optimal scale of production is large, a willingness to employ professional managers became important. Chandler famously ascribed British relative decline against the United States in the late nineteenth century to a preference for family firms rather than professional management. As originally constructed, however, the argument has attracted much criticism, and indeed has spurred a vibrant literature on the merits of family-owned and -managed business.[59]

The early literature from the Harvard Center and others on entrepreneurs and firms in non-Western countries was weakened by assumptions that deviations from American managerial practices should be a priori regarded as a sign of failure, or evidence of irrational cultural values. Much of the early literature on Latin American entrepreneurship in the nineteenth century blamed lack of economic growth on an alleged commercial and speculative ethos of the region's entrepreneurs. The diversified business groups which appeared during and after the nineteenth century in Latin America and elsewhere were regarded as inherently inefficient, and driven by social and political motivations rather than business logic. However, while the predominance of family-owned, diversified business groups with strong links to political elites is uncontested, later research has provided a better understanding of the rationality behind organizational structures such as diversified business groups arising from weaknesses in capital markets, shortage of managerial resources, and high transactions costs. Within such conditions, business groups can be, and often are, the most effective forms of business organization. In other words, they are characterized as examples more of productive than of redistributive entrepreneurship.[60]

Somewhat similarly, Indian firms in the newly created modern textile industry of the mid-nineteenth century innovated institutionally by abandoning the partnership form favored by their British counterparts and forming joint stock companies linked into wider groups by equity, debt, and cross-directorships. The resulting "managing agency" system, long disparaged in the literature as an idiosyncratic morass of conflicts of interest, is now seen as an effective organizational response to economic conditions, and was subsequently copied by British expatriate firms active in India.[61]

Indeed, as entrepreneurs in developing countries began catching up with their Western counterparts, they were often successful in developing hybrid organizational forms well adapted to their local contexts. In China, the new modern business enterprises which appeared in the early twentieth century typically combined the formal organization of Western-style corporations with traditional, well-established business practices from China's pre-industrial past. A study of the rapid growth of Shanghai's print machinery industry from the late nineteenth century has shown that in this industry, unlike in others such as textiles, Chinese entrepreneurs were so successful that they were able to replace foreign machine imports with products from the local machine industry.[62]

However, the preeminence of ethnic and religious minorities in entrepreneurial activity does point towards some combination of cultural and institutional explanations of retarded entrepreneurship. As many Asian, African, and Latin American countries began to industrialize, minorities or immigrants were especially important in new firm creation. These included Chinese in

Southeast Asia, Indians in East Africa, Lebanese in West Africa, Italians in Argentina, and French in Mexico.[63] Their success was often ascribed to particular ethical or working practices, but their role is more plausibly explained as a demonstration of the challenges faced by entrepreneurs in societies where trust levels were poor, information flows inadequate, institutions weak, and capital scarce. In such situations, small groups with shared values held major advantages as entrepreneurs. If, in addition, they established an intermediary role between "more local locals" and Western firms, they could secure easier access to knowledge and information from and about Western countries.

The prominent role of a few groups in modern industry in India from the nineteenth century has received much attention. The role of the tiny Parsee community around Bombay has been variously described as the result of close relations with the colonial authorities, "outsider" minority status, and a "Protestant–style" work ethic.[64] The Marwaris were far less close to the British. Indeed, a number of families, like the Bajaj who financed and supported Gandhi's campaign of civil disobedience against the British, became active in the Independence struggle. Other explanations have been found in unique cost-accounting methods and the work ethos which seems to feature in most accounts of minority successes.[65]

Wolcott has combined both cultural and institutional factors to explain the preeminence of Indian minorities. She relates the situation to India's caste system, and argues that the payoffs to entrepreneurship differed across caste lines. Members of the moneylending and trading castes like the Marwaris could enforce contracts through reputation, and membership deterred cheating. As a result, they were efficient at providing financial and other resources to entrepreneurs within their own castes. However, the large number of potential entrepreneurs outside these groups lacked privileged access to these informal financial networks, which reduced their incentives to engage in productive entrepreneurship.[66]

The ethnic clustering in modern entrepreneurship in India, and elsewhere, was striking, but as Roy has suggested, another way to look at such clustering is geographically. Before 1914 Bombay and Calcutta accounted for half the modern factories in India, and even more of related services such as banking and insurance. Unlike in other cities in India, they had grown through the activities of the East India Company, and were outward-oriented and cosmopolitan. In these two port cities, Roy observes, "modern Indian business enterprise and business families congregated and recreated a globalized world with strong Indian characteristics."[67]

The emergence of hubs such as Bombay, and modern entrepreneurship in general, took place within the context of the wider politico-economic environment. With perhaps the single exception of Britain in the eighteenth century, governments have contributed to entrepreneurship and firm growth not only by providing (or not providing) institutional rules of the game, but also through a wide range of policy measures. The role of the state in catching up from economic backwardness has been debated since the writings of Gershenkron decades ago.[68] However, the ways in which governments facilitated entrepreneurial perception and exploitation of opportunities has not been the primary emphasis of this research. Yet it is difficult to account for the rapid economic growth of the United States in the nineteenth century without mentioning government policy. The Federal government purchased, or annexed, much of the present-day territory of the country, and then largely gave it away. State governments were active promoters of infrastructure investment. High levels of tariff protection widened the market opportunities for entrepreneurs and firms by shutting out cheaper imports from Europe.[69] The Japanese government was prevented by Western countries from tariff protection, but it subsidized the first modern factories before privatizing them. It distorted markets by favoring *zaibatsu* through subsidies and the allocation of business. The government was not center-stage in the first wave of Meiji industrialization, as many of its interventions were poorly managed or not purposeful, but it provided a broadly favorable context for entrepreneurship.[70]

We can see the impact of the wider political economy in other settings. Explanations for why ethnic Chinese business became disproportionately important in Southeast Asia typically stress cultural factors, including the role of the family, dialect groups, and the Confucian value system. With respect to the latter, it has often been argued that social trust, the social obligations that bind family and lineage, was strengthened by Confucian belief, and that that provided the bedrock of commercial networking. Yet while some or all of these features may be significant, the growth of Chinese entrepreneurship in Southeast Asia also has to be placed within a wider political economy context. From the fourteenth century, the region's rulers favored foreign over local merchants because the latter might pose a political threat. Through the seventeenth century local trading communities, whether Malay or Filipino, continued to flourish, but the Chinese role was strengthened by the arrival of Western merchants, for the Chinese positioned themselves as intermediaries. By the late nineteenth century, the Chinese had secured the position of revenue farmers across the region, in both colonial and non-colonial areas. This made them indispensable for local and colonial governments, while providing a source of funds for their business interests.[71]

There are other examples of the importance of public policy in shaping entrepreneurial opportunities and outcomes in the nineteenth century. Take the fundamental shift in comparative advantage in the global copper industry away from Chilean dominance in the mid-nineteenth century to US dominance by the 1890s. By the end of the century, US firms were not only out-competing Chilean ones in the export market for copper but were also undertaking FDI in production in South America. The competitive advantage of US firms was developed by an array of public policies that supported the development of the infant industry in the United States. Industrial mining and smelting of copper prospered in the nineteenth century not because of free enterprise, but precisely because of its opposite, which was the extent and quality of government.[72]

Conversely, when local governments were able to change the rules of the game for their firms, the result was often if not always the creation of productive business enterprises. Take the case of late nineteenth-century Uruguay. Its banking market had been dominated by British banks. However in 1896 a local bank was formed to which the government gave the sole right of note issue. By 1914 it had captured a large share of the domestic banking market. This formed part of a wider story of the growth of viable and successful locally owned banks in Latin America. In Argentina, a first wave of local banks failed disastrously in the early 1890s. However a second generation, which explicitly adopted many of the prudent lending practices which characterized British banks and combined them with more entrepreneurial policies of opening numerous branches, was much more successful and by 1914 had captured well over half the Argentinian banking market.[73]

Less direct forms of geopolitical power also played a growing role in expanding opportunities for international entrepreneurs from powerful countries, especially after the turn of the century. For instance, "Dollar Diplomacy," an official US government policy first implemented in the early twentieth century, provided State Department support for US enterprises operating in Latin America. Such diplomatic (and often implicit military) backing was often important for entrepreneurs and firms making large fixed investments abroad or negotiating special concessions from a host government. In the case of certain forms of cross-border entrepreneurship, such as in natural resources, infrastructure, and agriculture, diplomatic influence and assistance were often critical for attaining the kinds of concessions needed to do business.[74]

It was within the context of Western geopolitical power that European and US firms surged abroad to the Rest looking for commodities and markets. By 1914 world FDI was not only substantial compared with world output, but was also primarily located in the non-Western world. Latin America and Asia were especially important as host regions, representing 33 and 21 percent respectively of the total world stock of FDI.[75] If domestic entrepreneurship in many developing countries struggled to get traction, it needs to be explained why foreign entrepreneurship did not exercise a more productive effect on local business systems.

The industrial composition of this FDI provides a partial answer. Possibly one-half of total world FDI was invested in natural resources, and a further one-third in services, especially finance, insurance, and transporting commodities and foodstuffs. Manufacturing FDI primarily went to serve the markets of the West, while most FDI in the Rest was in either resources or services.

Yet the establishment and maintenance of mines, oil fields, plantations, shipping depots, and railroad systems involved the transfer of packages of organizational and technological knowledge to host economies. Given the absence of appropriate infrastructure in developing countries, foreign enterprises frequently introduced not only technologies specific to their activities, but also social technologies such as police, postal, and education systems. In so far as lack of financial resources handicapped local firms, foreign banks contributed to building modern financial infrastructures. The British overseas banks which operated in Asia, Africa, and Latin America may have been focused on trade finance and found it safer to lend to expatriates than locals, whose creditworthiness was hard to assess, but they were more flexible in their lending policies than was once thought.[76] Moreover it is not evident that availability of finance was the major handicap to entrepreneurship in the Rest. There were high levels of Chinese investment in foreign shipping and insurance companies, banks, and manufacturing companies before 1914, and Chinese businessmen sat on the boards of companies.[77]

Perhaps a greater positive impact came from the building of transport and distribution infrastructure, which enabled entrepreneurs to access world markets for the first time. British, French, and other civil engineering and construction firms built railroads, ports and harbor facilities, bridges, urban sanitation systems, dams, and electricity and gas works all over Latin America, Asia, and parts of Africa. Between the late nineteenth century and 1914 residents of most of the world's cities were provided with access to electricity in their homes or at work, or else in the form of street lighting.[78] A global communications network based on submarine cables was put in place. In so far as access to markets had been a constraint, these investments relieved it.

However, spillovers and linkages to local entrepreneurs were limited by the nature of global capitalism at the time. Many natural resource investments were enclavist. Minerals and agricultural commodities were exported with only the minimum of processing. Most value was added to the product in the developed economies. Foreign firms were large employers of labor at that time, but training was only provided to local employees to enable them to fill unskilled or semiskilled jobs The French-controlled Suez Company, which built and operated the Suez Canal in Egypt between 1854 and 1956, had a major stimulus on the Egyptian economy, but until 1936 the Egyptian staff were almost exclusively unskilled workers.[79]

The nature of the industries and these employment practices meant that the diffusion of organizing and technological skills to host economies was far less than to developed economies. Diffusion worked best when there were already established firms which could be stimulated to become more competitive by foreign firms, or had the capacity to absorb workers who moved on from foreign firms. This was the case in Japan, where – for example – the long-established textile machinery manufacturer Toyoda was able to recruit workers from the US auto companies Ford and General Motors in the interwar years to build its new Toyota subsidiary. The process was facilitated by nationalistic government policies focused on removing the US-owned firms from the country.[80]

Nor were foreign companies typically transformers of domestic institutions. While theoretically they may have been channels to transfer aspects of the institutional arrangements in their home countries to their hosts, for the most part they reinforced local institutions. This was most directly seen in the concession system. In order to entice firms to make investments in mines, railroads, and so on, foreign firms were often given large concessions often involving freedom from taxation and other requirements over very long periods. It is not easy to imagine alternative options. Local entrepreneurs typically lacked knowledge of and access to foreign markets where these products were sold. Their ability to hire foreign managers was constrained by reputation as much as by capital. However in some cases local dictators also preferred to give contracts and concessions to foreign entrepreneurs rather than to local ones so as not to build up powerful domestic rivals.

Concessions worked to lock in already suboptimal institutional arrangements even when they had positive economic outcomes. In Mexico, President Diaz's contracts and concessions to the British engineering contractor Weetman Pearson were effective in securing major infrastructure improvements in railroads, ports, and the drainage of Mexico City, and Pearson also laid the basis for the successful Mexican oil industry. Yet Pearson's very success strengthened the autocratic and crony-capitalist regime of Diaz.[81]

Elsewhere the downsides of the concession system were even more apparent. A prime example is the malign influence of United Fruit, the US banana company, in central American countries such as Guatemala. This country had emerged as an independent nation in 1821 with an unequal social hierarchy based on race. The white population was positioned at the top, owned the majority of the land, and controlled the political system through a series of dictators. The second class consisted of so-called "*ladinos*"– the mixed-race population or Westernized Indians. At the bottom was the majority of the population, of Mayan descent. Guatemala had an unstable political system after independence from Spain in 1821. In 1898, General Manuel Estrada Cabrera took power, and stayed in power by repeated reelections of questionable legitimacy until 1920. During his presidency, he encouraged investment in infrastructure, promoted the export of goods, and gave United Fruit its first concessions for banana cultivation. The country was transformed into a "banana republic," with bananas dominating the export economy. Cabrera and his successors saw United Fruit as a vehicle to modernize the country through its investments in railroads, telegraph lines, and housing, as well as plantations. However, the plantation system also reinforced the unequal social structures in Guatemala, which served as a massive obstacle to the development of a more entrepreneurial culture. Moreover, because the position of United Fruit was supported by the United States government, change was made even harder to achieve. When during the early 1950s the democratically elected government of Jacobo Arbenz sought to achieve agrarian reform, with the specific aim of developing a market economy, it was overthrown in a CIA-inspired coup, a military dictator was put in its place, and United Fruit was restored to its lands.[82]

The nature of the first global economy, then, meant that there was limited diffusion of entrepreneurship and organizing capabilities from Western firms in developing countries. Their primary impact was often to lock in countries as resource providers, and to reinforce institutional constraints on domestic entrepreneurship rather than removing them. This partly explains why the domestic entrepreneurial response to globalization was weaker than might have been imagined, since at its heart lay a lagged understanding of the opportunities offered by the new global economy combined with problems in building effective business organizations which could absorb foreign technological and organizational skills. Public policy was one way to break constraints on local entrepreneurs – it was certainly effective in promoting the growth of the United States – but few governments in developing countries had either the autonomy or the capacity to pursue effective public policies.

However by 1914 the evidence, patchy as it might be, suggests that the lag was being addressed in India, China, and some countries in Latin America. The business enterprises being built, whether Japanese *zaibatsu*, Latin American business groups, or hybrid Chinese manufacturing firms, were often not US-style managerial corporations, but they were quite effective responses to local conditions.

GLOBALIZATION CONSTRAINED

The outbreak of World War I in 1914 began a process which saw the meltdown of the first global economy. The levels of integration in capital and commodity markets fell back sharply to levels seen in the mid-nineteenth century. During the 1930s high tariffs and tight exchange controls closed down the global economy in favor of regional trading blocs and currency areas. This represented a reversal of globalization, although as noted in Chapter 1, the term "de-globalization" may be too exaggerated a description. There was, however, certainly a new interest in the nationality of ownership, and a growing resentment beyond the West at the ownership of assets by foreign firms. The Russian Revolution in 1917 was followed by the sequestration of foreign property. By the 1930s political nationalism was rampant. The Mexican nationalization of foreign oil companies in 1938 was a landmark event which asserted national sovereignty over natural resources.[83]

In part, the growth of policy restrictions on global capitalism should be seen as the result of a revolt of the people who had not done well out of the globalization of the previous decades. Nineteenth-century-style global capitalism had made some Western countries rich, and left the remainder more aware that they were relatively poor. It had frequently strengthened inequalities, and had locked countries into positions of being resource-providers. There were many other losers, such as the peoples subject to the indignities of colonialism, Muslims who perceived their religion and its values as denigrated by Western colonialism, and so on.

The two world wars and the Great Depression caused enormous damage to global welfare, but were not without their benefits for entrepreneurs and firms in developing countries. They expanded market opportunities for such firms by cutting supplies from Europe, or protecting local firms from foreign competition. Japan's precocious modern industrial growth, underwritten by large state spending, was rescued from a likely meltdown by World War I, which enabled its textile and other industries to break into other Asian markets. In India, and other European colonies, the war accelerated a shift of political power to local people as nationalism accelerated. Foreign firms for the first time began to consider Indians and Africans for filling managerial posts – not through a sudden conversion to the merits of diversity in the workforce, but because they were short of money and locals were cheaper than expatriates.[84]

There was a strong growth of Indian-owned business from World War I. Modern industrialization spread from the small confines of parts of western and eastern India to many other regions of India. A major turning point was the entry of the Marwaris into industry. During the war Ghanshyam Das Birla led the Marwari community into its first sustained manufacturing investments. He was offended by the racism he encountered from the British, but he also studied and learned from them about modern business methods. During the interwar years the Marwaris and others greatly expanded their manufacturing investments, sometimes by buying the shares of British companies. Indian entrepreneurs invested in new industries such as sugar, paper, shipping, and chemicals, and challenged the British incumbents in jute and coal.[85]

There was also a significant growth of modern Chinese entrepreneurship, despite numerous institutional and infrastructural failings, and the determined efforts of the Nationalist Party governments of the interwar years to regulate and control the economy.[86] Zhang Jian founded the Dasheng textile mills in

Nantong in 1895, and this business evolved during the interwar years into a diversified business group in textiles, flour and oil milling, land development, and shipping.[87] In an important study of the pharmaceutical and Chinese medicine industry, Cochran has explored how Chinese entrepreneurs employed innovative advertising, retailing, and other strategies to build large businesses both in China and in Southeast Asia.[88]

There was evidence in the Middle East, too, of local entrepreneurs establishing modern business enterprises. In Egypt, under British occupation from the 1880s, new entrepreneurs drawn from various nationalities, including Egyptian and British, became active in economic diversification and industrialization, often in quite imaginative ways. Bank Misr was the creation of Egypt's dynamic business innovator, Tal'at Harb, who endeavored to promote new directions in the Egyptian economy after World War I. Influenced by the great German banks of the nineteenth century and believing that a large-scale, heavily capitalized, and Egyptian-run bank could lead the country out of its economic dependence on cotton exports, Tal'at Harb founded the bank and used its capital to create a host of Misr companies, including in textile manufacturing, shipping, and air travel. Bank Misr finally crashed in 1939 after becoming overextended and experiencing some serious managerial failures.[89]

In Turkey, also, modern entrepreneurship appeared. The Republic of Turkey was established in 1923 out of the ruins of the former Ottoman Empire, and was led by the modernizing general Kemal Atatürk. In the nineteenth-century Ottoman Empire, business had been primarily in the control of religious and ethnic minorities such as Greeks, Armenians, and Jews, many of whom were killed or fled the country following traumatic events during and after World War I. The new government offered subsidies and other support to aspiring entrepreneurs, and during the 1930s established public enterprises to drive modern economic growth and employed selective policies that led to the dispossessing of non-Muslim businesses. Within this context, Vehbi Koç was one of a new generation of Islamic Turks who began to build businesses. Beginning in grocery and leather, he moved into construction, securing multiple government contracts during the 1930s, as well as acting as a distributor for Ford automobiles. After making very large profits from truck importing during World War II, a war Turkey stayed out of until just before the end, Koç began to build what became Turkey's largest diversified business group during the postwar decades.[90]

These entrepreneurial pioneers across the Rest faced multiple challenges. Chinese firms, for example, had to deal with chronic political instability, and the Japanese military attack on the country after 1931. Many countries were badly affected by the Great Depression and secular decline in commodity prices. Building managerial competences was hard. Family businesses, as most of the ventures were, faced constant tensions as they grew in scale and needed expertise beyond the family. Often, even as nationalistic sentiments rose, local entrepreneurs simply faced a credibility gap even from their compatriots that they could be as competent as Western firms. Given the challenges, however, the catch-up of business in parts of the Rest during the interwar years was perhaps even more striking.

During the post-1945 decades a new global economy began to emerge in the capitalist countries of the West and Japan as trade barriers and exchange controls were lowered. However, much of the Rest either opted out of global capitalism or else sought to highly regulate it. As the European colonial empires were dismantled, there was often an aggressive reaction against the businesses of the former colonial power, and sometimes all foreign investment. The relatively small number of expropriations without compensation until the 1970s – when a period of large-scale expropriation began – reflected the power and determination of the United States to protect foreign investments, but Western countries were unable to reestablish an international legal regime which guaranteed the property rights of international investors. The 1970s saw the end of Western ownership of much of the world's natural resources, including oil, minerals, and plantations.

The postwar political environment was not well designed for the diffusion of entrepreneurial skills or organizational capabilities to the Rest. As political risk and government restrictions mounted, Western MNEs focused investment, trade, and knowledge flows on other developed countries. These countries offered the primary markets for advanced technological and consumer products. In new advanced-technology industries, MNEs located different parts of the value chain in different countries. In semiconductors, for example, from the 1970s firms such as Intel placed assembly stages in developing countries, but the higher-value-added activities were located in developed countries.[91] Overall, by 1980 two-thirds of world FDI was located in Western Europe and North America. Britain alone hosted more foreign direct investment than the whole of Africa and Asia combined. Within the developing world, there was enormous concentration of inward FDI. In Asia, for example, most FDI was located in a handful of Southeast Asian countries.[92]

This was the classic era of the large M-form (multidivisional) corporations which served as the powerhouse of innovation in high-technology manufacturing industries. US-based firms were preeminent in new technologies such as computers, and they typically sought to maintain innovation and other value-added activities within firm boundaries.[93] There was geographical clustering of knowledge also. During the 1950s and 1960s an unusual convergence of technological skills, educational institutions, and venture capital in California's Silicon Valley, combined with a pleasant climate, encouraged the emergence and clustering of numerous entrepreneurial firms which were to dominate innovation in many parts of the IT industry.[94]

MNEs concentrated innovation in their home countries. This may not always have been the case. There is aggregate evidence from patent data that the internationalization of technological activity by large manufacturing firms was quite extensive by the interwar years but then declined.[95] After 1945 US and Japanese firms especially did their innovation at home. European companies conducted more innovation in foreign laboratories, but they were located overwhelmingly in other European countries or the United States. The firms with the most dispersed innovatory technology were in "traditional" industries such as food, drink, and tobacco, building materials, and petroleum. In computers, aerospace, and motor vehicles, there was a strong propensity to concentrate technological activities at home.[96] Few MNEs undertook basic R&D in developing countries. A rare exception, discussed further in Chapter 8, was Unilever's affiliate in India. In general, however, cutting-edge advanced technological knowledge was locked within the boundaries of large Western firms, or else in clusters located primarily in the United States, notably Silicon Valley.

Nevertheless, there were some spillovers from MNEs in developing countries in the middle decades of the twentieth century. Large Western firms such as Unilever, Shell, and Citibank became important sources of management training in developing countries and important diffusers of management knowledge. The local managers recruited by these firms sometimes joined local firms, or launched startups. As Chapter 8 shows, Unilever was at the forefront of recruiting "locals" to management positions in India and other developing countries from the 1950s. Citibank was also a large recruiter and trainer of managerial talent in developing countries.[97]

A second spillover came from the emulation of foreign business models. As is discussed further in Chapter 3, Avon, the leading American direct seller in the beauty industry, began expanding to developing countries from the 1950s. The model proved especially relevant to developing countries as it enabled thousands of women salespeople to earn extra income from direct selling, and to become quasi-entrepreneurs in the process. The evident success of the business model spawned local competitors during the 1960s and 1970s, for example Brazil's Natura, which grew to be that country's largest beauty company.[98]

Yet between 1945 and 1980 many countries in the Rest looked to models other than firms like Avon or global capitalism in general to catch up. At one extreme, the Communist regimes in the Soviet Union, Eastern Europe, China, and elsewhere cut themselves off from global capitalism and sought to overcome the constraints on the modern economic growth of their countries by making heavy investments in human capital, and by forcibly mobilizing resources to promote heavy industries. This Communist model had very mixed results. There were significant achievements in improving educational levels and the manufacture of capital goods. However, such overall gains were outweighed by catastrophic policies towards agriculture, the closing of economies to flows of international trade and knowledge, and the creation of institutions which distorted incentives and promoted corruption. Occasionally quasi-capitalist firms were permitted – East Germany allowed some quasi-Mittelstand firms in toys and musical instruments because of their export importance, but for the most part the institutional and cultural consequences of a business system based on a relationship between large state-owned enterprises and central planners was negative. China's vast and inefficient state-owned firms became a long-term drag on that country's economic performance.[99]

At the other extreme, there were a handful of cases of developing countries which fully embraced global capitalism. Virtually from the state's full independence in the mid-1960s, Singapore had one of the most open policy regimes towards foreign MNEs anywhere in the world. Foreign-owned companies drove an export-led, labor-intensive export strategy which transformed the country in three decades from a poor island state to one of the world's richest countries in terms of per capita income. However the country relied on the state to develop local firms. A number of state-owned companies, including Singapore Airlines, became successful, globally competitive business enterprises. Singapore Airlines developed a competent management which used imaginative marketing strategies and bold investment strategies to create a world-class airline, implausibly located in a country with no domestic air market, providing a role model for the much later success of airlines based in a number of Arabian Gulf states. Singapore was less successful at promoting private sector entrepreneurship. The water treatment company Hyflux, founded by female entrepreneur Olivia Lum in 1989, which had revenues of $450 million by 2013, was sufficiently atypical to attract constant media attention.[100]

The role of MNEs in driving Singapore's fast economic growth rested on rather specific circumstances. Singapore's initial export strategy coincided both with the new strategies of MNEs in electronics and other industries to embark on policies of world-wide sourcing, and with anti-MNE policies in much of the rest of the developing world. It had a long tradition as a commercial entrepot, had a majority population of overseas Chinese with network links elsewhere in the region, and inherited from the British both a set of legal and other institutions, and a wide knowledge of English. Above all the government pursued policies, including repressive controls over wages and political dissent, in an unusually effective fashion.[101] The level of authoritarianism could probably only have been achieved in a small island.

A less successful version of this strategy was followed by neighboring Malaysia. Malaysia attracted vast investments from electronics companies into free trade zones established after 1971. This was successful in creating exports and jobs. Malaysian employment in electronics grew from 600 in the mid-1970s to 300 000 in 1995. By 2000, electronics accounted for over a quarter of Malaysia's manufacturing employment. However linkages with the surrounding economy were weak and not capable of stimulating local entrepreneurship. This reflected tensions within the country following racial riots between the majority Malays and minority ethnic Chinese in the late 1960s. The Malay-controlled government, concerned that foreign MNEs should not strengthen local Chinese business interests, allowed foreign companies to have 100 percent ownership of subsidiaries provided they exported their entire output, thus tacitly discouraging joint ventures with local firms. During the 1980s, 80 percent of the intermediate products used in electronics manufacturing in the export-processing zones were imported from abroad. This meant that the industry imported almost as much as it exported in the 1980s. Local firms supplied basic items such as cardboard boxes. Low-value-added components – where Malaysian factories usually added only about 30 percent of the value of the product – accounted for around 80 percent of the country's electronics sector in the 1980s. Little design or R&D was undertaken in Malaysia, partly because of a shortage of graduate scientists and skilled technicians.[102]

Most countries fell between the Singapore and Communist models. Japan and South Korea developed trade and investment policy regimes which enabled their firms to access foreign knowledge through licensing and joint ventures, while ensuring that foreign firms were largely prevented from investing in their countries. In Japan, although firms such as Toyota were developing highly innovative management methods which would eventually enable them to sweep away their US competitors, they were also allowed to grow to scale behind high levels of tariff protection, and to export on the basis of an undervalued currency. Government policies were not exogenous to firms – they played a large role in lobbying governments to get the policies they wanted, for example, on the entry of foreign firms into Japan.[103]

The remarkable growth of South Korea from being one of the world's poorest countries in 1960 to becoming the home of global champion firms in a range of manufacturing industries is particularly striking. The story does not fit the institutional model well, for the period of industrial takeoff coincided with a repressive military dictatorship. The regime banned trade unions and pursued a protectionist industrial policy which favored a small number of large family-owned business groups known as *chaebol*, including Samsung, Hyundai, Daewoo, and Lucky-Goldstar. It was not the protection of property rights or constrained executives which promoted growth, but "good-for-growth" dictators.

The chaebol were the principal forces behind South Korean rapid growth as a major force in electronics and automobiles. Hyundai, until its breakup in 2001, was the largest chaebol. The firm was founded by Chung Ju-yung in

1947 as a construction firm, and Chung remained directly in control of the company until his death in 2001. From a humble beginning, the firm grew rapidly, entering automobiles from the 1960s, shipbuilding from the 1970s, and electronics from the 1980s. Each stage of growth was shaped by government policy, which provided timely assistance in terms of favorable financing, and domestic market protection. In return, Hyundai built new factories, provided desperately needed jobs, and earned valuable foreign exchange by exporting. Widely condemned as crony capitalism after the 1997 Asian financial crisis, the system also delivered fast economic growth rates over decades and world-class firms.[104]

In many other developing countries, governments intervened to enable their countries to modernize. There were major, and frequently under-estimated, advances in literacy rates, which were very low at the end of the colonial period in most of Asia and Africa, and in women's political and other rights. Industrial policies were less successful. Many long-established, locally owned business sectors were destroyed in the new era of state planning and controls. The process could be seen at a micro level in the case of the Bolivan tin industry. Before 1914 the Bolivian entrepreneur Simon Patiño displaced the foreign companies which had initially developed the Bolivian industry to become the largest Bolivian producer of tin concentrates. This output was at first sold to smelters in Britain and Germany. In 1916 Patiño secured control of the British smelter. The high physical asset specificity of the smelters required to deal with Bolivia's lode ores provided an incentive for this strategy. In 1929 Patiño also obtained control of one of the two Malayan smelters. Patiño himself moved abroad during the 1920s, registering his main corporate vehicle in the United States, possibly to raise capital. During the 1930s he formed one of three companies which accounted for almost half of the world's mining and tin smelting outside the Soviet Union, and he was prominent in forming the long-standing tin cartel. But in 1952 Bolivia became the first country to take over its tin industry. Although the Patiño group remained important in the marketing and smelting of tin, it was fragmented because of the loss of the ownership of the mines.[105]

The same phenomenon was evident in Africa. By the 1960s the large-scale private sector in Egypt had been entirely dismantled. Nigeria's business communities, which had appeared as dynamic forces in the postwar decades, became engaged in ethnic and regional rivalry that badly damaged their businesses. In Africa, the most successful firms were seen in South Africa, which underwent fast economic growth between 1950 and 1973. However, these firms grew in the context of the institutionalized racism in the form of the apartheid system adopted after 1948. This forced millions of blacks off their farms and out of urban areas, denying them education. These decades saw the creation of giant industrial groups, often closely linked to the government, although the economy as a whole began to experience poor performance from the 1970s.[106]

In many developing countries, state intervention continued to encourage local entrepreneurs to grow large businesses, using political contacts rather than technological capabilities. This did not necessarily prevent the creation of large firms, although it usually provided a weak foundation for international competitiveness. An example might be the Charoen Pokphand (CP) Group, which became the largest Thai-owned MNE. It was founded in 1921 by recent emigrants from China as a small venture selling imported vegetable seeds. It became a major animal feeds manufacturer after World War II. In 1971 a joint venture with a leading US poultry-breeding firm became the basis for the creation of a modern integrated chicken business in Thailand. Further diversification followed into real estate and retailing, often through joint ventures with Western firms. However the firm's major growth in telecommunications was achieved through CP's close contacts with leading Thai politicians, while its rapid growth in China after 1979 – where it became one of the largest foreign investors – was based on strong ethnic ties.[107]

There is general agreement that import substitution regimes of this era resulted in inefficient industries which were sheltered from international markets, and often burdened by webs of planning regulations and corruption. Yet capacities were created, albeit inefficient ones. Take the case of Brazil. In the early 1950s Brazil still had only the beginnings of an industrial base. Virtually all the motor vehicles used in Brazil were imported as knocked-down kits and assembled locally. During the second half of the 1950s an industrial policy was pursued which threatened assemblers with market closure if they did not manufacture locally. Even more critical was the policy towards the level of local content which meant that firms were forced to produce the "technological heart" of their vehicles in Brazil, which was definitely not on their agenda. Although the large US automobile manufacturers Ford and General Motors initially declined to commit themselves, Germany's Volkswagen, which was just embarking on global expansion, decided to begin making its Beetle car there. By 1968 eight foreign firms manufactured 280 000 vehicles in the country. A further surge of growth resulted in annual production of over one million vehicles by 1980. The level of protectionism had resulted in low productivity, and it was entirely foreign-owned as early ambitions that a locally owned industry would develop did not come to fruition. Still, Brazil had acquired the tenth-largest automobile industry in the world.[108]

It would also appear that import substitution regimes provided local firms with opportunities to achieve scale within their domestic markets. CEMEX, now the world's third-largest cement company, was founded in Mexico in 1906, and was able to grow in a rather sheltered environment, slowly becoming a regional player and then, in the 1970s, a national player.

In India, the era of the so-called "License Raj" also enabled firms to grow within their domestic market. Arguably, it laid the basis for the country's subsequently successful IT services sector. Postwar India had growing numbers of engineers owing to the many national institutes, engineering universities, and regional colleges established after 1947. However, it had little choice but to be totally dependent on US computer makers. During the 1960s and 1970s a handful of locally-owned firms were established to develop and run applications software for Indian companies and research institutions that had brought or leased mainframes from IBM and other US companies. Tata, which had remained India's largest business group, established the first of these firms, Tata Consulting Services, in 1968. This and other ventures remained small, however, until 1977, when, after the Indian government tightened the laws on foreign ownership of firms, IBM and other US firms divested.

The departure of IBM opened new opportunities for local firms. TCS developed a relationship with another US computer maker, Burroughs, which provided an important channel of new technology. In 1982 the startup Infosys was founded by the dynamic entrepreneur Narayana Murthy. The Indian firms built a strong trade association, NASSCOM, which sought to enhance and certify the quality of Indian firms. By the time policy regulation got underway in 1991, which gave Indian IT firms a freer hand in establishing marketing offices abroad and serving foreign clients, it had built strong organizational capabilities. The software industry became focused on Bangalore, where the British had established India's first aircraft factory during World War II, and which was the home of two of India's premier institutes of higher education in pure science. As at Silicon Valley, there was also a pleasant climate, at least before pollution began to increase. The government's establishment of a Software Technology Park, or export zone, in Bangalore in 1990, and an influx of expertise and contracts from the many expatriate Indians employed in Silicon Valley, were other influential factors in the growth of the Bangalore cluster.[109]

A similar tale could be told about other Indian industries. Both long-established business groups and new entrepreneurial firms were able to emerge in the import substitution era, despite the formidable battery of government controls and restrictions, and despite a considerable number of firms experiencing problems because of family succession issues. The highly protected domestic market itself created profitable opportunities for incumbents, although a serious tradeoff was widespread corruption. Many new business groups were created, including those by Marwari families such as the Goenkas and Khaitans, who built business groups by acquiring former British assets. Although the productivity and effectiveness of Indian firms was highly constrained by planning controls and other bureaucratic obstacles, once policies were changed after 1991 they had the scale to improve rapidly. It was a different legacy from that of the state-owned companies in China.

The era of constrained globalization, then, was challenging for the catch up of the Rest. During the interwar years there were significant examples of strong locally owned business enterprises developing in India, China, Egypt, and elsewhere. After World War II, many governments opted for state-led industrialization programs which frequently disrupted local firms, while blocking or discouraging foreign MNEs. Protectionism and restrictions on foreign firms did provide a context for new local firms to emerge, although these policies also provided incentives for firms to build skills in political contacts rather than technology. The growth of some of the larger business enterprises in the Rest, such as the South Korean chaebol and large South African corporations, took place in the context of authoritarian and repressive regimes, far removed in most respects from the institutional arrangements postulated by North and others as best for capitalist development.

By 1980 the gap in income levels between the rich nations and the Rest was bigger than in 1914. Japan was the only case of a spectacular catchup, with a number of other smaller East and Southeast Asian economies following at a distance. Elsewhere, state interventionist regimes had encountered growing problems of macroeconomic instability and hyperinflation by the 1970s. These problems provided the background for the shift back to liberal polices beginning in the following decade.

THE SECOND GLOBAL ECONOMY

The world spectacularly re-globalized from the 1980s, even if in some respects – such as immigration – it remains less globalized than before 1914. Among the most dramatic changes has been a worldwide policy embrace of global capitalism as emerging markets countries abandoned state planning and import substitution and sought export-led growth.

The fast economic growth seen in China and India, and certain other regions of the Rest also, provided strong support for Baumol's argument that shifts in the rules of the game can stimulate productive entrepreneurship. It is, once more, less supportive of the institutional argument. China's resurgence began under another good-for-growth dictator, Deng Xiaoping, who had little concern with controls over the executive, human rights, political rights, or intellectual property protection. In some respects, however, China is a showcase for the transforming impact of global capitalism, as foreign firms played a key role in starting China's economic growth, and accounted for a high percentage of China's exports. By the 1990s inward FDI accounted for 13 percent of gross domestic capital formation in China.[110]

Debates continue about how exactly China's experience should be interpreted. Huang argued nearly a decade ago that it said as much about the highly inefficient domestic firms which failed to capitalize on opportunities, in part because of continuing government interference in the allocation of financial resources, as it did about the transforming impact of global capitalism.[111] More recently it has become less evident that this argument can be sustained, given the growing global competitiveness of a cluster of Chinese firms, often state-owned. For a time there appeared to be an interesting "natural experiment" with Asia's two largest economies. While China embraced FDI, India made a mirror-image choice. Foreign companies played only a limited role in the Indian economy, while powerful globally competitive firms developed. However, more recently, there has been more inward investment in India than previously.

While MNEs played a dynamic role in China's economic growth, as they had earlier for Singapore, it is less apparent that this was a general phenomenon. Policy regimes everywhere shifted towards openness, and many countries started to offer incentives to MNEs to invest, rather than passing laws to block them. However, most research on the impact of foreign MNEs was sobering. There remained little or no aggregate evidence of spillovers from MNEs to local firms in the same sector, especially in developing countries. There was convincing evidence of positive linkages between MNEs and suppliers in many developing countries. Foreign affiliates were often more demanding in their specifications and delivery targets, while more willing to provide assistance and advice to local firms.[112] However in countries where export-oriented FDI was concentrated within free trade zones, linkages with local firms were often weak. MNEs needed to cross the "border" in order to source locally, and they often preferred to source in neighboring countries.

One explanation for limited spillovers was that MNEs had clear incentives to minimize leakages to real or potential competitors. In many developing countries local firms also continued to lack the capabilities to compete with large MNEs, and the greater the technology gap the harder this discrepancy was to make up. In branded consumer goods, such as cosmetics, foreign entry often resulted in local firms retreating into the lower end of the market, competing on cost rather than innovation. Research increasingly suggests that large MNEs struggled even with transferring organizational knowledge across borders, even within their own firm. As such corporations grew in complexity, the organizational obstacles to knowledge diffusion may have expanded.[113]

Nor was there evidence that MNEs were any more able, or willing, to change growth–restricting institutions. For example, the development of business in many of the poorest countries is handicapped by high corruption levels. Before the 1980s many MNEs probably contributed to these. More recently, most have been less willing than local firms to engage in bribery and tax evasion, in part because of the threat to corporate reputation as well as home country regulations such as the Corrupt Practices Act in the United States, but they do not have the capacity to change societal norms for the most part. In important markets, foreign firms typically will lend support to institutional norms, as seen in the willingness of US firms such as Cisco, the internet networking company, to facilitate the Chinese government's censorship of the internet and curbing of political dissent.[114]

A further limitation on the impact of MNEs was that as firms moved resources across borders in pursuit of profitable opportunities, not social good per se, they were more likely to reinforce trends than counter them. Despite the availability of technologies which permit the dispersal of economic activities, the second global economy saw a strong trend towards the geographical clustering of higher-value-added activities, whether they are in Silicon Valley, Bangalore, the City of London, or coastal regions of China.

In some instances, especially where the knowledge component of activities was not great, MNE strategies were footloose as a result. The experience of Mexico's *maquiladoras* – foreign-owned factories that assemble imported components for export – provided one example. These originated in 1965, when the United States and Mexico started a Border Industrialization Program, designed to reduce regional unemployment in the northern territories of Mexico. US-owned firms including GE, RCA, IBM, Coca Cola, and Ford were the first to locate their production in Mexico. There was a rapid growth of production following the 1982 Mexican debt crisis, when wage rates fell sharply. Employment in the maquiladoras rose from 100 000 in 1982 to 500 000 in 1992. The implementation of NAFTA in 1994 resulted in a further boost. By 2000 employment had reached 1.3 million, and the sector accounted for over 40 percent of total Mexican exports. However there were two downsides. First of all, there were practically no Mexican spinoffs from all this investment. Second, the investment was vulnerable to greater attractions elsewhere. Between 2001 and 2004 employment the Mexican maquiladoras fell by 200 000 as firms shifted factories to China, although rising wage costs in China substantially reversed this trend over the following decade.

Nevertheless, certain aspects of global capitalism have evolved in ways which delivered more opportunities for firms and entrepreneurs based in the Rest. An important development was the disintegration of the boundaries of M-form firms during the 1970s and 1980s as many large US and European-owned M-form corporations suffered from growing managerial diseconomies and low rates of innovation caused by size and diversification.[115] The result was divestment of "non-core" businesses, outsourcing of many value-added activities once performed within corporate borders, and the formation of alliances with other firms which acted as suppliers and customers, or as partners in innovation. The second global economy became more complex than previously as a result. While large corporations remained powerhouses of innovation spending and market power, they formed components of a world-wide web of inter-firm connections.

The disintegration of production systems and their replacement by networks of inter-firm linkages lowered barriers for new entrants. The growth of outsourcing to contract manufacturers, for example, created many opportunities for such firms. In China networks of small and medium-sized enterprises flourished as original equipment manufacturers, establishing influential positions in world supply chains in the fields of low or mid-level technology. The growth of Galanz was one example. Founded in 1978 as a company that dealt in the trading of duck feathers, Galanz began producing OEM Toshiba-branded microwave ovens in 1993. Galanz later purchased the appliance division from Toshiba. By the following decade Galanz had become the world's largest microwave manufacturer. Within a network-type global economy, firms from emerging markets were able to piggyback on incumbent Western or Japanese firms as customers through subcontracting, linkages, and leverages. Although they lacked the size and technological capabilities of incumbents there was the potential to grow by leveraging resources from others through joint ventures and contract relationships.[116]

If a major constraint for firms based in the Rest was not only the existence of entrepreneurial opportunities but also the building of organizational capabilities to exploit them, then a number of developments during the second global economy alleviated this challenge, and facilitated "accelerated internationalization."[117]

First, diaspora assumed a renewed importance as transferors of entrepreneurship and capital, and means by which firms could access management talent. The revitalized use of diaspora reflected changes in policies in China and India especially, making them more attractive locations to do business and encouraging diaspora to return. After 1980, ethnic Chinese firms based in Hong Kong and Taiwan, and later elsewhere, became the leading foreign investors as China liberalized its economy. They enjoyed connections (*guanxi*) in China, which reduced the transactions costs of investment by offering contacts with public authorities and inside information, and were welcomed by the Chinese government.

During the 1990s the Indian diaspora began to serve the same function in India. Although the Indian diaspora had its origins in the nineteenth century, when merchants and laborers had emigrated to other parts of Asia and Africa under the umbrella of the British Empire, a professional diaspora left India during the 1960s, often to the United States, seeking greater economic opportunities. Many engineers settled in Silicon Valley and made up a quarter of the workforce by the 1990s. As the Indian economy has grown from the 1990s, there has been a significant reverse flow back to India. This was assisted by the Indian government's new policy in 2003 of granting dual nationality to some overseas Indian residents abroad. These diaspora links provided valuable connections between Silicon Valley and Bangalore, encouraging business connections and capital flows.[118]

Second, both business schools and management consultants provided much easier access to new management knowledge, and they have played important roles in building organizational capabilities in firms. In postwar Europe both US management consultancies and business schools were influential diffusers of American managerial knowledge to Europe and other developed countries. The impact on emerging markets only became stronger later. McKinsey opened in India in 1992. From the 1990s leading US business schools have internationalized their faculty and student body. During the 1950s and 1960s, although the Harvard Business School helped develop business schools in Turkey, India, Nicaragua, and the Philippines, it remained primarily an American school in its ethos and teaching. However the percentage of US-born faculty decreased from 75 percent in 1980 to 66 percent in 2000. The student body moved from being almost entirely white American males in the 1950s to being one-third international in 2000.

Many of the most successful companies from emerging markets used the leading US consulting firms to advise on strategy, sent senior managers on executive programs at the top business schools, and recruited MBAs as graduates. None of this meant that such firms evolved as replicas of US firms, but it did mean that they had faster and better access to information about the latest managerial ideas in ways which were impossible 50 years before.

It is possible to see the influence of such conduits of managerial knowledge on the growth of global firms based in emerging markets such as CEMEX. After the 1980s the firm began to diversify from Mexico following the appointment of a new generation of the Zambrano family. Lorenzo Zambrano, the architect of a new international strategy, had been educated at Stanford Business School, and sought strategy advice from Boston Consulting Group. Responding to the Mexican economic crisis, CEMEX began to expand internationally, initially in the US, but then, when blocked by an anti-dumping judgment, to Europe. CEMEX was a leading user of information technology. In 1987 CEMEX created a satellite system to link the Mexican plants it had begun to acquire. By the late 1990s it ranked as the third most profitable company in the world, and was the third-largest cement company after Holderbank and Lafarge. By the following decade it was the largest cement company in the United States.[119]

A final, important, factor in the growth of MNEs from some emerging markets has been support from their host governments. Both the nature and motives of this support have varied widely. Emerging-market governments have sought to intervene in many ways to help their firms overcome the information, transaction, and resource constraints faced by their domestic firms.[120] Some governments, especially China, have used state-owned firms as national champions to pursue strategic objectives.[121] As governments from emerging markets often establish ties with governments of other emerging countries, firms sometimes leverage these contacts to facilitate their international growth.[122] In many countries, firms formed contacts and associations at multiple levels of their home economy – city, provincial, and national.[123]

The opportunities from a network-style world economy, the growth of organizational capabilities, and state support were not discrete factors in the growth of the new generation of MNEs based in emerging markets. These factors often combined to spur the growth of individual firms. This was evident in the growth of the internet router company Huawei Technologies, which was established in 1988 in the Shenzhen economic zone of China by Ren Zhengfei, a former major in the People's Liberation Army. It began as a small startup business selling telephone exchange equipment imported from Hong Kong, but grew rapidly after it began to make telecom equipment in the mid-1990s. By the new century it had become a leading supplier of digital switches and routers in China, and had secured 3 percent of the world market for routers by producing equipment at lower prices than its Western competitors.

The firm's initial growth was facilitated by the founder's close association with the People's Liberation Army and credit from the state-owned development bank. Wireless networking was a strategic industry for the Chinese government, not least because the equipment was the hardware which enabled the government to censor information and monitor activity on the internet. However Huawei's growth was not a simple story of growth based on political contacts and support. Ren Zhengfei implemented a clever strategy of building businesses in remoter and outlying cities in China before targeting the major cities where Cisco and others had built a market since the 1990s. He then repeated the strategy globally, first selling to countries like Russia, Brazil, and Thailand, before moving to more advanced markets, especially in Europe. Huawei also invested heavily in research, creating research centers in numerous locations around the world including Bangalore and Silicon Valley. Innovation was supported by an aggressive corporate culture which rewarded talent. The firm also benefited from alliances with Western firms, with whom it collaborated as well as competed. In 2003 Huawei formed a joint venture with 3Com, then a leading US-owned router firm, designed to facilitate sales to US corporate customers. In 2007 Bain Capital, the private equity firm, and Huawei reached an agreement to acquire 3Com altogether for $2.2 billion, but this was blocked by opposition from the Committee on Foreign Investment in the United States, an agency chaired by the secretary of the Treasury.[124] Although the US government continued to hinder Huawei's growth in the

United States, this did not prevent fast global expansion elsewhere. By 2012 Huawei was a $32 billion company active in 140 countries, selling high-end internet networking equipment.[125]

The growth of powerful globally active MNEs from the Rest was a singular feature of the second global economy. Huawei and CEMEX were the tip of a growing iceberg of emerging market giants such as Tata in India, Brahma, Embraer, Sabó, and Aracruz in Brazil, and Grupo Bimbo and Univision in Mexico.[126] In more aggregate terms, the share of FDI from emerging markets in total outward FDI rose from 8.3 percent to 15.9 percent between 1990 and 2009.[127]

CONCLUSION

This chapter has sought to integrate the role of entrepreneurship and firms into debates on why the Rest was slow to catch up with the West following the Industrial Revolution and the advent of modern economic growth. It has been suggested that poor human capital development and deficient institutions are important explanations, but not sufficient ones. The emphasis on national-level institutions seems particularly unhelpful, given strong regional variations in business activities between countries. The impact of institutions on the allocation of entrepreneurship between productive and redistributive activities takes the analysis to a deeper level, without entirely solving the problem, as the slow development of modern business in colonial India, and its skewed ownership, indicates. Entrepreneurs were also actors and not simply responders to institutions and resource endowments. They could train their own workers and they introduced investor protection into their own byelaws.

It is evident that once the process of modern economic growth had started, catchup was surprisingly difficult in much of the Rest, if less so in regions neighboring the original North Sea industrializers. The societal and cultural embeddedness of the new technologies was an important factor. Evidently, the challenges were sufficiently great in the Rest during the first global economy for some minorities to hold significant advantages in capital-raising and trust levels which enabled them to flourish as entrepreneurs. They also benefited from a greater willingness to interact with Western firms and colonial governments. Generally, as the first global economy got underway, MNEs proved important facilitators of globalization, but they were a disappointing diffuser of organizational skills and information to the Rest, and had limited importance in relieving the institutional, human capital or other constraints faced by local entrepreneurs.

There is considerable evidence of emergent modern entrepreneurship and business enterprise by the interwar years, in Asia, Latin America, and Africa.

Japan was a spectacular case of a more general process. This generation of entrepreneurs were sometimes facilitated by nationalistic governments and sentiments, and in China and elsewhere they were quite effective, combining local and Western practices to produce hybrid forms of business enterprise. However, many governmental policies after 1945 designed to facilitate catch-up ended up crippling emergent business enterprises without putting any effective alternatives in place. Many policy regimes ended up favoring redistributive rather than productive entrepreneurship, although it was noteworthy that they also provided some shelter for local firms to develop without being crippled by competition from the West. Evidently individual businesses had the agency to invest in managerial and technological competences in this era, or alternatively simply to focus on rent-seeking.

The second global economy has provided more opportunities for catchup by the Rest. Firms from emerging markets had the opportunity to access the global networks which in part replaced large integrated firms. There were new ways for firms in the Rest to access knowledge and capital. The rapid international growth of MNEs based in emerging markets was a striking departure from the past. However, global capitalism is also a system which rewards winners, and it has facilitated clustering in favored locations. Innovation has remained heavily clustered in the advanced countries, especially the United States. Western and Japanese firms have powerful incumbency advantages. Falling tariff and other barriers meant that a new generation of firms based in the Rest might find it harder to reach scale than their predecessors who could grow in the much-derided era of import substitution.

NOTES

1. This previously unpublished paper originated as the annual Heckscher Lecture at the Stockholm School of Economics in 2006.
2. Kenneth Pomeranz, *The Great Divergence*, Princeton, NJ: Princeton University Press, 2000.
3. Stephen Broadberry and B. Gupta, "The early modern great divergence: wages, prices and economic development in Europe and Asia, 1500–1800", *Economic History Review*, **59** (1) (2006), pp. 2–31; Jan Luiten van Zanden, "The skill premium and the 'great divergence,'" *European Review of Economic History*, **13** (1) (2009), pp. 121–53; Robert C. Allen, Jean-Pascal Bassino, Debin Ma, Christine Moll-Murata and Jan Luiten van Zanden, "Wages, prices, and living standards in China, Japan, and Europe, 1738–1925," *Economic History Review*, **64** (1) (2011), pp. 8–38; Bozhong Li and Jan Luiten van Zanden, "Before the great divergence? Comparing the Yangzi delta and the Netherlands at the beginning of the nineteenth century," *Journal of Economic History*, **72** (4) (2012), pp. 956–89.
4. Agustin S. Bénétrix, Kevin H. O'Rourke and Jeffrey G. Williamson, "The spread of manufacturing to the periphery 1870–2007: eight stylized facts", mimeo, July, 2012.
5. A.D. Chandler, *Strategy and Structure*, Cambridge, MA: Harvard University Press, 1962; idem, *The Visible Hand*, Cambridge, MA: Harvard University Press, 1977, and idem, *Scale and Scope*, Cambridge, MA: Harvard University Press, 1990. See also William

Lazonick and David J. Teece (eds), *Management Innovation: Essays in the Spirit of Alfred D. Chandler, Jr.,* Oxford: Oxford University Press, 2012.

6.   James Foreman-Peck and Leslie Hannah, "Extreme divorce: the managerial revolution in UK companies before 1914," *Economic History Review,* **65** (4) (2012), pp. 1217–38.

7.   Douglass C. North, *Institutions, Institutional Change, and Economic Performance,* Cambridge: Cambridge University Press, 1990, p. 97.

8.   Avner Greif, *Institutions and the Path to the Modern Economy: Lessons from Medieval Trade,* Cambridge: Cambridge University Press, 2006, p. 30.

9.   Douglass C. North, *Understanding the Process of Economic Change,* Princeton, NJ: Princeton University Press, 2005.

10.   Douglass C. North and Barry R. Weingast, "Constitutions and commitment: the evolution of institutional governing public choice in seventeenth-century England," *Journal of Economic History,* **49** (4) (1989), 803–32. For the subsequent debate on this issue, see Steven C.A. Pincus and James A. Robinson, "What really happened during the Industrial Revolution," NBER working paper 17206, July, 2011.

11.   Stanley L. Engerman and Kenneth L. Sokoloff, "Colonialism, inequality, and long-run paths of development," in Abhijit Vinayak Banerjee, Roland Bénabou and Dilip Mookherjee (eds), *Understanding Poverty,* Oxford: Oxford University Press, 2006, pp. 37–61; idem, *Economic Development in the Americas since 1500,* New York: Cambridge University Press, 2012.

12.   Daron Acemoglu, Simon Johnson and James A. Robinson, "Reversal of fortune: geography and institutions in the making of the modern world income distribution", *Quarterly Journal of Economics,* **117** (4) (2002), pp. 1231–94.

13.   Rafael La Porta, Florencio Lopez-de-Silanes, Andrei Shleifer and Robert W. Vishny, "Law and finance," *Journal of Political Economy,* **106** (6) (1998), 1113–15; Rafael La Porta, Florencio Lopez-de-Silanes, Andrei Shleifer and Robert Vishny, "Investor protection and corporate governance," *Journal of Financial Economics,* **58** (1–2) (2000), pp. 3–27.

14.   Richard A. Easterlin, "Why isn't the whole world developed?" *Journal of Economic History,* **41** (1) (1981), pp. 1–19.

15.   Claudia Goldin, "The human-capital century and American leadership," *Journal of Economic History,* **61** (2) (June 2001), 263–91. See also Claudia Goldin and Lawrence Katz, *The Race Between Education and Technology,* Cambridge, MA: Harvard University Press, 2008.

16.   Edward L. Glaeser, Rafael La Porta, Florencio Lopez-De-Silanes and Andrei Shleifer, "Do institutions cause growth?" *Journal of Economic Growth,* **9** (3) (2004), pp. 271–303.

17.   Kent Deng, "A critical survey of recent research in Chinese economic history," *Economic History Review,* **53**, 1 (2000), 1–28; David Faure, *China and Capitalism,* Hong Kong: Hong Kong University Press, 2006, ch. 2.

18.   Justin Yifu Lin, "The Needham puzzle: why the industrial revolution did not originate in China," *Economic Development and Cultural Change,* **43** (2) (1995), pp. 269–92.

19.   Max Weber, *The Protestant Ethic and the Spirit of Capitalism,* Oxford: Oxford University Press, 2011.

20.   Joel Mokyr, *The Lever of Riches,* Oxford: Oxford University Press, 1990, ch. 9.

21.   Steven Sass, "Entrepreneurial historians and history: an essay in organized intellect," PhD dissertation, John Hopkins University, 1977.

22.   David S. Landes, "French entrepreneurship and industrial growth in the nineteenth century," *Journal of Economic History,* **9** (1) (1949), pp. 245–72.

23.   David S. Landes, *The Wealth and Poverty of Nations,* New York; W.W. Norton, 1998.

24.   The classic work is Martin Wiener, *English Culture and the Decline of the Industrial Spirit, 1850–1980,* Cambridge: Cambridge University Press, 1981.

25.   Michael S. Smith, *The Emergence of Modern Business Enterprise in France, 1800–1930,* Cambridge MA: Harvard University Press, 2006.

26.   Alexander Gershenkron, "Social attitudes, entrepreneurship, and economic development: a comment," *Explorations in Entrepreneurial History,* **6** (4) (1954), pp. 245–72.

27.   Joseph Schumpeter, "The creative response in economic history," *Journal of Economic History,* 7 (2) (1947), pp. 149–59.

28. Angus Maddison, *Monitoring the World Economy 1820–1992*, Washington DC: Organization for Economic Co-operation and Development, 1995.
29. William J. Baumol, "Entrepreneurship: productive, unproductive, and destructive," *Journal of Political Economy*, **98** (5) (1990), pp. 893–921.
30. David S. Landes, Joel Mokyr and William J. Baumol (eds), *The Invention of Enterprise: Entrepreneurship from Ancient Mesopotamia to Modern Times*, Princeton, NJ: Princeton University Press, 2010.
31. Noel Maurer, *The Power and the Money: The Mexican Financial System, 1876–1932*, Stanford, CA: Stanford University Press, 2002.
32. Yovanna Pineda, "Financing manufacturing innovation in Argentina, 1890–1930," *Business History Review*, **83** (3) (2009), pp. 539–62.
33. Tirthankar Roy, "Did globalization aid industrial development in colonial India? A study of knowledge transfer in the iron industry," *Indian Economic and Social History Review*, **46** (4) (2009), pp. 579–613.
34. Edward Beatty, "Approaches to technology transfer in history and the case of nineteenth century Mexico," *Comparative Technology Transfer and Society*, **1** (2) (2009), pp. 167–200; idem, "Bottles for beer: the business of technological innovation in Mexico, 1890–1920," *Business History Review*, **83** (2) (2009), pp. 317–48.
35. Mario Cerutti, "Estudios regionals e historia empresarial en Mexico (1840–1920): una revision de lo producido desde 1975," in Carlos Davilla (ed.) *Empresa e historia en América latina*, Bogotá: Tercer Mundo/Colciendas, 1996); Carlos Davilla, *Empresas y empresarios en la historia de Colombia: siglos XIX y XX*, Bogotá: Norma/Uniandes, 2003.
36. For the Meiji Restoration, see Andrew Gordon, *A Modern History of Japan: from Tokugawa Times to the Present*, New York: Oxford University Press, 2003; Seiichiro Yonekura and Hiroshi Shimizu, "Entrepreneurship in pre-World War II Japan: the role and logic of the Zaibatsu," in Landes et al., *Invention*, pp. 506–07.
37. William D. Wray, *Mitsubishi and the NYK, 1870–1914: Business Strategy in the Japanese Shipping Industry*, Cambridge, MA: Harvard University Press, 1984.
38. Joel Mokyr, "Intellectual property rights, the Industrial Revolution, and the beginnings of modern economic growth," *American Economic Review Papers and Proceedings*, **99** (2) (2009), pp. 349–55; Josh Lerner, "150 years of patent protection," NBER working paper 7478, 2000.
39. Winfried Ruigrok and Rob van Tulder, *The Logic of International Restructuring*, London: Routledge, 1995, pp. 213–14.
40. Petra Moser, "Patent laws and innovation: evidence from economic history," NBER working paper 18631, December 2012.
41. Faure, *China*, ch. 4; William C. Kirby, "China unincorporated: company law and business enterprise in twentieth-century China," *Journal of Asian Studies*, **54** (1) (1995), pp. 43–63.
42. Aldo Musacchio, "Can civil law countries get good credit institutions? Lessons from the history of creditor rights and bond markets in Brazil," *Journal of Economic History*, **68** (1) (2008), pp. 80–108.
43. A.G. Hopkins, "Big business in African studies," *Journal of African History*, **28** (1) (1987), pp. 119–40.
44. Ina B. McCabe, Gelina Harlaftis, and Ioanna P. Minoglou (eds), *Diaspora Entrepreneurial Networks: Four Centuries of History*, Oxford: Berg, 2005; Gijsbert Oonk, *The Karimjee Jivanjee Family: Merchant Princes of East Africa 1800–2000*, Amsterdam: Pallas, 2009.
45. Susan Wolcott, "An examination of the supply of financial credit to entrepreneurs in colonial India," in Landes et al., *Invention*, pp. 443–68.
46. Dwijendra Tripathi, *Oxford History of Indian Business*, New Delhi: Oxford University Press, 2004; Claude Markovits, *Merchants, Traders, Entrepreneurs: Indian Business in the Colonial Era*, New York: Palgrave Macmillan, 2008.
47. Tirthankar Roy, *The Economic History of India 1857–1947*, New Delhi: Oxford University Press, 1947, ch. 7; idem, "Economic history and modern India: redefining the link," *Journal of Economic Perspectives*, **16** (3) (2002), pp. 117–18.
48. Ronald P. Dore, "Education; Japan," in Robert E. Ward and Dankwart A. Rustow (eds), *Political Modernization in Japan and Turkey*, Princeton, NJ: Princeton University Press,

1964, pp. 176–204. A more critical study was provided in Koji Taira, "Education and literacy in Meiji Japan: an interpretation," *Explorations in Economic History*, **8** (4) (1971), pp. 371–94.

49. Ulf Olsson, "Securing the markets: Swedish multinationals in a historical perspective," in Geoffrey Jones and Harm G. Schröter (eds), *The Rise of Multinationals in Continental Europe*, Aldershot: Edward Elgar, 1993, pp. 100–102.

50. Deng, "Critical."

51. Stanley L. Engerman with Elisa Mariscal, "The evolution of schooling, 1800–1925," in Stanley L. Engerman and Kenneth L. Sokoloff (eds), *Economic Development in the Americas since 1500: Endowments and Institutions*, Cambridge: Cambridge University Press, 2012, pp. 121–67.

52. Michael Y. Yoshino and Thomas B. Lifson, *The Invisible Link: Japan's Sogo Shosha and the Organization of Trade*, Cambridge, MA: MIT Press, 1986.

53. Tripathi, *Oxford.*

54. Morris D. Morris, "Large-scale industrial development," in Dharma Kumar and Meghnad Desai (eds), *Cambridge Economic History of India*, Cambridge: Cambridge University Press, 1983, pp. 553–676.

55. North, *Understanding*, pp. 42, 46.

56. Geert Hofstede and Michael Harris Bond, "The Confucius connection: from cultural roots to economic growth," *Organizational Dynamics*, **16** (4) (1988), 4–21; Geert Hofstede, Gert Jan Hofstede, and Michael Minkov, *Cultures and Organizations: Software of the Mind*, 3rd edn, New York: McGraw-Hill, 2010.

57. Yat Hoong Yip, *The Development of the Tin Mining Industry of Malaya*, Kuala Lumpur: University of Malaya Press, 1969; Jean-Jacques van Helten and Geoffrey Jones, "British business in Malaysia and Singapore since the 1870s," in R.P.T. Davenport-Hines and Geoffrey Jones (eds), *British Business in Asia since 1860*, Cambridge; Cambridge University Press, 1989, pp. 165–6; John Hillman, *The International Tin Cartel*, London: Routledge, 2010, ch. 3.

58. Mark Casson, *The Economics of Business Culture*, Oxford: Clarendon Press, 1991; idem, *Entrepreneurship and Business Culture*, Cheltenham: Edward Elgar, 1995; Mark Casson and Andrew Godley (eds),*Cultural Factors in Economic Growth*, New York: Springer, 2000.

59. Andrea Colli and Mary Rose, "Family capitalism," in Jones and Zeitlin, *Oxford Handbook*, pp. 194–218.

60. Tarun Khanna and Yishay Yafeh, "Business groups in emerging markets: paragons or parasites?" in Asli M. Colpan, Takashi Hikino and James R. Lincoln (eds), *Oxford Handbook of Business Groups*, Oxford: Oxford University Press, 2010; Tarun Khanna and Krishna G. Palepu, "The future of business groups in emerging markets: long-run evidence from Chile," *Academy of Management Journal*, **43** (3) (2000): Geoffrey Jones and Tarun Khanna, "Bringing history (back) into international business," *Journal of International Business Studies*, **37** (4) (2006), pp. 453–68.

61. Tripathi, *Oxford.*

62. Christopher A. Reed, *Gutenberg in Shanghai: Chinese Print Capitalism 1876–1937*, Honolulu: University of Hawaii Press, 2004; Wellington K.K. Chan, "Chinese entrepreneurship since its late imperial period," in Landes et al., *Invention*, pp. 489–91.

63. For the role of French immigrants in Mexican Textiles, see Aurora Gómez-Galvarriato, "Networks and entrepreneurship: the modernization of the textile business in Porfirian Mexico," *Business History Review*, **82** (3) (2008), pp. 475–502.

64. Ashok Desai, "The origins of Parsi entrepreneurship," *Indian Economic and Social History Review*, **5** (4) (1968), pp. 307–18; Christine Dobbin, *Urban Leadership in Western India: Politics and Communities in Bombay City, 1840–1885*, Oxford: Oxford University Press, 1972; idem, *Asian Entrepreneurial Minorities: Conjoint Communities in the Making of the World-Economy 1570–1940*, Richmond: Curzon Press, 1996.

65. Omkar Goswami, "Then came the Marwaris: some aspects of the changes in the pattern of industrial control in Eastern India", *Indian Economic and Social History Review*, **22** (3) (1985), pp. 225–49; Thomas A. Timburg, *The Marwaris, from Traders to Industrialists*, New Delhi: Vikas, 1978.

66. Wolcott, "Examination," pp. 443–68.
67. Tirthankar Roy, "Beyond divergence: rethinking the economic history of India," *Economic History of Developing Regions*, **27** (1) (2012), p. S62.
68. Alexander Gershenkron, *Economic Backwardness in Historical Perspective*, Cambridge, MA: Belknap Press, 1962.
69. Geoffrey Jones and R. Daniel Wadhwani, "Entrepreneurship," in Geoffrey Jones and Jonathan Zeitlin (eds) *Oxford Handbook of Business History*, Oxford: Oxford University Press, 2008, pp. 513–14.
70. Steven Tolliday (ed.), *The Economic Development of Modern Japan*, 1868–1945, vol. 1, Cheltenham, UK and Northampton, MA, USA: Edward Elgar, 2001, pp. xiv-xv.
71. Rajeswary Ampalavanar Brown, *Chinese Big Business and the Wealth of Nations*, London: Palgrave, 2000.
72. William W. Culver and Cornell J. Reinhart, "Capitalist dreams: Chile's response to nineteenth century world copper competition," *Comparative Studies in Society and History*, **31** (4) (1989), pp. 722–44.
73. Geoffrey Jones, *British Multinational Banking 1830–1990*, Oxford: Clarendon Press, 1993.
74. Emily S. Rosenberg, *Financial Missionaries to the World: The Politics and Culture of Dollar Diplomacy, 1900–1930*, Cambridge, MA: Harvard University Press, 1999.
75. John H. Dunning and Sarianna M. Lundan, *Multinational Enterprises and the Global Economy*, Cheltenham, UK and Northampton, MA, USA: Edward Elgar, 2008, pp. 172–6.
76. Jones, *British Multinational Banking*; Frank H.H. King, *The Hongkong Bank in Late Imperial China, 1864–1902: On an Even Keel*, Cambridge: Cambridge University Press, 1987.
77. Yen-Ping Hao, *The Commercial Revolution in Nineteenth-Century China: The Rise of Sino-Western Mercantile Capitalism*, Berkeley, CA: University of California Press, 1986.
78. William J. Hausman, Peter Hertner and Mira Wilkins (eds), *Global Electrification*, New York: Cambridge University Press, 2008.
79. Caroline Piquet, "The Suez Company's concession in Egypt, 1854–1956: modern infrastructure and local economic development," *Enterprise & Society*, **5** (1) (2004), 107–27; Daniel R. Headrick, *The Tentacles of Progress: Technology Transfer in the Age of Imperialism, 1850–1940*, New York: Oxford University Press, 1988.
80. Mark Mason, *American Multinationals and Japan*, Cambridge, MA: Harvard University Press, 1992.
81. Priscilla Connolly, "Pearson and public works construction in Mexico, 1890–1910," *Business History*, **41** (4) (1999); Lisa Bud-Frierman, Andrew Godley and Judith Wale, "Weetman Pearson in Mexico and the emergence of a British oil major, 1901–1919," *Business History Review*, **84** (2) (2010), pp. 275–300.
82. Stephen Schlesinger and Stephen Kinzer, *Bitter Fruit: The Story of the American Coup in Guatemala*, Cambridge, MA: Harvard University, David Rockefeller Center for Latin American Studies, 1999.
83. Jones, *Multinationals*.
84. See Chapter 8.
85. Tripathi, *Oxford History*.
86. Madeleine Zelin, *The Merchants of Zigong*, New York: Columbia University Press, 2005; Kai Yiu Chan, *Business Expansion and Structural Change in Pre-War China*, Hong Kong: Hong Kong University Press, 2006.
87. Elisabeth Koll, *From Cotton Mill to Business Empire*, Cambridge, MA: Harvard University Press, 2003.
88. Sherman Cochran, *Chinese Medicine Men: Consumer Culture in China and Southeast Asia*, Cambridge, MA: Harvard University Press, 2006.
89. Eric Davis, *Challenging Colonialism: Bank Misr and Egyptian Industrialization, 1920–1941*, Princeton, NJ: Princeton University Press, 1983; Robert L. Tignor, *State, Private Enterprise, and Economic Change in Egypt, 1918–1952*, Princeton, NJ: Princeton University Press, 1984; idem, "The Economic Activities of Foreigners in Egypt, 1920–1950: From Millet to Haute Bourgeoisie," *Comparative Studies in Society and History*, **22** (3) (1980), pp. 416–49.

90. Asli M. Coplan and Geoffrey Jones, "Vehbi Koç and the making of Turkey's largest business group", Harvard Business School case no. 9811081, 20 November, 2012.
91. Jones, *Multinationals*, p. 99.
92. Dunning and Lundan, *Multinational*, pp. 31–2, 175, 185–6; Jones, *Multinationals*, pp. 22–3, 33–5.
93. Alfred D. Chandler, *Inventing the Electronic Century*, New York: Free Press, 2001; Carl Dassbach, *Global Enterprises and the World Economy*, New York: Garland, 1989.
94. Christophe Lécuyer, *Making Silicon Valley: Innovation and the Growth of High Tech, 1930–1970*, Cambridge, MA: MIT Press, 2006.
95. John A. Cantwell, "The globalization of technology: what remains of the product cycle model?" *Cambridge Journal of Economics*, **19** (1) (195), pp. 155–74.
96. Daniele Archibugi and Simona Iammarino, "Innovation and globalization", in Francois Chesmais, Grazia Ietto-Gillies and Roberto Simonetti (eds), *European Integration and Global Corporate Strategies*, London: Routledge, 2000, pp. 95–120.
97. For the case of a Citibank manager who became an Indian IT entrepreneur, see R. Daniel Wadhwani, "Jerry Rao: diaspora and entrepreneurship in the global economy", Harvard Business School case no. 805017, February 2008.
98. See Chapter 3.
99. For an introduction to the economic history of the Communist world, see Gabriel Tortella, *The Origins of the Twenty First Century*, London; Routledge, 2010), Ch. 11. See also Andrei Yudanov, "USSR: large enterprises in the USSR – the functional disorder", in Alfred D. Chandler, Franco Amatori and Takashi Hikino (eds), *Big Business and the Wealth of Nations*, Cambridge: Cambridge University Press, 1997.
100. Greg Huff, *The Economic Growth of Singapore: Trade and Development in the Twentieth Century*, Cambridge: Cambridge University Press, 1997; S.Y. Wong, "The business and sustainability of water supply in Singapore: the case of Hyflux" in Jay D. Gatrell and Neil Reid (eds), *Enterprising Worlds*, Dordrecht, Germany: Springer, 2006, pp. 145–63; Rohit Deshpande and Hal Hogan, "Singapore Airlines: customer service innovation," Harvard Business School case no. 504025, April 2011.
101. Greg Huff, *The Economic Growth of Singapore: Trade and Development in the Twentieth Century*, Cambridge: Cambridge University Press, 1997; Hafiz Mirza, *Multinationals and the Growth of the Singapore Economy*, Beckenham: Croom Helm, 1986.
102. Rajah Rasiah, "The importance of size in the growth and performance of the electrical industrial machinery and apparatus industry in Malaysia," in Chris Nyland, Wendy Smith, Russell Smyth and Marika Vicziany (eds), *Malaysian Business in the New Era*, Cheltenham, UK and Northampton, MA, USA: Edward Elgar, 2001; Peter G. Warr, "Malaysia's industrial enclaves: benefits and costs," *The Developing Economies*, **25** (1) (1987), pp. 30–55.
103. Mason, *American*.
104. Alice H. Amsden, *Asia's Next Giant: South Korea and Late Industrialization*, Oxford: Oxford University Press, 1989; idem, *The Rise of "the Rest": Challenges to the West from Late-Industrializing Countries*, Oxford: Oxford University Press, 2003.
105. Charles F. Geddes, *Patiño, the Tin King*, London: R. Hale, 1972.
106. Charles H. Feinstein, *An Economic History of South Africa: Conquest, Discrimination and Development*, Cambridge: Cambridge University Press, 2005.
107. Rajeswary A. Brown, "Overseas Chinese investments in China – patterns of growth, diversification and finance: the case of Charoen Pokphand," *China Quarterly*, **155** (Sept.) (1998), pp. 610–36; Pavida Pananond, "The making of Thai multinationals: the internalisation process of Thai firms", unpublished PhD thesis, University of Reading, 2001.
108. Helen Shapiro, *Engines of Growth: The State and Transnational Auto Companies in Brazil*, Cambridge: Cambridge University Press, 1994.
109. Balaji Parthasarathy and Yuko Aoyama, "From software services to R&D services: local entrepreneurship in the software industry in Bangalore, India," *Environment and Planning A*, **38** (7) (2006), pp. 1269–85.
110. Erza F. Vogel, *Deng Xiaoping and the Transformation of China*, Cambridge, MA: Belknap Press, 2011.

111.   Yasheng Huang, *Selling China: Foreign Direct Investment During the Reform Era*, Cambridge: Cambridge University Press, 2003.
112.   Laura Alfaro and Andres Rodriguez-Clare. "Multinationals and linkages: an empirical investigation," *Economía*, **4** (2) (2004), pp. 113–70.
113.   Anil K. Gupta and Vijay Govindarajan, "Knowledge flows within multinational corporations," *Strategic Management Journal*, **21** (4) (2000), pp. 473–96; Nicolai Foss and Torben Pedersen, "Transferring knowledge in MNCs: the roles of sources of subsidiary knowledge and organizational context," *Journal of International Management*, **8** (1) (2002), pp. 1–19.
114.   Geoffrey Jones and David Kiron, "Cisco goes to China: routing an emerging economy," Harvard Business School case no. 805020, June 2012.
115.   Clayton Christensen, *The Innovator's Dilemma: When New Technologies Cause Great Firms to Fail*, Boston, MA: Harvard Business School Press, 1997.
116.   John A. Mathews, *Dragon Multinational: A New Model for Global Growth*, Oxford: Oxford University Press, 2002.
117.   John A Matthews and Ivo Zander, "The international entrepreneurial dynamics of accelerated internationalization," *Journal of International Business Studies*, 38 (3), pp. 387–403.
118.   Abhishek Pandey, Alok Aggarwal, Richard Devane and Yevgency Kuznetsov, "India's transformation to knowledge-based economy – evolving role of the Indian diaspora," *Evalueserve*, July, 2004; accessed at http://info.worldbank.org/etools/docs/library/152386/abhishek.pdf.
119.   Donald R. Lessard and Cate Reavis, "CEMEX: globalization "The CEMEX way," MIT Sloan Management case 09–039, March 2009.
120.   Tarun Khanna, Krishna Palepu and Jayant Sinla, "Strategies that fit emerging markets," *Harvard Business Review*, **83** (3) (2005), pp. 6–15.
121.   John Child and Suzana B. Rodriques, "The internationalization of Chinese firms: a case for theoretical extension?" *Management and Organization Review*, **1** (3) (2005), pp. 381–418.
122.   Jing-Lin Duanmu, "Firm heterogeneity and location choice of Chinese multinational enterprises," *Journal of World Business*, 47 (1) (2012), pp. 64–72.
123.   Chengqi Wang, Junjie Hong, Mario Kafouros and Mike Wright, "Exploring the role of government involvement in outward FDI from emerging markets," *Journal of International Business Studies*, **43** (7) (2012), pp. 655–76.
124.   "China fear scuppers $2 billion deal for 3Com," *Financial Times*, 21 February, 2008.
125.   "The company that spooked the world," *The Economist*, 4 August, 2012, pp. 19–23.
126.   Donald N. Sull and Martin Escobari, *Success Against the Odds*, São Paulo, Brazil: Elsevier, 2005.
127.   Ravi Ramamurti, "What is really different about emerging market multinationals?" *Global Strategy Journal*, 2 (1) (2012) 41–7.

3. Globalization and beauty: a historical and firm perspective[1]

OVERVIEW

This chapter uses the beauty industry to explore the impact of globalization over the long run. Beauty may seem an odd choice: the industry rarely features in the management literature. Yet the industry is large, with global sales of $426 billion in 2011.[2] Moreover, the industry sells products which (for better or worse) impact all of us as individual human beings, because it defines who is conceived as being attractive. As recent research has demonstrated, there is a "beauty premium" which enables people considered to be more attractive to earn higher incomes, get acquitted more often in jury trials, earn higher student evaluations, and much more.[3] In so far as the globalization of the beauty industry involved the globalization of what was considered to be attractive, the societal, cultural and individual impact was profound.

The modern beauty industry, involving factory production and the selling of brands, originated in nineteenth-century Europe and North America as a very local activity drawing on long-established craft traditions and beauty rituals. The use of beauty products themselves certainly did not originate in the nineteenth century. Indeed, every known human civilization for thousands of years has used beauty aids of one kind or another, lending support to the view that the use of cosmetic artifices rested ultimately on biological imperatives to attract and to reproduce.[4] In most past societies, however, access to beauty products was largely restricted to elites who had sufficient leisure and income. During the nineteenth century, industrialization began to enable products to be made in larger amounts, often more cheaply; transport improvements enabled entrepreneurs to seek markets beyond their immediate locality and so prompted the emergence of brands; and rising incomes, first of all in towns, enabled larger numbers of people to engage in discretionary spending, including that on beauty products.

The growth of the new beauty industry was initially modest rather than dramatic. Moral objections to the use of color cosmetics lingered in many Western societies, especially outside major cities, until well into the twentieth century. Limited access to piped water and indoor plumbing restricted the

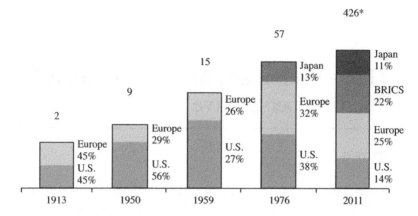

Note: The 1914–76 figures are for production. The 2011 figure is for retail sales. BRICS = Brazil, Russia, India, and China.

Source: Jones, Geoffrey, *Beauty Imagined: A History of the Global Beauty Industry,* Oxford: Oxford University Press, 2010, pp. 366–7; Global Market Information Database.

Figure 3.1   Growth of the global beauty market 1913–2011 (in US dollars)*

demand for toiletries such as soap and toothpaste, again into the twentieth century, even in affluent Western countries. Only one-fifth of Americans may have used a toiletry or cosmetic in 1916.[5]

There remain major uncertainties about the subsequent growth of the global beauty industry. Few countries, except the United States and Japan, collected statistical data on the industry – often products could be found included into other categories, especially soap and detergents. Figure 3.1, which provides an estimate of the growth of the industry in today's US dollars between 1913 and 2011, is thus best seen as a broad approximation.

Despite uncertainties about numbers, however, Figure 3.1 offers what seems to be a broadly accurate view of the expanding world market for beauty in real terms. The market was initially dominated by the rich Western countries in Europe and the United States, although there is every reason to assume that elsewhere beauty products were being made at home and in the informal sector. It is known that during the 1920s production and consumption soared in the affluent United States, and there is good evidence that the elites in large cities in Latin America and Asia, such as Buenos Aires, Tokyo, and Shanghai, also became significant consumers. In 1950, as Europe and most of Asia slowly recovered from the destruction of World War II, the United States may have accounted for over half of the world industry. The Japanese market grew rapidly thereafter; it had become the world's second-largest after the United States by 1976.

During recent decades, the growth of beauty sales in emerging and transition markets has been phenomenal. During the 1980s the beauty market in China was close to zero, as the regime of Mao Zedong had suppressed cosmetics production, while Russian consumers could access only the products made under the central planning regime in the Soviet Union. Three decades later Brazil, China, Russia, and India – the so-called BRIC economies – were the world's third-, fourth-, eighth-, and fourteenth-largest beauty markets. Collectively they represented almost one-fifth of the entire world market in 2011.

With this broad picture of the evolution of the world industry in mind, this chapter now proceeds chronologically. It examines the international growth of the industry from the nineteenth century, with a focus on the products and the beauty ideals it was marketing.

Beauty and the first global economy

The growth of the world beauty market was closely linked to the globalization wave which began in the nineteenth century, and which saw accelerating amounts of multinational investment. Beauty firms were minuscule entrepreneurial enterprises compared with consumer products giants like Singer Sewing Machine, but it was striking how many of the first generation of beauty entrepreneurs were also committed from the start to selling their brands in foreign countries. This commitment rested, ultimately, on a perception of the universality of beauty in human societies, as well as the international ambitions of the entrepreneurs themselves. Born into an age when international travel and communications were much easier than ever before, many pioneering entrepreneurs in the nineteenth century also started businesses in countries other than their birthplaces. These included such iconic figures in the American cosmetics industry as Elizabeth Arden, Max Factor, and Helena Rubinstein.

Both French and British perfume houses, for example, had built large export businesses by the middle of the nineteenth century. Parisian and London perfume houses, such as Piver, Guerlain, and Rimmel, opened retail shops in foreign countries to sell their brands. French perfume houses, led by the pioneering Grasse firm of Chiris, began a worldwide search for new flowers and plants. This started a transformation of the range of scents available to perfumiers.[6] As a mass production and mass marketing branded soap business emerged during the second half of the century, leading British and American firms such as Lever Brothers and Procter & Gamble also energetically pursued international markets.

While perfume and soap were at the forefront of globalizing beauty, firms making smaller emergent product categories also sought international markets.

In skin care, the American firms Pond's and Chesebrough both developed strong international markets for their mass skin creams. At a higher price point, Polish-born Helena Rubinstein had built a network of beauty salons selling her creams in Melbourne, London, and Paris before 1914. She moved to New York following the outbreak of World War I, where she began to develop another business. In a further as yet small product category, hair dyes, Eugène Schueller invented the first safe synthetic hair color formula in Paris in 1907, which provided the basis for a new company called L'Oréal. Within a decade, the still small company was selling its hair dyes in neighboring countries.[7]

As firms advertised their brands, there were frequent assertions of the universality of beauty. The German fragrance house Muehlens, which was very active internationally, proclaimed in an advertisement for its perfumed soap in the United States in 1897 that its virtues were "upheld by beautiful women everywhere." An advert by the leading Swedish toothpaste manufacturer Barnängen maintained that "Men around the world use Vademecum."[8] Yet brands, and their emotional associations, were not value-free. They carried with them strong assumptions from the societies and countries in which they emerged concerning what it meant to be beautiful.

Before these and other Western firms began exporting, beauty had always been a craft which was very local in its products and traditions. There was no global standard of what it meant to be beautiful. Societies had always varied considerably both over time and between geographies in how they sought to enhance their attractiveness through use of cosmetic aids, as well as hairstyles and clothes, and in their views more broadly of what constituted beauty. Both males and females, for example, have in some contexts made extensive use of cosmetics. Indeed, in some societies it was the male body rather than the female which represented the beauty ideal of the society. As Western culture and influence expanded during the nineteenth century, Europeans and Americans began to become increasingly curious if not respectful about the rest of the world, writing in scientific journals about the apparent differences in beauty ideals.[9] In 1871 Charles Darwin confidently asserted in his book *The Descent of Man* that, "it is certainly not true that there is in the mind of man any universal standard of beauty with respect to the human body."[10]

The international growth of the beauty industry soon challenged Darwin's view, and drove a worldwide homogenization of beauty ideals. Beauty ideals, assumptions, and routines which were prevalent in the West spread as global benchmarks. These ideals included the aspirational status of Paris as the capital of fashion and beauty. This reflected France's established reputation for luxury, which was greatly strengthened by the development of haute couture during the middle decades of the century. As the French perfume industry grew rapidly through technological and marketing innovation, its companies linked it firmly to this prestigious world of fashion.[11] One of the peculiarities of the emergent global economy was that country, or city, of origin assumed an ever greater importance as an indication of quality and prestige. In the case of beauty, France and Paris became the symbolic capital, joined much later by New York.

Beauty also came to mean white. Although before the nineteenth century Western people, with their long-established hostility to washing with water, had stunk, and were probably the dirtiest societies on earth, by the end of that century Western soap brands confidently associated cleanliness with "whiteness". Crude racial stereotypes were used to advertise soap and other toiletries, which were presented as components of the Western contribution to "civilizing" colonized peoples.[12] The British and US mass marketers of soap regularly claimed that using their soap would whiten the skin of people of color, thereby "civilizing" them.[13] Strikingly, the advertisements of traditional Greek soap firms proclaimed that they were capable of "turning even a negro white."[14]

The underlying assumptions of the beauty industry about ethnicity were seen most conspicuously in the United States, where African-Americans represented over one-tenth of the population before World War I, but where the commercial beauty industry made no provision for their distinctive hair texture or skin tones. The mainstream beauty industry did not cater to this market because racial stereotyping prevented the portrayal of non-whites as beautiful. This provided an entrepreneurial opportunity for African-American entrepreneurs, such as Annie Turnbo Malone and Madam C.J. Walker, who built large businesses concerned with the treatment of African-American hair, which is often tightly curled. Whether because of a desire to look more like white people or because of a wish to make their hair more "manageable," products to "straighten" African hair became a fertile area for African-American entrepreneurs.[15]

The beauty companies were interpreters, rather than creators, of ethnic and cultural assumptions in their societies. It was hardly surprising that at the peak of Western imperialism, white skin was considered superior, along with everything else in Western civilization. However, adroit marketing and branding strategies reinforced and diffused such values. Business enterprises were diffusers of the underlying assumptions behind their brands, not originators, but their role was nonetheless an important driver of the globalization of beauty ideals. These ideals diffused through specific firms' marketing strategies.

As Western beauty was globalized, non-Western countries, local ideals and practices were diminished, although at different rates and to different extents. This coercion was achieved not by force of arms, but by setting aspirations. Nineteenth-century Japan provides one example. After Japan was forced to open its doors to trade with the West, the modernizing Meiji government sought actively to change the cultural face of the Japanese people by banning traditional practices such as tooth blackening, eyebrow shaving, and male use of cosmetics.[16] Although the Japanese government sought to avoid Western colonization, and facilitated the creation of indigenous firms to compete with Western firms in industries such as shipping and banking, it took the lead in imposing more Western beauty ideals on its own people. When Japanese-owned beauty companies such as Shiseido and Lion emerged towards the end of the century, they looked to France and the United States for products and brand names.[17]

The momentum of homogenization continued after 1914. The international spread and appeal of Hollywood created a powerful new driver. During World War I the American movie industry pulled ahead of the French firms which initially dominated the cinema. By the 1920s the industry, now concentrated in southern California, was able to benefit from the size of its home market and control of distribution networks to dominate both the domestic market and international markets.[18] Movie theatres reached almost every American town, diffusing new lifestyles and creating a new celebrity culture around movie stars, which shaped perceptions of beauty, especially female beauty.[19]

Beauty companies formed part of the ecosystem of Hollywood and celebrity. The firm of Max Factor, based in Los Angeles, innovated in cosmetics for the needs of actors and actresses, and then commercialized those innovations, first in the United States and then elsewhere.[20] In 1925 Lever Brothers launched the perfumed Lux bar toilet soap, which was popuarized after 1928 with an advertising campaign asserting that nearly 100 percent of Hollywood screen stars used the brand. The association with the celebrities of the expanding film industry was reinforced by testimonials from actresses and directors.[21] Hollywood was a thoroughly capitalist enterprise, and was heavily dependent on export markets, so there was no narrow definition of beauty. By the 1930s the Hollywood studios were active recruiting actors and actresses all over Europe and Latin America, both to make their films seem exotic, and to enhance their international appeal. Female actresses were permitted a wide range of skin tones and hair colors. Diversity had strict boundaries, however. African-Americans or, with rare exceptions, Asians did not appear on screen.[22]

The beauty industry in the era of constrained globalization

The role of firms and entrepreneurs as preservers of globalization was very evident in consumer products such as beauty. The international consumer culture which had emerged before World War I proved surprisingly resilient during the rampant political and economic nationalism of the interwar years. Hollywood movies were still shown in Nazi Germany, in part because most studios declined to criticize such repressive regimes as they were important markets. Companies such as Max Factor and Unilever were closely associated with, and benefited from, the globalization of Hollywood through their use of stars to endorse their brands.

Globalization was sustained by the strategies of leading firms. In the more expensive product categories, the fragrance house Coty and cosmetics companies such as Elizabeth Arden and Helena Rubenstein built businesses on both sides of the Atlantic, and sometimes in prosperous cities elsewhere, especially Latin America. During the interwar years the sellers of mass-market creams and toiletries, such as Pond's and Unilever, expanded their exports and even manufacturing to parts of Asia and Latin America.[23]

After World War II, as Chapter 1 noted, much of the world opted out of global capitalism. The global beauty industry made few if any sales in the Communist world, and the highly protected markets in many developing countries also greatly constrained sales. However the beauty industry continued to internationalize where it was permitted to invest. It was now helped by new and powerful diffuser of a Western-orchestrated international beauty culture. Television reinforced the impact of Hollywood's role in diffusing Western, and especially American, ideals of lifestyle, fashion, and beauty. The United States became a major source of television programming for other countries, with programs dubbed or subtitled into local languages.

Television was also important in turning beauty pageants, which existed well before World War II, into international media events. A British-based Miss World pageant was launched in 1951. A US-based Miss Universe followed in 1952. Both pageants were televised in many countries. Feminine grooming was turned into a media spectacle which set expectations and defined aspirations.[24] At a global level, the paler skins and wider eyes favored in both these contests for the first few decades represented what has been termed a "Miss Universe standard of beauty."[25]

There were new international distribution channels, too, after World War II. The first duty-free shop opened at Shannon Airport in Ireland in 1946 to cater for transatlantic passengers who had to get off at the airport while their planes made refueling stops. The first duty-free counter at London's Heathrow airport appeared in 1959. As air travel expanded, duty-free grew, especially in Europe and Asia. Travel retail provided an important means to grow the market for more expensive fragrances, cosmetics, and skin care products because it exposed many new potential customers, including male international business travelers, to brands for the first time, and at prices without tax. Overcoming consumers' reluctance to buy international, rather than local, beauty products became easier as consumers themselves became more international.[26]

By the postwar decades, consumers could buy the same brands in many markets. By 1971 Max Factor manufactured in eight foreign countries and sold in 143.[27] Prestige perfume brands, such as Chanel or Guerlain, were widely sold in developed countries and to the elites of non-Western developing countries. Companies such as Unilever and Colgate-Palmolive sold their soap, toothpaste, and shampoo brands on five continents. Above all, aspirations had been globalized. Beauty and even hygiene was associated with Western white ethnicity, and with certain countries and cities, notably Paris and New York.

Homogenization constrained

Although this chapter has so far emphasized the role of the beauty industry in homogenizing beauty ideals, it is important to introduce a note of caution. At no point were globalization and homogenization entirely identical. As firms invested internationally, they shaped markets by transferring brands and products, but they had also to respond to markets. The ability of firms to dictate was constrained by their need to make profits, and in a consumer products industry profits were made by selling things consumers wanted to buy. Corporate advertising and marketing could certainly shape consumer preferences, but they were also shaped by inherited cultural and social norms which proved very resilient, even as globalization gathered pace.

As firms expanded internationally, they quickly learned that markets differed in their tastes and preferences. As the French fragrance company Coty sought to grow a US business in the decade before World War I, for example, the firm identified cosmetics and face powders as representing a greater opportunity than perfumes, and built a business based on them.[28] It was to become a familiar story in the industry – firms needed to make their products relevant to local consumers. Despite the spread of an international consumer culture, the markets for consumer products, whether movies or laundry soap, continued to exhibit local preferences reflecting inherited social and cultural values, linguistic differences, different climatic conditions and culinary traditions, differences in distribution systems, variations in political systems, and many other factors. Beauty, as an industry which sold deeply personal products which were applied to the body and affected personal confidence and perceived ability to attract, was an unlikely candidate for homogenization, and so it proved.

The challenge of making international brands locally relevant was complex, and firms adopted different strategies. As a general rule, the companies which sold premium and luxury brands sought to minimize local adaptation. They were essentially in the business of selling global aspirations associated with Paris, or later New York, to people who travelled. This meant that any adaption needed for local relevance had to be subtle, if as intended consumers were to associate the product with Paris, not with Detroit or Rotterdam. Premium brands which went very local, such as Coty in the US in the 1920s, risked diluting the appeal of their brands, and were often penalized. Coty's American business collapsed dramatically after the onset of the Great Depression.[29]

Armand Petitjean, the Belgian who founded the new company of Lancôme in Paris in 1935, experimented with a more subtle solution to seeking global relevance. He launched five fragrances sold in elegant bottles created by a renowned artist. The defining idea was to create a separate scent for women from each of the five continents by building an association between each scent and the flowers, spices, and cultural identity of each part of the world. A true beauty brand, Petitjean argued, had to be relevant to women everywhere.[30] It was an intriguing idea, which successfully launched his new brand, but did not provide a general solution to the dilemma faced by prestige brands as they went global. Too much local adaption continued to decimate even the most iconic brands. Strong brand equities such as Chanel No. 5 perfume could be, and were, eroded by poor marketing. Despite an iconic Catherine Deneuve advertising campaign at the iconic Chanel No. 5, aimed exclusively for the American market between 1968 and 1978, the brand was badly tarnished for years in the United States when it was decided to sell it through drugstores.[31]

In contrast, as mass brands were internationalized from the interwar decades, they were generally much more customized both in their formulation and marketing. Strikingly, toiletry companies such as Palmolive and Unilever used local celebrities rather than Hollywood stars in their advertisements. In interwar China and India, in particular, Western firms seem especially willing to use local celebrities and advertising images when selling mass brands such as Pond's, Nivea, and Lux, even though Hollywood celebrities were well known in those markets.[32]

Such localization reflected the substantial regional and national differences which persisted even in neighboring developed countries for the consumption of beauty products. There were, and remain, especially large variations between countries in usage of fragrances and scent preferences. French use of fragrances, for example, remained unusually high for a developed Western country. There was also a strong preference for prestige fragrances, and as a result the mass-market segment was smaller than elsewhere in postwar Europe, and especially the United States. During the 1970s over a quarter of the entire French beauty market was fragrances compared with 8 percent in Germany, and French per capita consumption was twice that of Britain and Germany. In contrast, in the United States, in the mid-1950s fragrances were still less than 1 percent of the total beauty market. In Japan, and East Asia generally, there was little demand at all for fragrances, a characteristic which has remained stubbornly persistent until the present day.[33]

There also remained significant differences between countries in the use of color cosmetics and skin care products. American women became famous for being highly "made-up." By the early 1960s an estimated 86 percent of American girls aged 14 to 17 already used lipstick. In Europe, overall acceptance of cosmetics remained lower for much longer. In much of Europe and

Japan skin products were more important than in the United States. During the 1960s three-fifths of the total Japanese beauty market was held by skin preparations. In Europe, skin products were used much more widely than color lines, although with major differences between countries. In 1963, while 75 percent of German women used a skin or face cream, only 54 percent of French women and 20 percent of Italians used one. While 73 percent of women in Britain used lipstick and 58 percent in France, a mere 25 percent of Italian women applied the product. On the other hand, Italians made much more use of eye make-up. "It is a general rule in Western Europe," one contemporary study observed, "that either the eyes or the mouth are emphasized but not both altogether."[34]

There were wide differences even in toiletries. While, broadly, shampoo consumption increased with per capita incomes, actual consumption varied widely at broadly similar levels. In the early 1980s per capita shampoo consumption in Venezuela and Argentina was three times that of Malaysia and South Africa, despite broadly similar incomes.[35] While the need to be "clean," and not to smell, became a social norm in all developed countries, and among social elites elsewhere, societies continued to differ widely in which products they used, and how frequently they used them, to achieve such a desirable goal. The United States emerged as obsessively "clean".[36] In Europe, there were regional differences. Per capita consumption of toilet soap was highest in northern European countries such as Britain, Germany, and the Netherlands. In France, Spain, and Italy it remained low until the 1960s, when a slow convergence in consumption patterns began.[37]

These variations in toiletry demand were striking in that these markets were largely dominated by the same large firms – Colgate-Palmolive, Henkel, Procter & Gamble, and Unilever. Yet these firms had to adapt to different cultural values, and variations in urbanization levels, access to piped water, and the availability and nature of washing facilities. Bathing consumed more soap than showering. Britain had a growing proportion of installed baths in houses – 90 percent in the early 1970s – but a low proportion of showers: less than one-fifth of households, whereas in Germany the majority of households had both baths and showers installed.[38] Germans had a special preference for bath preparations, with a particular liking for liquids with foaming properties, scented with herbal extracts such as pine. During the 1960s, 7 percent of total German beauty production was represented by this category. No other country had such a demand for perfumed soap baths and bath salts.[39]

MNEs proved not to be reliable enforcers or guarantors of homogenization. During the postwar decades most firms remained, by later standards, quite fragmented. The name L'Oréal was not even used in most of its foreign subsidiaries, for example. The company was named SAIPO in Italy, Golden in Britain, and Haarkosmetik u. Parfumerie in Germany.[40] It was common for the same product to be given different brand names in different countries. Companies marketed multiple brands using different brand names in different countries. Even the most "global" beauty brand was in practice typically very "local." It was the norm rather than the exception for brand positioning to vary between countries. In part, this reflected tensions and rivalries within large business organizations. Local managers frequently exaggerated the need for local adaptations, sometimes simply to defend their own turfs, but often also because their understanding of the market gave them a greater understanding of what would be successful in their own area.

However there were wide variations in this regard between firms, and even inside firms. Many of Unilever's large number of international brands in the postwar decades lacked consistent positioning or formulation, although it had more success maintaining consistency across countries in several large toiletry brands than in its much larger detergents and foods businesses. Lux toilet soap, which was sold on five continents by 1960 and was the largest-selling toilet bar soap, was marketed worldwide with a consistent brand positioning as the "soap of the stars."[41] It was the highly centralized P&G that experienced more problems with the less widely sold Camay bar soap. The former head of their export division later observed how P&G during the postwar decades "kept going from right to left on Camay ... I did not recognize the Camay in Australia or in Germany because they were different."[42]

Despite all this, though, even in cases when brand positioning was consistent, such as Unilever's Lux toilet soap, product formulation was usually adapted to local conditions. This was often required by government regulations as well as the cost and availability of raw materials, let alone local consumer preferences for scents, colors, and other features. The upshot was that the same brand and product often looked and smelled very different in different countries.

Wide differences between countries in their retail distribution systems provided both a major barrier to globalization and a constraint on homogenization, as retailers and sales channels had important voices on what was sold. In Europe, Italy, and Britain were almost at opposite extremes. In postwar Italy, the market was fragmented with the majority of outlets, most of which were individually owned, being small perfumeries, hairdressing salons, pharmacies, and grocery shops. While perfumeries accounted for over one-third of the outlets for cosmetics and toiletries around 1980, there were few department stores or supermarkets. In Britain at the same time, there were few perfumery shops, but supermarkets accounted for one-quarter of cosmetics and toiletries outlets, and pharmacies almost a half, of which the Boots chain of over 1100 retail pharmacies accounted for 30 percent. In Germany, specialist drugstores rather than pharmacies accounted for 35 percent of the market, and supermarkets only 11 percent. For much of the postwar period prestige cosmetics were sold exclusively through drug stores and perfumeries. It was only in 1981 that a major department store began to sell a prestige cosmetics range, that of Estée Lauder.[43]

In developing countries, Western firms were often obliged to make great adaptations in formulations. In India and many other developing countries, import and exchange controls obliged firms to use alternative, local ingredients. In Thailand, Unilever's Lux held one-half of the total bar soap market by the early 1980s, but unlike in Europe or the United States, the product had no tallow, and instead used local palm oil.[44] In the early 1970s, for example, Unilever employed the advertising agency J. Walter Thompson to help it expand the market share for Pepsodent in Kenya, then a mere 4 percent. Another Unilever brand, Signal, held 10 percent, but both were dwarfed by Colgate's four-fifths market share. Unilever wanted to reach new toothpaste users, rather than cannibalize its existing consumers, but careful thought had to be given to the marketing campaign. While the agency had run a campaign for the brand in Italy, claiming "Whiteness without scratching the teeth," this could not be used as attitude surveys indicated that Kenyans blamed yellow teeth (correctly) on the high natural fluoride levels in their water. The next campaign idea to claim that Pepsodent would deliver the "Big white smile of success" was abandoned when it was realized that the concept of "success" was hard to explain in the local language of Swahili. After several more experiments, the agency settled on a "Dangermouth" campaign which claimed that Pepsodent gave relief from the prospect of toothache. However figuring out the right campaign message remained as much an art as a science.[45]

SPIKY AND FLAT WORLDS IN THE SECOND GLOBAL ECONOMY

The new wave of globalization which began during the 1980s had a paradoxical impact on the beauty industry. On the one hand, the industry underwent unprecedented globalization, including the large-scale penetration of the US market by foreign firms, the spread of megabrands, and the reopening of China and Eastern Europe to the global industry. The impact of the globalization of celebrity culture, and the diffusion of the aspirational appeal of New York and Paris to a new generation of consumers in China, India, Russia, and elsewhere, was striking. Certain beauty ideals, especially for women, became widely diffused worldwide, including wide eyes, paler skins, and thin bodies.

This was an era of consolidation in the industry, in which global giants grew rapidly through acquisitions, and then rolled brands out fast and furiously. L'Oréal and Procter & Gamble were also emblematic of the scale of changes. During the 1980s both were primarily confined to their home regions. Within two decades the two firms became the largest in the industry, and together sold about one-quarter of all the world's beauty products.

In the 1980s L'Oréal was still primarily a European company, with a small business in the United States, and nothing at all in Asia. Over the following decade the firm bought leading US brands such as Redken, Maybelline, and SoftSheen-Carson, and subsequently acquired Japanese brands such as Shu Uemura and British brands such as The Body Shop. It opened businesses in Russia and then China, taking its French and recently acquired US brands into them. In the mid-1990s the company still had 63 percent of its business in Western Europe and 20 percent in North America. A decade later the Western Europe's share of sales had fallen to 46 percent, and North America's had risen to 27 percent, indicating the rapid growth of sales in the rest of the world.

In the case of Procter & Gamble, it had only a modest shampoo and bar soap business, mainly in rich countries, in the 1980s. Thereafter acquisitions of brands such as Max Factor, Clairol, Wella, and Gillette gave the firm a huge global beauty business. Within a decade from the mid-1990s, the US firm became the world's largest hair care and men's grooming products company, the second-largest in oral hygiene, and the third-largest in color cosmetics and bath and hygiene.[46]

These two firms, and others, responded to the opening of Russia, China, and other countries with a surge of globalization as exemplified by the rapid geographical diffusion of megabrands such as L'Oréal Paris, Pantene, Nivea, and Dove. The beauty companies, along with many other consumer products companies in this era, sought to refine their brand portfolios down to what they considered as "core" brands, which had large sales and could then be expanded across the world and to different product categories. The pace of the worldwide rollout of brands was unprecedented. When L'Oréal acquired Maybelline in 1996, the brand only had 7 percent of its sales outside America, and the company was based in Tennessee. L'Oréal rapidly moved the company to New York, transformed its products with its own technology and people, and rebranded it as Maybelline New York. The Maybelline New York brand was launched in 80 new countries within five years. A disciplined global brand image of American modernity – urban, relaxed and hip – was enforced, even though the make-up was formulaically adapted to skin types and weather across the globe. The fast rollout of the brand was achieved partly by buying prominent local brands, such as Miss Ylang in Argentina in 2000 and Colorama in Brazil in 2001, which were integrated into Maybelline.[47]

The merger of such prominent local brands into global behemoths would appear to provide compelling evidence of the further erosion of the local by the homogenized global. However there were other political, social, and cultural trends during these decades which worked in a different direction. During the 1960s and 1970s, the Civil Rights movement in the United States and decolonization in Asia and Africa defenestrated a world in which white and Western was automatically superior. As Western societies have grown more ethnically diverse, and as the rights of minorities have been recognized and even in rare cases celebrated, any imagined world of blond and blue-eyed white beauty has given way to a new multi-ethnicity in beauty ideals. In the United States, the narrative of the melting pot gave way to the image of the mosaic. The rapid economic growth of China and India, especially, but also some other emerging markets, has raised both awareness and the status of non-Western cultures and physical appearances. The impact is evident in the increasing worldwide popularity of Bollywood and other non-Western cinemas and the spread of "ethnic" cuisines.[48] In beauty, it appears to have stimulated a reassertion of local traditions, and a new confidence that Asians or Africans were just as beautiful as anyone else.

While the spread of megabrands might be seen as driving a further homogenization of beauty ideals, in fact the outcome was often more nuanced. While the core claims, and usually the core technologies, of such global brands were the same worldwide, companies paid growing regard to making sure that the form in which such claims and technologies was delivered, whether in jars or creams, and the scents which were employed, were relevant to consumers in each market. Global marketing campaigns increasingly incorporated considerations of cultural and ethnic differences in markets. Mass consumer brands had always tended to contain substantial local content in their presentation, but now even prestige brands reflected the trend.

A major example came from the strong preference for skin whitening products in Asia. While during the postwar decades Japan and other countries emulated Western preferences for suntanning, this fashion declined hugely towards the end of the century. In its stead, there was a reversion to traditional preferences for very pale skins, and the products which promised to deliver such skins. Shiseido launched a successful Whitess essence cream in 1989, and many Western companies such as Chanel, Christian Dior and Yves Saint-Laurent also sold whitening cosmetics for the Japanese market by the middle of the 1990s.[49]

Western firms transferred their Japanese expertise lightening creams as businesses were built in China, where a similar historical preference was strong. Lancôme, for example, rapidly established itself as the leading prestige brand in China after its launch in 1999, primarily because of skin-lightening products. Although globally Lancôme sought to maintain a consistent brand image, the historical development of the brand meant that it needed to communicate its values in different ways in different regions. By the first decade of the new century, two-thirds of the brand's sales in Asia were skin care products, but in the United States half its sales were make-up and most of the remainder skin care. In Europe, sales were more evenly balanced between skin, make-up and fragrance. While in the United States the brand heavily emphasized efficacy in fighting things like wrinkles, in Europe marketing carried more emotional images about skin, while in Asia the brand emphasized its impact on the purity and lightness of skin.[50]

The Lancôme story was evident in the Chinese, and other East Asian, markets as a whole. Western and Japanese brands retained the enormous aspirational value compared with local Chinese brands which they had secured after entering the country during the 1980s, but a strong consumer demand for increasing local content became apparent. This included both using local models in advertisements. Luxury brands as a whole remained wary of too much localization, and cautious about using local models, but a search for local relevance became increasingly noticeable as the twenty-first century progressed. In China, as well as Japan, South Korea, and Taiwan, prestige advertisements in beauty magazines began to take the form of a Western global spokesmodel at the front of a magazine, but with three to six pages of local models near the end. There was also a growing demand for local content. While Chinese consumers embraced the aspirational values of leading American and French beauty brands, they have also wanted their Western shampoos to include local ingredients like ginseng.[51] In 2012 Estée Lauder raised the stakes in localization in China by launching a new prestige skin line called Osiao, aimed specifically at local consumers. The new line was developed and tested at the firm's research institute in Shanghai, and sought to combine "the best of Eastern tradition with Western dermatology."[52]

Globalization now also served as a diffuser of non-Western beauty norms. A case in point was Unilever's highly successful skin whitener, Fair and Lovely, launched in India in the 1970s.[53] The brand was so successful that it held well over half of India's $200 million skin-lightening market in the first decade of the new century. Unilever also began to globalize, or at least regionalize, the brand. It was launched in Sri Lanka in 1992, and then in nearly 40 countries in Asia, Africa, the Caribbean, and the Middle East over the following two decades. Unilever, a leading Western consumer products company, is now globalizing a non-Western vision of beauty. There are major issues of legitimacy here: the brand's association of fairness with female beauty, a long-established tradition in India which predates the British colonial era, and claims that its use enables women to find a better husband or job, would do more than raise eyebrows if it was used to promote sales in the United States and Europe. In India itself there has been substantial criticism that such advertising is both racist and demeaning to women, as well as to men who have also been increasingly buying such creams.[54] Nevertheless the brand can be seen as part of a wider trend of the globalization, or regionalization, of brands which has proved a strong trend over the last two decades.[55]

The rediscovery of local ideals and ingredients previously swept away by the era of industrialization, or at least an imagined view of such local traditions, also provided new opportunities for local firms in an industry where US and Western European firms so long dominated. Korres, a Greek firm which in the 1990s grew from a single Athens pharmacy making natural products using traditional knowledge of herbs and flora in the country, has expanded rapidly throughout Europe and the United States over the last decade. In Brazil, now the world's third-largest beauty market, locally owned Natura Cosméticos was market leader in the country by 2013. This 40-year old direct-sales company pursued a remarkable social and environmental agenda, which included sourcing ingredients from indigenous peoples in the Amazon. One of its founders ran as the vice-presidential candidate for the Green Party in the Brazilian presidential election in 2011. From the 1990s the company also opened businesses elsewhere in Latin America, and even in France, the capital of beauty, although further attempts to build businesses in developed markets were put on hold after 2008.[56]

In China, too, local firms such as Shanghai Jawha are building brands using past traditions. This firm had its origins in 1898, and its first brand, ShanghaiVive (Two Girls) excelled in a market otherwise dominated by foreign products. The company fell on hard times during the era of Mao Zedong, when it was reduced to making household cleaning products, but in recent years it has flourished again in beauty. The Herboralist brand, launched a decade ago, builds on the traditional Chinese herbal ingredients used in Chinese medicine to enhance the condition of the skin. More recently the ShanghaiVive brand has been revived, its packaging and marketing drawing heavily on images of style and opulence in old Shanghai. Shanghai Jawha, like Natura, has sold its products in France, and expressed global ambitions.[57]

It remains to be seen how far such global ambitions by firms from Brazil and China will be realized. Japanese companies such as Shiseido pursued global markets from the 1960s, if not longer, only to find Western consumers skeptical, and have increasingly reverted to a focus on their regional market, where their brands find relevance with consumers, and to buying Western brands. Between 2010 and 2012 alone Shiseido bought the pioneering Californian minerals brand Bare Escentuals, while Pola Orbis acquired the Chicago brand H20 and the Australian natural brand Jurlique. South Korean firms such as AmorePacific have repeated the Japanese story more recently as they struggled to sell their brands in the West.[58] Natura also, over time, pulled back from its strategy to build markets in Europe and the United States, and for some years after 2008 focused its primary attention on the fast-growing Latin American regional market, before in 2012 acquiring control of the medium-sized Australian brand Aesop, which had developed an international business for its upscale skincare products.[59]

While globalization in the past, then, led to a homogenization of beauty ideals and practices, today there is a strong revival of local traditions, real or imagined. Globalization is also enabling alternative visions of beauty, whether Chinese or Brazilian, to be offered to consumers worldwide, both by local firms and by Western firms anxious to offer their consumers more choices. When, or if, Shanghai and Rio de Janeiro will become as globally relevant as beauty capitals as Paris and New York, remains to be seen. However, it is evident that there is a new pluralism in beauty markets worldwide. This is facilitated by the breakdown of once rigid distribution channels, as specialty stores, television shopping channels, and e-commerce offer consumers more choices. The web and social networking has also empowered consumers of beauty products to make more choices compared with two decades ago. They have far more knowledge, and more confidence in themselves, and the power of corporate behemoths to dictate beauty standards has waned. Brand managers today ignore bloggers at their peril.

CONCLUSION

This chapter has explored the impact of globalization on worldwide beauty ideals and practices. As the world globalized, there was an unmistakable homogenization of beauty ideals and practices around the world. In the age of imperialism, Western and white beauty ideals emerged as the global standard. This was historically contingent on the unique circumstances prevailing at that time, but once the standard was in place, the strategies of business enterprises helped to reinforce it..

As the beauty companies built international markets through exporting and foreign direct investment, they diffused perceptions of beauty and not simply skin creams and lipsticks. Firms turned societal and cultural ideals into aspirational brands, artfully taking norms around the world, in part through using their marketing skills to make them appear locally relevant. The momentum behind this standard was reinforced by the impact of Hollywood and other drivers of an international consumer culture, despite the spectacular breakdown of the first global economy due to world wars, the Great Depression, and the spread of nationalistic regimes. Beauty companies formed an important component of a wider business ecosystem, which included movie studios, pageant organizers, and fashion magazines.

Yet the process of homogenization, powerful as it was, was never complete. The local was never entirely subsumed by the homogenized global. Convergence and homogenization was stronger in aspirations than in preferences for particular products or scents, which remained more persistently local, despite the spread of global brand names. Moreover, the MNE firm was never a monolith, in beauty or any other industry, while fundamental cultural and social values and preferences proved deeply ingrained.

The more recent era of globalization since the 1980s has coincided with a strong revival of interest in local traditions and practices, which is particularly noticeable in some of the fastest-growing emerging markets, such as China. As a result, the leading firms in the industry now find themselves struggling with the challenge of how to respond to consumers who require increasingly nuanced mixtures of the global and the local in the brands they buy. The strong market positions of a number of very large companies mean that we are seeing to some extent an "orchestrated" diversity, but the current fragmentation of distribution channels, the empowerment of consumers through the web, and the rise of new entrants has also set constraints on the ability of large corporations to orchestrate. If Henry Kissinger was right that globalization in the past was another name for Americanization, or at least Westernization, this is not the case now. In beauty, as in many other things, globalization is no longer a one-way street. Beauty is at the epicenter of the contradictions in today's world, which is simultaneously getting flatter every day, and more spiky, as the local reasserts itself, and the wealth of countries and regions beyond the West grows incessantly.

NOTES

1. This chapter is a revised version of Geoffrey Jones, "Globalization and beauty: a historical and firm perspective," *Ou Mei yan jiu [EurAmerica]*, **41** (4) (December) 2011, 885–916. It draws on Geoffrey Jones, *Beauty Imagined: A History of the Global Beauty Industry*, Oxford: Oxford University Press, 2010. Archival documents were consulted in the following archives: records of Avon held at the Hagley Museum and Library, Wilmington, DE (AVON); the records of J. Walter Thompson held by The History of Advertising Trust, Norwich, Britain (HAT/JWT); the records of Procter & Gamble held in Procter & Gamble archives, Cincinnati (P&G); records of Unilever NV held in Unilever Archives, Rotterdam (UAR).
2. The definition of the beauty industry used here includes fragrances, hair and skin care products, color cosmetics, bath and shower products; oral care, and baby care. It does not include services such as salons and hairdressers, medical products and surgery such as Botox and plastic surgery, or fashion.
3. Giam P. Cipriani and Angelo Zago, "Productivity or discrimination? Beauty and the exams," *Oxford Bulletin of Economics and Statistics*, **73** (3) (2011), pp. 428–47; Naci Mocan and Erdal Tekin, "Ugly criminals", *Review of Economics and Statistics*, **92** (1) (2010), pp. 15–30; Markus M. Mobias and Tanya S. Rosenblat, "Why beauty matters", *American Economic Review*, 96 (1) (2006), pp. 222–35; Daniel S. Hamermesh and Jeff Biddle, "Beauty and the labor market," *American Economic Review*, **8** (5) (1994), pp. 174–94.
4. Jones, *Beauty*; Fenja Gunn, *The Artificial Face: A History of Cosmetics*, New York: Hippocene Books, 1973; Edwin T. Morris, *Fragrance: The Story of Perfume from Cleopatra to Chanel*, New York: Charles Scribner, 1984; Annick Le Guérer, *Le Parfum: Des origines à nos jours*, Paris: Editions Odile Jacob, 2005; B.V. Subbarayappa, "The tradition of cosmetics and perfumery," in B.V. Subbarayappa (ed.), *Chemistry and Chemical Techniques in India*, New Delhi; Munshiram Monoharlal Publishers, 1999; Ping Wang, *Aching for Beauty: Footbinding in China*, Minneapolis, MN: University of Minnesota Press, 2000.

5. Kathy Peiss, *Hope in a Jar*, New York: Henry Holt, 1998, p. 50.
6. Jones, *Beauty*, pp. 22–4, 34.
7. Ibid., pp. 49–50.
8. Ibid., p. 35.
9. "Facts for the curious – female beauty", *Scientific American*, 30 August 1851.
10. Charles Darwin, *The Descent of Man, and Selection in Relation to Sex*, 1871; reprint, Princeton, NJ: Princeton University Press, 1981.
11. Jones, *Beauty*, pp. 26–7; Eugenie Briot, "From industry to luxury: French perfume in the nineteenth century," *Business History Review*, 85 (2) (2011), pp. 273–94.
12. Timothy Burke, *Lifebuoy Men, Lux Women*, Durham, NC: Duke University Press, pp. 17–34.
13. Anne McClintock, *Imperial Leather: Race, Gender and Sexuality in the Colonial Context*, New York: Routledge, 1995, pp. 207–31; Juliann Sivulka, *Stronger than Dirt*, New York: Humanity Books, 2001, pp. 98–106.
14. Evridiki Sifneos, *Soap Making in Lesvos*, Athens: Livani, 2002, p. 71.
15. Peiss, *Hope*, pp. 67–70.
16. Mikiko Ashikari, "The memory of the women's white faces: Japaneseness and the ideal image of women," *Japan Forum*, **15** (1) (2003), pp. 55–79.
17. Jones, *Beauty*, pp. 61–2.
18. Gerben Bakker, *Entertainment Industrialised: The Emergence of the International Film Industry, 1890–1940*, Cambridge: Cambridge University Press, 2008.
19. Lois. W. Banner, *American Beauty*, Chicago, IL: University of Chicago Press, 1983, p. 283.
20. Fred E. Basten, *Max Factor: The Man Who Changed the Faces of the World*, New York: Arcade, 2008, p. 46.
21. Tom Reichert, *The Erotic History of Advertising*, New York: Prometheus, 2003, pp. 118–9; Linda Scott, *Fresh Lipstick: Redressing Fashion and Feminism*, New York: Palgrave Macmillan, 2005, pp. 184–6.
22. Sarah Berry, "Hollywood exoticism: cosmetics and color in the 1930s," in David Dresser and Garth S. Jowett (eds), *Hollywood Goes Shopping*, Minneapolis, MN: University of Minnosota Press, 2000.
23. Jones, *Beauty*, ch. 4.
24. Stephen Gundle, *Glamour: A History*, Oxford: Oxford University Press, 2008, pp. 257–8.
25. Penny van Esterik, "The politics of beauty in Thailand," in Colleen Ballerino Cohen, Richard Wilk and Beverly Stoeltje (eds), *Beauty Queens on the Global Stage: Gender, Contests, and Power*, New York: Routledge, 1996, pp. 215.
26. Jones, *Beauty*, pp. 209–10.
27. Max Factor Annual Report 1971, P&G.
28. Jones, *Beauty*, p. 37.
29. Ibid., p. 110.
30. Ibid., p. 128.
31. "Chanel SA", in www.fundinguniverse.com/companiy-histories/Chanel; accessed 14 October 2012.
32. Jones, *Beauty*, p. 147.
33. Avon, Boca Raton Conference, May, 1979, Series 1: Administration. Subseries C: Conferences, 1973–1978; Frost & Sullivan, *The Cosmetics and Toiletries Industry Market*, New York, 1972.
34. Avon, Boca Raton Conference, May 1979, Series 1: Administration: Subseries C: Conferences, 1973–1978; Jones, *Beauty*, p. 190; S.A. Mann, *Cosmetics Industry of Europe 1968*, Park Ridge, NJ: Noyes Development Corporation, 1968, pp. 2, 54.
35. Geoffrey Jones, "Blonde and blue-eyed globalizing beauty, c1945–c1980," *Economic History Review*, **61** (1) (2008), pp. 125–54.
36. Katherine Ashenburg, *The Dirt on Clean*, New York: North Point Press, 2007, p. 275.
37. UAR, The Toilet Soap Market in Europe, March 1981, ES 81 222C.
38. Ibid.
39. Mann, *Cosmetics*.
40. Geoffrey Jones, *Renewing Unilever: Transformation and Tradition*, Oxford: Oxford University Press, 2005, pp. 38–42.

41. Jones, *Renewing*, pp. 142–6, 165–6.
42. Procter & Gamble, *Samih Sherif*, oral history, 8 September, 1996; "Samih Sherif: entrepreneur extraordinaire," *Moonbeans*, Procter & Gamble internal newsletter, 1988, pp. 3–6.
43. Frost and Sullivan, *Marketing Strategies for Selling Cosmetics and Toiletries in Europe*, New York, 1983), pp. 308–33.
44. Jones, *Renewing*, p. 164.
45. HAT/JWT, John Lindesay-Bethune to J. Armstrong, 28 May, 1971; memo by Jasper Armstrong, 7 September, 1971, Box 705, Pepsodent.
46. Jones, *Beauty*, pp. 302–8.
47. Ibid., p. 308; Geoffrey Jones, David Kiron, Vincent Dessain and Anders Sjöman, "L'Oréal and the globalization of American beauty," Harvard Business School case no. 805086, February, 2006.
48. Anandam P. Kavoori and Aswin Punathambe (eds), *Global Bollywood*, New York: New York University Press, 2008.
49. Mikiko Ashikari, "Cultivating Japanese whiteness. The "whitening" cosmetics boom and the Japanese identity", *Journal of Material Culture*, **10** (1) (2005), pp. 73–91.
50. Jones, *Beauty*, p. 324.
51. Ibid., p. 326.
52. Andrew McDougall, "Estée Lauder to release first China-focused skin care brand," *Cosmetics Design Europe*, 4 October, 2012.
53. Jones, *Beauty*, p. 174.
54. Amy Kazmin, "Indian men turn to the lighter side of skincare", *Financial Times*, 27 June, 2011.
55. Julien Cayla and Giana M. Eckhardt, "Asian brands and the shaping of a transnational imagined community," *Journal of Consumer Research*, **35** (2) (2008), pp. 216–30.
56. Geoffrey Jones, "The Growth Opportunity That Lies Next Door." *Harvard Business Review*, **90** (7–8) (2012), pp. 141–5.
57. John Deighton and Leora Kornfeld, "Herborist," Harvard Business School case no. 510126, 12 August 2010.
58. Jones, *Beauty*, pp. 314–5.
59. Jones, "Growth Opportunity".

4. US MNEs in British manufacturing before 1962[1]

OVERVIEW

This chapter maps the growth of US MNEs in Britain before 1962 on the basis of a unique database. US MNEs began to establish both distribution and production facilities in Britain in the 1850s. By the 1900s US-owned companies were already important in a number of sectors. The role of US affiliates in British manufacturing grew in size and significance as the twentieth century progressed. They were clustered in products involving either high technological content or advanced marketing skills, and in which their market share was very high. By the mid-1960s, US affiliates were estimated to account for over 50 percent of the British market for automobiles, vacuum cleaners, electric shavers, razor blades, breakfast cereals, potato chips, sewing machines, custard powder, typewriters, and a considerable range of other products. They held between 30 and 50 percent of the market for computers, rubber tires, soaps and detergents, instant coffee, watches, refrigerators, and washing machines.[2] US-owned firms accounted for 49 percent of the value of prescriptions to Britain's National Health Service, compared with the 27 percent share held by British-owned firms.[3]

Individual US companies controlled large market shares. In the mid-1960s, Kodak produced over 90 percent of the film sold; Heinz accounted for 87 percent of baby foods and 62 percent of soups and baked beans sold; Kraft and Swift accounted for 75 percent of the processed cheese market; and IBM accounted for 40 percent of computer sales.[4]

If US MNEs were important for Britain, Britain was also important for US MNEs. US-owned companies were or appeared to be paragons of efficiency compared with their British-owned counterparts after World War II. In 1954, total labor productivity of US affiliates in Britain was estimated to be almost 33 percent higher than that of all British manufacturing industry.[5] In turn, Britain was an extremely important location for US manufacturing MNEs. Before World War II, Canada was the largest host for US FDI in manufacturing, but Britain was the second-largest host economy. By 1929, US FDI in British manufacturing had reached $268.2 million – more than that invested in

Germany, France, Italy, and Spain combined. By 1940, it had only grown marginally to \$275.3 million, compared with a rapid growth of US FDI in Germany from \$138.9 million to \$206.3 million, but Britain remained the largest host in Europe. Overall, Britain hosted approximately 15 percent of the total US manufacturing direct investment in 1940.[6] For US manufacturers, Britain retained its position as the second-largest host after Canada, and the largest European host, through the 1950s, and in 1962 accounted for 19 percent of US outward FDI worldwide.[7]

There were multiple reasons why Britain was such an attractive location for American companies. Investment was market-oriented rather than resource-seeking. Britain was a high-income market – in 1950 British GDP per head remained well ahead of that of almost every European country apart from the small neutral states of Switzerland and Sweden – with many similarities to the United States. It was the center of the sterling area, with sterling a major world trading currency into the 1950s. In addition, Britain's similar language and culture to the United States reduced the information costs and uncertainty faced by US investors. As a result, US MNEs often used Britain, like Canada, in the first stage of their foreign expansion before proceeding to markets with higher uncertainty levels.[8] This preference for either physically close or culturally similar investment locations, which Mira Wilkins has termed the "nearby factor," is a widely observed feature in the history of international business.[9]

The history of US-owned businesses in Britain has been discussed in a number of important studies from the pioneering work of Frank A. Southard in 1931 onwards.[10] However the absence of inward FDI data, meant that our knowledge of the dimensions and characteristics of this American investment has not been robust. The database on which this chapter relies, therefore, has sought to put our knowledge of the evolution of US investment into Britain on a firmer footing.

COUNTING MNEs

MNE activity can be aggregated in one of two ways. The most widely used measure is direct investment. MNEs are defined as enterprises engaged in foreign direct investment (FDI), which involves not only an export of capital but also the exercise of managerial control. There are a number of conceptual problems with using FDI as a proxy for MNE investment, starting with the fact that transferring capital across borders is one of the least significant functions of MNEs. A focus on financial flows diverts attention from the key role of MNEs as transferors of technologies and organizational systems.[11] Statistical measures of FDI rest on arbitrary assumptions about the amount of equity required to "control" a foreign company. In practice, it is often difficult to define "control" and thus to distinguish between direct and portfolio investment. Measures of the flow of FDI may not include the reinvestment of earnings – a key means by which MNEs finance themselves – while measures of stock are quite often based on the historical value of an investment and are not updated at market prices.[12]

While the growth of US MNE activities in Britain can be shown from FDI data, the limitations of this measure are also evident. The United States remains the only country to possess plausible FDI estimates for the period before the 1960s. As Wilkins has noted, the estimates for the 1930s and 1940s are "terrible" because of lack uniformity in accounting practices, exchange rate problems, and general inconsistencies.[13] Although the post-1950 US data are much better, on the British side there are no data at all for inward FDI into Britain until the early 1960s.[14]

An alternative means of quantifying MNEs is to focus on companies rather than capital. The most ambitious research along these lines remains the MNE Enterprise project at the Harvard Business School directed by Raymond Vernon (hereafter the Vernon database). This pioneering project compiled data on the 10 000 foreign subsidiaries of 187 US manufacturing MNE parents active between 1900 and 1967. The sample was chosen using the twin criteria of whether the enterprise appeared in the *Fortune 500* Largest US Industrial Corporations for the year 1964, and whether, at the end of 1963, the US parent held equity interests in manufacturing enterprises located in six more foreign countries, such equity interest in each case amounting to 25 percent or more of the total equity.[15] The database was updated in a second phase to include over 19 000 subsidiaries and extended to 1975.[16] The Vernon database provided an impressively large sample of firms and, not surprisingly, it has been widely employed.[17]

The Vernon database, however, is not without its drawbacks. The limitation of the study to US firms manufacturing in at least six countries meant the exclusion of "smaller" companies which manufactured overseas, or bigger ones which chose to focus on less than six foreign markets. The methodology of tracing back the antecedents of contemporary MNEs excluded from the sample the many MNE investments which were made by US firms but did not, for one reason or another, continue into the mid-1960s, although the Vernon team did search historical records for earlier entries and exits.

This new database study has employed a different methodological approach. It forms part of a larger project which has sought to identify all foreign firms which established a manufacturing presence in Britain between 1850 and 1962. Firms with distribution operations only were excluded. There was no requirement that such firms had to have factories in any other country. Firms were identified through research in company histories, trade directories, newspapers, annual reports, official records, and other sources. Dates and other details were crosschecked to try to achieve maximum accuracy. Both British and non-British sources were consulted extensively.[18]

This chapter focuses exclusively on US-owned MNEs in Britain, and confines its focus to the period between 1907 and 1962.[19] It is believed that the database contains detailed information about a high percentage of the total population of US firms which invested in British manufacturing in this time period, although the exact size of this corporate population can probably never be known. The good news is that the numbers are not too out of line with the various existing estimates. The database identifies 222 US-owned manufacturing subsidiaries in Britain in 1935, while a Department of Commerce estimate for 1940 found that 233 US companies were manufacturing in Britain.[20] The UK's Board of Trade estimated that 637 US-owned companies were manufacturing in Britain in 1965, while the database identifies 493 active in 1962.[21] The wider definitions employed in this study allow it to include more companies than the Vernon database. In *Scale and Scope*, Chandler uses the Vernon database to identify 22 new US investments in Britain between 1900 and 1917, 42 between 1918 and 1929, 93 between 1930 and 1948, and 544 between 1949 and 1971.[22] The new database has identified a considerably larger number of firms.

A company database of this kind has both advantages and disadvantages. Compared with an aggregate statistical measure of capital such as FDI, it provides much more nuanced information about corporate strategies. But there are problems of interpretation arising especially from the size distribution of firms. In the database, every direct investment is counted as equal, without regard to employment, sales, or asset size. In practice, there has always been a wide variation in size (however measured) in MNE investments. Dunning's 1958 study showed that a mere nine of the sample of 205 US firms identified as active in British manufacturing in 1953 accounted for 43 percent of total US-controlled employment. At the other end of the spectrum, 111 firms accounted for less than 9 percent of employment.[23] The distortions caused by this problem can best be seen in the transportation sector, in which the number of US companies investing in Britain appears quite small, although they included the corporate giants of Ford and General Motors.[24]

The solution to this problem is to weight for firm size, but data on subsidiary size is extremely hard to locate. Table 4.1 provides an analysis of firm size by employment of the US-owned subsidiaries at the three benchmark dates – 1907, 1935, 1962 – used in the database.

The evidence from the database confirms the wide size dispersion of US manufacturers in Britain. In 1907, the largest identified employer was Singer. Its factory employment at that date was approximately 10 500, while the company employed a further 10 000 workers in the extensive distribution and

*Table 4.1   Firm size by employment of US-owned manufacturing
            subsidiaries in Britain 1907, 1935, and 1962*

Employment (number of persons)	1907	1935	1962
50 and under	1	5	11
51–100	–	19	14
101–200	3	14	16
201–500	–	21	37
501–1000	2	14	36
1001–2000	1	7	22
2001–5000	3	7	21
5001–20000	–	5	10
Over 20000	1	1	3
Unknown	32	129	323
Total no. of firms	43	222	493

Source: Database.

marketing operation which made it Britain's second-largest multiple retailer.[25]
In contrast, the smallest known US employer in 1907 was Pfister & Vogel
Leather Company, which established selling operations in Britain in 1902 and
soon afterwards built a factory at Leicester employing 40 workers. In 1962,
Ford had by far the largest British labor force with 61 000 workers. In contrast,
the smallest known US employer was Analytical Measurements Ltd, which
produced pH meters in Richmond, Surrey with seven workers.

Unfortunately, it is the size of the unknown figure shown in Table 4.1 which
is most striking. A search for alternative size indicators such as asset size or
capital proved even less successful. Part of the problem was the inclusion in
the study of many smaller companies, as information about smaller companies
is usually harder to locate than that about larger ones. Certainly, the implications of the wide size dispersion and the large "Unknown" figure need to be
firmly borne in mind in the following analysis of the trends shown in the database.

EVOLUTION AND ENTRY PATTERNS

The arrival of the first US MNEs in British manufacturing in the middle of the
nineteenth century has been explored in many studies. Colt, the hand-gun
manufacturer, and J.R. Ford, a rubber footwear manufacturer, opened British
factories in the 1850s. The Colt investment lasted only until 1856, and that of

Entrepreneurship and multinationals

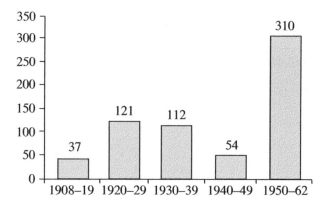

Note: Excludes US MNE acquisition of preexisting US-owned plant in Britain.

Source: Database.

Figure 4.1   Establishment of new US-owned manufacturing subsidiaries in Britain, 1908–62 – number of companies

J.R. Ford until 1869, but the 1860s saw more sustained investments. The most important was that of Singer Sewing Machines, which opened a factory in Glasgow, Scotland in 1867. The trickle of subsequent US investments began to accelerate after 1890.[26] At the 1907 benchmark date the database identifies 43 US affiliates with manufacturing operations in Britain. In 1935 the number was 222, and in 1962 it had grown to 493.

Between 1908 and 1962 a total of 634 new US-owned manufacturing subsidiaries were established in Britain. Figure 4.1 shows the overall time-trend.

The decade between 1908 and 1919 covers the last prewar years of the wave of US investments in British manufacturing which had begun in the 1890s. It includes the arrival of the Ford Motor Company, which opened a factory at Manchester in 1911, as well as a small number of wartime investments made before the United States entered World War I in 1917. During the 1920s there was a large surge in the number of new US manufacturing affiliates established, which formed part of a general surge in US FDI in manufacturing.[27] New US entrants to Britain included General Motors, Goodrich, Goodyear, Firestone, Monsanto, Otis Elevator, and Gillette. The considerable number of new US investments made in the 1930s, which include Procter & Gamble, Hoover, Mars, and Coca Cola, is more surprising. It contradicts the picture of stagnation suggested by the FDI data, and the widely accepted view that US manufacturing activities abroad in the Depression decade were "far less than in the 1920s."[28]

Instead, it appears that it was World War II and its aftermath that reduced new US subsidiary creation in Britain. Altogether less surprising is the surge of MNE investments after 1950. As Vernon described when he developed the product cycle model to explain the growth of US manufacturing FDI in post-war Europe, the United States had innovated in a range of products which were then diffused to foreign markets as the product matured.[29] The dollar shortage throughout Europe encouraged US firms to replace exports by FDI. In Britain, the new US arrivals ranged from Texas Instruments and Hewlett-Packard to Campbell Soup. This was the classic era of the worldwide hegemony of US manufacturing MNEs. In Britain's case, there was a particular surge of new US investments around the beginning of the 1960s. Some 117 of the total of 310 new subsidiaries identified opened in the years 1960–62 alone.

A closer look at the evolution of US MNEs in Britain is available in Table 4.2, which analyzes new subsidiaries by product group as well as decade of entry. This larger sample modifies, to some extent, the existing picture of the

Table 4.2   Establishment of manufacturing subsidiaries in Britain by US industrial enterprises, 1908–62 (by 2-digit SIC code) – number of cases

Industry	1908– 19	1920– 29	1930– 39	1940– 49	1950– 62	Total
Food (20)	2	7	13	3	20	45
Tobacco (21)	0	1	0	0	1	2
Textiles (22)	0	0	3	1	1	5
Apparel (23)	1	2	4	0	4	11
Lumber (24)	1	0	1	1	0	3
Furniture (25)	0	1	0	0	0	1
Paper (26)	0	1	1	1	5	8
Printing and publishing (27)	0	3	2	1	3	9
Chemicals (28)	6	22	31	8	77	144
Petroleum (29)	0	3	0	0	1	4
Rubber (30)	0	6	1	3	6	16
Leather (31)	1	1	0	1	0	3
Stone, clay and glass (32)	2	2	3	0	8	15
Primary metals	2	4	5	1	12	24
Fabricated metals (34)	3	14	8	5	20	50
Machinery (35)	6	22	14	15	80	137
Electric machinery (36)	4	16	14	4	39	77
Transportation (37)	3	8	4	1	7	23
Instruments (38)	3	5	7	5	20	40
Miscellaneous (39)	3	3	1	4	6	17
Total	37	121	112	54	310	634

Source: Database

industrial distribution of US companies investing in Britain. Both the Vernon data used by Chandler and the present study demonstrate clearly that US FDI was highly concentrated by product group.[30] But while the Vernon data stressed machinery as the leading sector for US investment before World War I, Table 4.2 indicates that in the prewar decade chemicals was almost as important. In the 1920s, machinery and chemicals, followed by fabricated metals and electric machinery, appear as the most important sectors, while the Vernon data suggests a relatively greater role for the food industry. In the 1930s and 1940s, Table 4.2 again highlights the importance of chemicals followed by machinery and electric machinery, while the Vernon data suggests that chemicals was followed in importance by food products. Both datasets point to the greater importance of chemicals, machinery, and electrical machinery after 1950, though again food appears less prominently in the present study than in the Vernon data.

The industrial distribution of the US MNEs entering British manufacturing is examined in more detail in Table 4.3, which analyzes by three-digit SIC code the eight product groups for which there were 20 or more entries between 1908 and 1962. These groups include 540 cases, or 85 percent of the total number of entries.

The heavy concentration of US investments in a relatively small number of products stands out. Within chemicals, pharmaceuticals appears as the largest category, especially after 1930, followed by industrial chemicals and chemicals for agriculture and industry. In transportation, investments in motor vehicles and components were preeminent. There were also noteworthy changes over time reflecting technological shifts. The sudden appearance of electronic components as an avenue for US investment after 1950 is the clearest example. Overall, a mere 18 product lines (3-digit SIC code) accounted for 54 percent of the 634 new entries.

In the language of the economic theory of MNEs, US companies possessed ownership advantages over their British competitors which they sought to exploit through FDI. The ownership advantages possessed by the US MNEs in Britain and elsewhere are the staples of much business history literature. They arose from the American superiority in mass production and science-based industries derived from the three-pronged investments in manufacturing, marketing, and management classically described by Chandler.[31] US investment was concentrated in those industries – machinery, chemicals, branded foodstuffs, transportation – in which large US corporations with professional managerial hierarchies had appeared. US firms had secured first-mover advantages over most of their British competitors in these capital-intensive sectors.[32] British capitalism had its own strengths which provided the ownership advantages to support Britain's own position as the world's leading direct investor before 1945,[33] but US corporations held technological and organiza-

*Table 4.3   Establishment of US manufacturing subsidiaries in Britain,
1908–62 (by 3-digit SIC code) – number of cases*

	1908– 19	1920– 29	1930– 39	1940– 49	1950– 62	Total
Food (20)						
meat products (201)	0	2	0	0	7	9
sugar, chocolate (206)	1	1	1	0	4	7
animal feed/misc. (209)	0	2	3	1	4	10
spirit distilling/soft drinks (208)	0	0	4	0	3	7
Other	1	2	5	2	2	12
Chemicals (28)						
pharmaceuticals (283)	2	7	11	5	24	49
soaps/detergents (284)	0	6	7	1	4	18
organic industrial chemicals (286)	3	2	5	2	19	31
chemicals for agriculture industry (287)	0	2	2	0	16	20
Other	1	5	6	0	14	26
Primary metals (33)						
non-ferrous (333) metals	2	3	3	1	8	17
Other	0	1	2	0	4	7
Fabricated metals (34)						
cans/packaging (341)	0	3	0	0	5	8
cutlery/hardware (342)	2	4	2	3	4	15
bolts/nuts (345)	0	0	3	1	0	4
misc. fabricated metals (349)	0	4	2	1	7	14
Other	1	3	1	0	4	9
Machinery (35)						
mining/construction (353)	1	4	0	3	15	23
machine tools (354)	1	2	3	3	14	23
textiles, food, printing, dry-cleaning industries (355)	1	5	6	2	20	34
general industrial machinery (356)	2	4	4	1	15	26
office/computing (357)	0	4	0	2	6	12
Other	1	3	1	4	10	19
Electric machinery (36)						
records/radio/consumer (365)	2	5	3	2	8	20
electrical components (367)	0	1	0	0	24	25
miscellaneous (369)	0	2	6	1	1	10
Other	2	8	5	1	6	22
Transportation (37)						
motor vehicles (371)	3	6	4	1	4	18
Other	0	2	0	0	3	5
Instruments (38)						
engineering/scientific (381)	1	0	2	1	7	11
measuring and control (382)	1	1	4	0	9	15
Other	1	4	1	4	4	14

Source: Database.

tional advantages in the capital-intensive industries associated first with the Second Industrial Revolution, and subsequently with the post-1945 high-technology industries such as pharmaceuticals and electronics.

It was the concentration of US MNEs in a limited range of products which accounted for their importance in the British economy. US affiliates accounted for less than 6 percent of total British manufacturing output in 1957. The sales of US affiliates as a percentage of total manufacturing sales in Britain rose from 5.6 percent in 1957 to 7.4 percent in 1962.[34] However, their concentration in high-technology and branded products gave US affiliates an importance in the British economy far greater than the picture presented by their share in the British manufacturing sector as a whole.

MODE OF ENTRY

Historically, as manufacturing companies sought to sell to foreign markets, their engagement in these markets frequently grew in complexity over time. At first, they would export, but later they would sometimes employ agents, very often invest in distribution facilities, and finally move into production. A variant of this pattern involved licensing technology to local producers. Internalization theory has provided an explanation of shifts from one mode to another. The frequency of transacting is a key variable. While discrete or low-volume transactions can be mediated through markets, recurrent transactions encourage the use of intermediate modes such as licensing and agents, or else hierarchical modes such as sales and production branches. Both the use of agents and of licensing incur the risk of opportunistic behavior and involve monitoring costs, which increase with the frequency of transactions, encouraging a shift to hierarchical modes.[35]

This pattern is strongly evident in the overseas expansion of US firms as a whole, and in their investments in Britain.[36] The database shows, however, strong firm-specific patterns in this evolution. US firms active in Britain progressed through these stages at different speeds. Often a lengthy period of time was involved. Coro Inc., a jewelry manufacturing company, established a marketing subsidiary in Britain in 1933. By 1946 a small assembly operation employed 18 people, but it was not until 1959 that fullscale manufacture started.[37] Sudden exogenous events, such as the British adoption of trade protectionism in 1931 or, at the end of the 1950s, the return to international convertibility of sterling, served as triggers which encouraged clusters of firms to shift modes at broadly the same time.

Table 4.4 examines the choice of mode when a US firm decided to begin manufacture in Britain. It includes details of the 68 cases when US companies acquired manufacturing firms in Britain which were already owned by another

Table 4.4   Mode of entry into Britain by US industrial enterprises, 1908–62

	Total subsidiaries	Acquisition of US-owned co.	Total new subsidiaries	Greenfield	Acquisition	Unknown
1908–19	37	0	37	27	10	0
1920–29	128	7	121	70	49	2
1930–39	122	10	112	84	26	2
1940–49	57	3	54	36	17	1
1950–62	358	48	310	161	136	13
Total	702	68	634	378	238	18

Source: Database.

US-owned firm. Typically, these acquisitions were the result of merger and acquisition activity in the United States.

Between 1908 and 1962, 38 percent of new US entrants were the result of the acquisition of an existing British firm. However, the ratio of acquisitions to greenfield investments in each period was not constant. While the proportion of new subsidiaries formed as a result of acquisitions of British firms was 27 percent in 1908–19 and 38 percent in 1950–62, the proportion was high in the 1920s (40 percent) and fell sharply in the 1930s (23 percent), before rising a little in the 1940s (31 percent). The Vernon database suggests a higher ratio of acquisitions to total entries in the postwar period. For 1951–66, this ratio for Britain was 64 percent and for Europe as a whole 54 percent.[38] The discrepancy with the present study may reflect the growing number of acquisitions in the first half of the 1960s – 64 of the 136 acquisitions between 1950 and 1962 occurred in 1960–62 alone – as well as the larger number of smaller firms covered in the present study.

A number of theoretical propositions on entry mode have been put forward over the years which elucidate some of the long-term trends shown in Table 4.4. Dubin, one the earliest scholars who undertook detailed analysis of acquisition versus greenfield using the Vernon database, suggested that firms initially going abroad preferred to enter foreign markets via an acquisition in order to reduce uncertainty while large MNEs were more willing to undertake greenfield investments. The high ratio of acquisitions even in 1908–19 might support such a proposition, as well as the corollary that when FDI was based on major innovations – as was the case with many of these early investors – the lack of suitable partners simply ruled out acquisitions. Dubin, Knickerbocker and others also suggested that late entrants in oligopolistic markets preferred acquisitions in order to speed up their response to the entry of "leaders" in foreign markets, and that higher acquisition rates were to be anticipated in faster-growing markets because of their being a quicker means of entering such markets. These predictions may explain the high level of acquisitions in the 1920s – when an oligopolistic "bunching" of new US investments was a prominent feature of industries such as tires – and again in the 1950s, when a surge of new US entrants were seeking to establish themselves in the British market, and oligopolistic bunching was again evident. The 1950s were also a period when the British market was growing reasonably fast, although not as fast as most Western European markets.[39]

The database reveals that in some periods a significant proportion of US acquisitions were of British firms with which a preexisting connection existed. These connections included such intermediate modes as licensing agreements and subcontractor and supplier relationships. This was the case for at least 20 percent of the 26 acquisitions in the 1930s and of the 72 acquisitions in the 1950s. In 1952, for example, H.H. Robertson began manufacturing in Britain by acquiring the company which had previously manufactured its metal sheets and ventilators under license. In 1954, Corning Glass Works started its production activities in Britain by acquiring 40 percent of James Jobling Ltd, a long-established licensee for its glassware.[40] The significance of such preexisting connections is not identified in the Vernon or other studies, and the phenomenon merits further investigation, especially since it appears to have been inconsistent over time. Less than 10 percent of the 49 US acquisitions in the 1920s and 64 acquisitions in 1960–62 were of British firms with a preexisting connection to American enterprises.

One problem with hypothesizing about choice of entry mode is that multiple influences were at work. The economic environment was an important one. Theory suggests that acquisition may be a suitable method of entry when a target market is static or declining, as additional production capacity is not required, while greenfield strategies become more attractive when a market is growing. Britain did not experience the collapse of economic activity seen in the United States in the wake of the Great Depression. Indeed, working Britons in the 1930s experienced rising real incomes, partly as a result of falling world prices for imported foodstuffs and other primary products. As a result, there was a flourishing market for precisely the consumer goods which many US MNEs wanted to manufacture in Britain.

Britain's shift from free trade, albeit tempered from World War I onwards by a growing number of trade restrictions in particular industries, to full-scale protectionism in 1931 was a major exogenous shock. It posed an immediate threat to well-established market shares built up through exporting strategies. One example was Hoover, which had established a marketing company to distribute its vacuum cleaners in 1919, but was now suddenly threatened by tariffs. Hoover initiated manufacturing soon after the British abandonment of free trade, opening a London factory in 1932. Hoover's example was followed by others. Among the US branded food manufacturers building new factories in Britain in the 1930s were Mars, Shredded Wheat, Quaker Oats, and Kellogg. The latter had established a large market for breakfast cereals since it began importing into Britain in the early 1920s.[41] Coca Cola and Pepsi Cola also established concentrate manufacturing plants in Britain in 1935 and 1939 respectively. The greenfield investments made in the 1930s were mostly in such branded food products, as well as in those segments of the chemical industry where there were no British competitors to acquire. When appropriate British targets existed, acquisition strategies were still employed. National Distilleries of America built up a presence in the Scotch whisky market by acquiring firms such as Train & McIntyre, in which a controlling interest was taken in 1937.[42]

Given the differences in entry mode between the two interwar decades, the hypothesis that exchange rate regimes were an influence has to be investigated. Table 4.5 explores this issue by analyzing mode of entry on the basis of the three exchange rate regimes seen in these years: general floating rate (before 1925), gold exchange standard (1926–31) and managed float (until 1939).[43]

The relationship between currency movements and MNE modes of entry has received limited attention. The early work of Aliber pointed to a financial influence on investment decisions by suggesting that firms from countries with strong currencies had an advantage in capital-raising compared with those from countries with weak currencies. This theory would suggest, among other things, that the timing (at least) of acquisitions would be influenced by currency factors.[44] In so far as a relationship can be discerned in the interwar years, it appears that US acquisitions peaked when sterling was valued highly against the dollar. During the first half of the 1920s sterling was "cheaper" against the dollar than it had been before World War II . However, the British return to the gold standard in 1925 at a rate of £1 = $4.86 began a period when the British currency was widely regarded as being overvalued by around 10 percent. When Britain was forced to abandon the gold standard in 1931, the pound fell to $3.5 within a year, although thereafter the exchange rate moved

Table 4.5　Mode of entry by exchange rate regime 1920–39

Period	No. of acquisitions	% of total	No. of greenfield investments	% of total
1920–1925	20	27	36	23
1926–1931	37	49	46	30
1932–1939	18	24	72	47
Total	75	100	154	100

Source:　Database.

up again, and was approximately $4.9 on average between 1934 and 1938. US firms made most of their interwar acquisitions when the pound was "overvalued," while sterling's devaluation was followed by the collapse in acquisition activity. Only four acquisitions were made between 1932 and 1934. However, it is difficult to develop a plausible hypothesis to link entry modes with nominal exchange rates given that both acquisitions and greenfield investments involve buying local assets, although in different markets. More generally, as the export of technology and management is a more important function of MNEs than the export of capital, it is unlikely that short-term currency movements will fundamentally influence long-term investment decisions.

It is possible that it was the exchange rate regime rather than the nominal exchange rate which influenced modes of entry. It is often asserted that flexible exchange rates discourage international capital mobility. Eichengreen refuted this view for the interwar years in a study on the performance of fixed and flexible exchange rate regimes.[45] However, it is noteworthy that virtually a half of all the acquisitions made in a 20-year period occurred in five years of fixed exchange rates. An examination of volatility in the monthly real exchange rate between the US and Britain shows that both the first half of the 1920s and the years after 1931 were extremely unstable periods compared with the intervening gold exchange period. Real exchange rate volatility declined again in the post-1949 era of fixed exchange rates.[46] This evidence suggests that, whatever the effects on overall FDI flows, fixed exchange rates may have influenced US MNE mode of entry into Britain by encouraging acquisitions of domestic firms. If acquisitions are regarded as a less risky means of entering a market, as suggested earlier, this is difficult to explain. However, although acquisition strategies do offer a faster entry into a market than greenfield investments, they can also be regarded as riskier in some respects. Risks arise both from the acquisition itself – sellers of a firm typically have better information than buyers – and also from post-acquisition problems of managing a preexisting firm. If US firms in the interwar years did consider acquiring British firms as a risky business, low exchange rate volatility might have encouraged them to adopt a more adventurous strategy by reducing one of the risks involved in it.

However, the strongest correlation with the shifts in entry mode in the interwar years shown in Table 4.5 appears to be with trends in the British capital markets. The 1920s saw an unprecedented merger wave in Britain, which peaked in the second half of the decade. The US acquirers formed part of this restructuring of British business through mergers, and were no doubt encouraged to consider acquisitions as an option by the high level of activity. Conversely, merger activity in Britain fell to subdued levels in the 1930s and 1940s, before starting to rise in the 1950s, leading to another giant merger wave in the 1960s.[47] Although other factors were at work, the entry modes of

Table 4.6   Percentage of acquisitions in total new US entrants in Britain 1908–62 (by 2-digit SIC code)

Industry	1908–19	1920–29	1930–39	1940–49	1950–62	1908–62
Food (20)	0	14	23	100	55	40
Chemicals (28)	33	45	13	25	30	28
Primary metals (33)	100	75	0	0	42	42
Fabricated metals (34)	0	29	38	40	55	40
Machinery (35)	67	32	29	27	51	44
Electric machinery (36)	0	50	29	50	36	36
Transportation (37)	67	63	50	100	86	70
Instruments (38)	0	60	29	20	40	35
All SIC codes	27	40	23	31	44	38

Source: Database.

US MNEs appear to have been strongly influenced by overall trends in the British market for corporate control.

In a longer perspective, there were industry-specific influences on the choice of entry mode. Table 4.6 provides a crude test for such differences by showing the ratio of acquisitions to total new US entrants for the eight largest product groups shown in Table 4.3 and for all SIC codes.

Table 4.6 appears to confirm industry-specific differences in choice of entry mode. Over the period as a whole, transportation, and to a lesser extent machinery, primary metals, and food, had higher ratios of acquisitions to total entries than the average industry, while chemicals had lower ratios. The analysis by decade only partly confirms this general picture, but especially in the earlier decades the total number of entries was so small that the ratios have no statistical significance. In this respect, the 1950–62 column is the most meaningful, as it contains the greatest number of entries. Chemicals and machinery had about the same number of entries, but the latter made far more use of acquisition than the former.

There are a number of possible explanations for such industry differences. Transactions cost theory points to the nature of the assets possessed by firms. If these assets are deeply embedded in a firm's labor force and are consequently tightly bound to a firm's organization, it is likely that they cannot be combined with those of an acquired foreign company. Instead, the firm must recreate a replica of itself by means of a greenfield investment. This suggests that the greater the research and development intensity of a foreign investor, the higher the probability that it will enter through a greenfield investment. Conversely, if the main assets of a firm consist of superior organizational ability or technical expertise that can be separated from the organization, a company can combine these assets with those embodied in an acquired foreign firm.[48] On the whole, Table 4.6 lends support to these predictions. Greenfield entry strategies were the most prominent in the more "research-intensive" industries such as chemicals, and not in machinery or food.

At the level of the individual firm, greenfield and acquisition strategies would be combined as a viable business was constructed. Procter & Gamble entered Britain by acquiring the Newcastle soap manufacturer Thomas Hedley in 1930. However, the US company proceeded to invest heavily to modernize the acquired factory, and within a few years had built an entirely new factory at Manchester as the firm rapidly gained market share in the British soap market from Unilever.[49] Pfizer, one of a cluster of US entrants into the British pharmaceutical industry after World War II, entered Britain with a greenfield investment and then made acquisitions. The firm opened an office in London in 1951 to facilitate the marketing of antibiotics, and began training sales representatives. Two years later a small factory opened in Kent. Initially only packaging operations were undertaken, but by 1955 bulk manufacture of products had begun. Research laboratories were in operation by 1958. In the same year, Pfizer acquired a British company – Kemball Bishop & Co. – with a London factory. Three years later it acquired Exning Biological Institute, a British research operation, which gave the US company an extensive line of veterinary vaccines and serums, dairy hygiene products, and other animal health products. In 1962 a new purpose-built manufacturing facility was opened in Wales. By then, the marketing of the first product of Pfizer's British-based research – a slimming biscuit – had begun.[50]

EVOLUTION OF SUBSIDIARIES

The MNE investments of US firms in Britain grew in complexity over time. Table 4.7 shows the growth of multi-plant and multi-product operations.

A proxy for this complexity is multi-plant operation. Typically, a US MNE started manufacturing in Britain with a single plant, and over time further plants would be built or acquired. The move to multi-plant manufacturing could be rapid. By the early 1880s Singer was operating three separate factories in Glasgow. In 1885, these were subsequently closed when the firm opened a large new modern plant at Kilbowie (later renamed Clydebank) west of Glasgow. This was the largest sewing machine factory in the world and the largest single factory in Britain.[51] In this case and similar instances, a shift from multi-plant to single-plant operation was not a retrograde step, but an indication of the growing scale of the business. In 1907 the number of US multi-plant operations was still limited to three firms, of which two were partly British-owned. British American Tobacco (BAT), a joint venture estab-

Table 4.7   Numbers of plants and products of US-owned manufacturing subsidiaries in Britain 1907, 1935, and 1962

	1907	1935	1962
No. of US parents	42	204	381
No. of US subsidiaries	43	222	493
Total no. of plants	48	264	728
Single plants	40	199	374
Multi-plants	8	65	354
Single product[a]	29	153	345
Multi product	14	69	148

Note: [a] Product defined using 3-digit SIC code.

Source: Database.

lished in 1901 which was two-thirds owned by American Tobacco and one-third by Imperial Tobacco, had four manufacturing plants. Two plants were operated also by Bryant and May, a British company in which Diamond Match had taken a 54.5 percent share, but which had also reverted to full British control by 1914. The only wholly owned US subsidiary with multi-plant operations was Standard Oil's Vacuum Oil (later Mobil), which had lubricating oil facilities in London and Liverpool.

A substantial increase in multi-plant operations occurred in the interwar years, often as a result of acquisition strategies. Corn Products established a marketing subsidiary in Britain in 1903, and then in 1920 acquired 40 percent of a corn-milling and glucose-refining firm in Manchester. Within 2 years Corn Products had acquired all the equity. In 1935 Corn Products bought Brown and Polson, a large Scottish manufacturer, which owned three corn-grinding mills in Scotland.[52] ITT, Procter & Gamble, Heinz, United Shoe Machinery, General Motors, and Briggs Bodies were among the other US MNEs with multi-plant operations in 1935. By 1962 multi-plant operation by US firms was widespread.[53]

The number of US-owned subsidiaries which were multi-product grew over time, and there was an increase in the range of products, although it was unusual before World War II to find firms manufacturing extremely unrelated product lines. More "typical" – from the 1935 benchmark list of multi-product operations – was Yale and Towne. This company established a sales branch in Britain in 1894, and then made its first move into British manufacturing in 1929 when it purchased the UK's largest lock manufacturer, H. & T. Vaughn. In 1935, Yale and Towne began to manufacture mechanical handling equipment at a second British plant. On a much smaller scale was the O-Cedar Corporation, which produced on a single site at Slough (between London and Reading) a range of cleaning goods, including household mops and brushes as well as chemical and cleaning products, even though its total work force only amounted to 60 employees.[54] Subsequently, the number of multi-product companies expanded much further, although (in so far as valid comparisons are possible) there would appear to have been no marked contrast between the degree of product specializations produced by the average US-owned firm and British industry as a whole.[55]

EXIT PATTERNS

An advantage in using a company-focused database rather than FDI data is that it demonstrates that MNE activity was a continuous process of entries and exits, growth and decline. This may not seem a revolutionary finding, but the frequent association of MNEs with big business, as well as the emphasis in much of the theoretical literature that MNEs must possess "advantages" to operate in foreign countries, have tended to focus research more on entry than exit patterns, though from her earliest studies onwards Wilkins has been consistent in pointing out that MNE growth patterns over time have never been continuous or "inevitable."[56] Table 4.8 examines the issue of divestment by analyzing the US subsidiaries which are known to have ceased manufacturing.

The large number of exits in the 1930s is not surprising. Many American corporations experienced financial difficulties in their domestic business and reined in their foreign ambitions. Others were apprehensive about the spread of political instability and fascism, and sought to divest, provided they could remit funds out of a country. A substantial number of US MNEs are known to have divested their British and other European operations in this decade, even though some of them simultaneously opened new plants in Latin America and elsewhere. In some cases, US divestment in Britain was accompanied by licensing agreements with British firms.[57] A comparison of the number of exits to the number of entries for each decade shows the consequences of the unstable conditions prevailing during the Depression and World War II . Both in 1908–19 and in 1950–62 the proportion of exits to entries was around 11 percent, and in the 1920s it fell to 6 percent, but in the 1930s and 1940s it rose to 28 percent.

There was a concentration of exits by product group. Not surprisingly, given their size in the overall sample, the greatest number of exits came in machinery, electric machinery, and chemicals. But in relating the number of exits to entries, apparent industry differences emerge.

Table 4.8 *US-owned subsidiaries which ceased manufacturing in Britain,*
1908–62 (by 2 digit SIC code)ᵃ – number of casesᵇ

Industry	1908–19	1920–29	1930–39	1940–49	1950–62	Total
Food (20)	0	3	0	2	1	6
Tobacco (21)	0	0	0	0	1	1
Textiles (22)	0	0	0	0	1	1
Apparel (23)	0	0	0	0	2	2
Paper (26)	0	0	0	0	1	1
Chemicals (28)	1	0	7	2	3	13
Rubber (30)	0	1	3	0	1	5
Leather (31)	0	0	1	0	0	1
Stone, clay and glass (32)	0	0	0	0	1	1
Primary metals (33)	0	1	0	1	0	2
Fabricated (34)	0	1	1	2	2	6
Machinery (35)	0	0	4	4	10	18
Electric machinery (36)	2	1	7	2	7	19
Transportation (37)	0	0	5	0	0	5
Instruments (38)	1	0	0	2	3	6
Miscellaneous (39)	0	0	3	0	0	3
Total	4	7	31	15	33	90

Note: ᵃThere were no exits for product groups not listed.
ᵇIncludes US subsidiaries founded before 1908.

Source: Database.

While the proportion for the population as a whole from 1908 to 1962 was 14 percent, it was less than 10 percent in chemicals and 25 percent in electric machinery. The case of transportation – where the proportion of exits to entries was 22 percent – was distinctive in that all five exits came in the 1930s. These were Bendix-Perrot Brakes, in which a majority share was sold to British interests in 1932; J.G. White & Co., in which control was again transferred to British interests in 1933; Willys Overland Crossley, which was liquidated in 1933; Westinghouse Brake Co., which was sold to British interests in 1935; and the Pressed Steel Co., which was also sold to British interests in 1936. However, the transportation sector remained, as noted above, the home of some of the largest and most Significant US MNEs in Britain. The database's list of the ten largest known US-owned manufacturing employers in the country in 1935 includes Ford (8600 workers), GM-owned Vauxhall (6350) and Briggs Bodies, the Ford supplier (5000).

The Vernon database suggested that, for US affiliates worldwide between 1951 and 1975, a higher proportion of subsidiaries founded by merger subsequently existed than those established through greenfield investment.[58] This is surprising if acquisitions are regarded as less risky than greenfield invest-ments, but fits well with the opposite view. The evidence from the database points in the same direction as Vernon's findings. Of the 90 US exits between 1908 and 1962, 36 originated through acquisition. The percentage of acquired firms to total exits was, therefore, 40 percent, or slightly higher than the percentage of acquisitions in total new entrants shown in Table 4.6. However, there were strong decadal variations. While all four exits in 1908–19 origi-nated as greenfield investments, the numbers of acquired firms subsequently exiting were as follows: 1920–29, 2 out of 7 (29 percent); 1930–39, 17 out of 31 (55 percent); 1940–49, 3 out of 15 (20 percent); and 1950–62, 14 out of 33 (42 percent).[59] The 1930s stand out as a time when more than half of all the exits had originated as acquisitions.

US firms "exited" by various routes. Only a relatively small number – 10 out of the total of 90 – were entirely liquidated. These were spread evenly over the whole period, with a slight peak in the 1930s when three subsidiaries were closed in the context of the general divestment from Europe at the time. An example was the Pfister and Vogel Leather Company which in 1930–31 put all of its European subsidiaries – including the British one – in liquidation.[60] This category also included a number of ventures which lasted decades before being wound up. An example was the Oliver Typewriter Manufacturing Company, which entered Britain as a distributor at the turn of the century before establishing a factory at Croydon, near London, in 1928. The subsidiary subsequently developed a large export business before going into voluntary liquidation in 1960.[61]

Far greater numbers were "anglicized" in one of two ways. In 38 cases control over the US subsidiary fell into British corporate hands. This fate awaited many US joint ventures with British firms. A major example was British American Tobacco (BAT). After the US Supreme Court ruling against American Tobacco in the antitrust case of 1911, the US firm began to sell its shares in BAT, and by the end of World War I the company – and its large manufacturing and marketing operations in Europe, China, and elsewhere – had fallen under British control.[62] In the remaining 42 cases ownership passed into the hands of the British public through a share issue. Sometimes this process of anglicization proceeded slowly. When Associated Electrical Industries was formed in Britain in 1928 as one of the country's three largest electrical companies, it was secretly controlled by GEC. However, in the mid-1930s, GEC began to dispose of stock and by 1953 the shareholding was down to 25 percent, at which point the remainder was sold off.[63]

A significant proportion of US MNEs in Britain were fairly short-lived. Among the new entrants of 1908–19, 22 percent were no longer under American control within two decades. Of the new entrants of the 1920s, 14 percent did not survive for two decades. And of the new entrants of the 1930s,

20 percent did not survive for two decades. An example of a short-lived and unsuccessful company before World War I was National Phonograph. National Phonograph was a wholly owned British subsidiary of National Phonograph Inc., of the United States, formed in 1903 to sell records and phonographs which had been made in America. Between 1904 and 1908, these products were manufactured in Antwerp, where the US company had established a subsidiary, and the British company imported products from Belgium for sale in Britain. In 1908, the Belgian manufacturing company was relocated to London. With the factory, skilled Belgian workmen and a Belgian managing director were relocated to London. This proved to be an unwise decision. The London factory had the wrong ventilation system. There was also industrial action and a large turnover of staff. Manufacture in London ceased and was relocated to the United States in 1909. Sales continued, but only until 1914, when the parent withdrew from Europe altogether.[64]

Investments of short duration could have long-term consequences for the British economy. In 1929, American Can's acquisition of the small British container manufacturer Ernest Taylor & Co. was intended to challenge the position of the British-owned Metal Box on the British market. But American Can's arrival prompted Metal Box to form a wide-ranging licensing agreement with its US rival, Continental Can. This resulted in radical improvements in the British firm's production technology and management. Although American Can sold its British company to Metal Box in 1931, thus becoming one of the shorter-lived US investments in Britain, the consequences for the British industry were considerable.[65]

This evidence on divestment rates and longevity demonstrates the risky nature of MNE investment, and in a wider sense suggests the need for caution when employing the concept of ownership advantages. While corporations such as Singer or, later, IBM entered Britain possessing large and distinct technological and/or organizational advantages over any local competitors, the scale of "advantage" held by many of the US firms investing in Britain was less impressive. Moreover the considerable number of divestments suggests that many US firms either overestimated the scale of their advantage in Britain or else underestimated the costs of FDI.

There were also cases where strong initial advantages were not sustained over time. There was often a diffusion of techniques and products to British competitors which diminished the initial advantages of US firms, and it is misleading to classify this process as a "failure" on the part of the US company. Indeed, some divestments occurred – as in the 1930s – as a result of US firms withdrawing from a mature market to seek more attractive returns elsewhere. In other cases, there was a real failure to sustain competitiveness. A prominent example was Ford, which did not end up by divesting but did experience a dramatic reversal of fortunes. Having secured a commanding market share in Britain over its local competitors by the early 1920s, managerial failure permitted powerful British automobile producers, especially Austin and Morris, to emerge and overhaul it. Ford's market share of British automobile production tumbled from 22 percent in 1921 to only 4 percent in 1929. In 1932, Ford opened the largest automobile factory in the world outside the United States at Dagenham, and the subsequent production of vehicles designed specifically for the British market was followed by a revival in the company's fortunes, but even in 1938 its market share was only 18 percent.[66]

CHARACTERISTICS OF US AFFILIATES IN BRITAIN

The database reveals some intriguing characteristics of US affiliates in Britain. Table 4.9 provides an analysis of their ownership structure.

The proportion of wholly owned subsidiaries to the total population of US affiliates firms (whose ownership structure is known) went up from 62 percent in 1907 to 69 percent in 1935, and remained around that level in 1962. This latter ratio matches quite well with the evidence from the Vernon database, which suggests that 72 percent of new US entries into Britain between 1951 and 1962 were wholly US-owned.[67] However, the high percentage of wholly-owned affiliates does not mean that there were not significant.

US investments employed other modes. Ford, for example, offered 40 percent of the equity of Ford of England to the British public in 1928, and the

Table 4.9 Ownership structures of US-owned subsidiaries in Britain 1907, 1935, and 1962[a] – number of firms

Ownership structure	1907	1935	1962
Wholly-owned	26	149	337
Joint venture (UK)	0	5	69
Joint venture (US)	1	0	4
Majority-owned	12	48	64
Minority-owned	3	13	10
Unknown	1	7	9
Total cases	43	222	493

Note: [a]Joint venture (UK) = joint venture between US and UK company. Joint venture (US) = joint venture between US companies. Majority-owned = over 50 percent of the equity held by a US company with remainder distributed to British equity market. Minority-owned = under 50 percent of the equity held by a US company with remainder distributed to British public.

Source: Database.

American parent only resumed full ownership in 1960. A prominent use of the joint venture form in the 1950s was the Haloid Co. (Xerox Corporation from 1960), which began its international expansion by forming Rank Xerox as a joint venture with Britain's Rank Organisation.

US MNEs as a whole had a long-term preference for wholly owned affiliates, which reflected a desire to retain full control over their intangible assets in product and/or process technologies. But the proportion of US wholly-owned subsidiaries in Britain appears a little higher than in other developed countries. The Vernon database shows that only 61 percent of new US entrants to Europe (excluding Britain) were wholly owned between 1951 and 1966, although the corresponding figure for Canada was 80 percent.[68] The less frequent use of joint ventures in Britain may have reflected the fact that this organizational form might be employed to economize on information requirements in foreign ventures, and was consequently often favored in unfamiliar host economies. Given the cultural proximity of the United States and Britain, US MNEs may have felt less of a need to share ownership than elsewhere in Europe. They may also have judged that British partners had in most cases little to add in terms of capabilities, which made cooperation with them rather redundant.

Table 4.10 examines industry-specific differences on ownership structures by comparing the ratio of wholly-owned subsidiaries with total subsidiaries for the eight largest product groups.

There is an expectation in the literature that firms in research-intensive industries are more inclined to seek 100 percent control ownership of their affiliates because of the danger of diffusion of their knowledge, and Dunning found support for this hypothesis in the case of US affiliates in Britain.[69] The evidence of Table 4.10 also points in this direction, though the small number of observations for some products in 1907 and 1935 makes the percentages shown of limited value. If the 1962 figures alone are taken, research-intensive industries such as chemicals and instruments do show a greater enthusiasm for

Table 4.10   Percentage of wholly owned subsidiaries in Britain, 1907, 1935, and 1962 (by 2-digit SIC code)

Industry	20	28	33	34	35	36	37	38	All products
1907		67	100	–	33	55	71	50	0	62
1935		100	67	86	67	63	68	70	58	69
1962		85	68	50	57	70	70	57	88	69

Source: Database.

Entrepreneurship and multinationals

Table 4.11   *R&D by US-owned subsidiaries in Britain, 1935 and 1962 (by 2-digit SIC code)*

Year	Total cases	Not known	No. R&D	R&D	20	23	24	28	29	30	32	33	34	35	36	37	38	39
1935	222	114	80	28	0	2	0	3	0	1	2	2	4	6	4	3	1	0
1962	493	226	132	135	4	2	1	40	2	3	5	5	12	20	18	8	13	2

Source: Database.

the wholly owned form than for primary and fabricated metals. However, over the whole period, it is the food industry which emerges with the strongest consistent preference for wholly owned subsidiaries. This is surprising, given that there is a correlation between high exporting activity and the wholly owned form, while the US food affiliates in Britain tended to focus on the domestic market (see below).[70] The concentration of US affiliates in branded products, however, appears to have provided a strong incentive towards retaining full ownership.

Britain appears to have attracted some R&D from quite an early date. Table 4.11 provides evidence on the number of US-owned subsidiaries which were known to undertake R&D in Britain.

There is little evidence of R&D activity by US affiliates in Britain at the time of the 1907 benchmark date, but in at least one case, that of Singer, such activity was evident. There is evidence of innovations in machine tools as well as sewing machine technology originating at the Glasgow factory and being diffused to the firm's operations back in the United States and elsewhere.[71]

By 1935 there was quite extensive R&D activity by US affiliates, supporting recent research that has suggested that US firms achieved high levels of internationalization of technological activity in the interwar years.[72] Kodak is credited with having established the first American industrial research laboratory abroad in 1928 when it established a facility at Harrow on the outskirts of London. By the end of the 1930s this laboratory was larger than the entire scientific effort of the US firm's British competitor – Ilford – and it was also engaged – unlike Ilford – in fundamental research work.[73] Ford also had extensive R&D operations in Britain in the 1930s.[74] General Motors, Gillette, Firestone, and Monsanto were among other US investors undertaking some R&D in Britain in the 1930s, though their strategies fluctuated. ITT's affiliate Standard Telephones & Cables established R&D facilities in 1927, but closed them in the early 1930s, though some adaptive research continued.[75] Overall, chemicals, machinery, electric machinery, and instruments accounted for 58 percent of the total known number of cases of R&D in 1935. Unfortunately, information on the quality and extent of R&D activity is thin for most firms, but it seems likely that few if any US affiliates could match the research activities of Kodak and Ford in Britain.

The database shows that, by 1962, a considerable number of US firms were engaged in R&D in Britain, two-thirds of which were located in chemicals, machinery, electric machinery, and instruments. By this date the list of US companies with sizeable R&D operations in Britain included Ford and General Motors, Esso, Monsanto, United Shoe Machinery, and Procter & Gamble, although most of the research undertaken remained adaptive rather than fundamental. The 1950s also saw the beginnings of substantial investment in R&D in pharmaceuticals by US affiliates. A pioneer was Parke, Davis & Co., which had manufactured pharmaceuticals in Britain since 1900. It established its first overseas research laboratory near London in 1951. This activity was subsequently to grow considerably in significance, as US companies were attracted to Britain by its flexible regulatory system and well-developed scientific and educational base. The "demonstration effect" of this US research effort in Britain proved important in stimulating Britain's pharmaceutical companies to engage in more intensive R&D.[76] Overall, in 1966 the British affiliates of US manufacturing firms spent $145 million on R&D in Britain, which was equivalent to about 10 percent of total privately financed R&D expenditure in that country.[77]

US investors were, from an early date, also interested in using Britain as an export platform to supply other markets. By 1965, US-owned manufacturing companies in Britain exported 25 percent of their output and sold the rest locally. Probably around half of their exports were intra-firm – i.e. to other parts of their company. US affiliates as a whole accounted for over 13 percent of total British manufacturing exports.[78] Table 4.12 shows the growth over time in the numbers of US firms engaged in exporting activities.

It is a general feature of MNE affiliates, at least since 1945, that they are on average more active in international trade than their indigenous counterparts. High export propensities are also often matched by high levels of imports, about which it is much harder to find information.[79] The most interesting

Table 4.12   Exporting by US-owned subsidiaries in Britain, 1907, 1935, and 1962

	Total cases	Exporting	Not exporting	Not known
1907	43	20	4	19
1935	222	91	15	116
1962	493	293	23	177

Source: Database.

feature of Table 4.12 is the considerable number of firms exporting even in the 1930s. The interwar years have been seen as a time when foreign affiliates increasingly focused on their domestic markets in response to stagnant trade flows and high tariffs.[80] Although the forces of political and economic nationalism were undoubtedly encouraging a trend towards the increased autonomy of affiliates in this period, it is also evident that – at least in the case of US affiliates in Britain – they never entirely opted out of the international economy.

Britain's position as the center of a worldwide empire, which included economies with high per capita incomes such as Australia, made it a potentially attractive site for US MNEs to service markets too small in themselves to have a manufacturing facility. The introduction of preferential duties in trade between Empire countries from the 1900s provided a new incentive to manufacture within the Empire. During the 1930s, a full system of imperial preferences was put in place and the sterling area – which included not only all the Empire (except for Canada and British Honduras), but also Argentina and Scandinavia and some other countries which were economically dependent on trade with Britain – came into being. The sterling area continued in some form until the early 1970s.[81]

The exports of US subsidiaries were never exclusively focused on the British Empire. Singer developed an extensive exporting business from its giant Glasgow factory. By 1881, three-quarters of the factory output was exported, and by 1905, the number had risen to 85 percent. Although British Empire markets were important, sales to other European countries were also very high.[82] In the interwar years, Ford's British subsidiary made substantial exports to Germany and the United States.[83] The formation of the European Common Market stimulated a surge of US investment into Britain which was seen as a convenient base to supply what looked like becoming a large regional market. By the early 1960s, it was becoming usual for US MNEs to use a British factory to supply their French and German sales subsidiaries.[84] In this respect, US business underestimated the scale of the British political and cultural differences with the rest of Europe, for it was not until 1973 that Britain joined the European Economic Community and thereafter began a new role as its most reluctant member.

Dunning's study found that, while US-affiliated firms as a whole accounted for around 12 percent of total manufacturing exports in 1953, there were considerable differences between products. While firms in certain lines of manufacturing such as refrigerators and sewing machines exported as much as three-quarters of their total output, the food and drink sector was much more focused on the local market.[85] The present study confirms this picture. In 1907, 60 percent of the known exporters were in the machinery (SIC 35) and electric machinery (SIC 36) product codes. In 1935 and 1962, chemicals (SIC 28) joined the other two product codes as the leading export sectors, accounting for 58 percent of known exports in 1935 and 74 percent in 1962. In contrast, the number of food firms known to export in 1907 and 1935 was only 1 and 5 respectively, although by 1962 the number had risen to 17.

These sectoral differences meant that there were sharp variations in the relative importance of exporting activities between US companies. In 1960 – a year for which data are available for quite a number of firms – GM-owned Vauxhall and Ford exported 48 and 46 percent respectively of their total sales. Caterpillar Tractors exported 60 percent of its sales. Burroughs Machines exported 42 percent of its sales of office machines, while Hoover exported 25 percent of its sales of cleaners and washing machines in 1960. In contrast, the exporting activity of the food companies was much less important. In 1960, Brown and Polson sold only 7 percent of its sales of soups, starch and glucose abroad, Heinz exported 5 percent of its sales of baked beans and pasta products, while General Food's Alfred Bird exported only 3 percent of its sales of custard and soluble coffee. For the limited number of companies for which market destination is available, the main export markets in the 1950s and the early 1960s were the British Commonwealth and the rest of Europe, though with wide inter-firm differences, reflecting not only products but also individual MNE strategies.[86]

Finally, US investors in Britain showed a distinct locational pattern. Table 4.13 shows the location by region of US-owned plants. It confirms the evidence of earlier studies that before World War II US MNE investment was heavily concentrated in the southern half of England, especially the South East region which included London.[87] Dunning's survey of US manufacturing

Table 4.13   Geographical locations of US manufacturing plants in Britain, 1907, 1935, and 1962

UK regions	1907	1935	1962
England			
Southeast	25	159	331
Midlands	9	37	86
North West	11	30	62
Other	2	18	80
Scotland	1	8	90
Wales	0	5	48
Northern Ireland	0	0	14
Unknown	0	7	17
Total	48	264	728

Source: Database.

affiliates in 1953 found that an area within 20 miles" radius of London accounted for over 46 percent of the total British employment in American firms.[88] This strong regional pattern was not an idiosyncratic US phenomenon, but reflected the geographical location pattern of similar British firms in each industry. During the interwar years it was the South East region which saw the most rapid industrial growth and the development of the new consumer goods, automobile and light engineering industries. These were the industries in which US investors were engaged.

After World War II, US companies showed a new interest in Scotland. There was a public policy influence on this locational shift. Parts of Scotland, especially around Glasgow and Dundee, were designated "development areas," where the government built plants or let them at favorable rates to British or foreign firms which invested in the area. For the most part these plants were on industrial estates with road, rail, and other infrastructure services supplied. The aim of this policy was to create more jobs in regions with high unemployment rates. Although it was not specifically targeted at US MNEs, new investors with no commitments to particular areas were likely to have been more influenced by incentives than many domestic British firms. Government officials tried to steer new inward investors to Scotland and other development areas when they entered Britain for the first time using exchange control regulations, which were the main policy used to regulate inward FDI.[89] However, there were other factors behind these postwar US shifts to Scotland, which in fact began to slow down just as more assertive regional policies began to be pursued in the late 1950s.[90] The region had a pool of skilled labor in engineering and shipbuilding, and the US investment in Scotland was very heavily concentrated in engineering. Whatever the motivation, the employment impact in a region of above-average unemployment was considerable. By the early 1970s, US affiliates accounted for 14 percent of Scotland's manufacturing labor force and for one-third of Scottish manufacturing exports.[91]

The case of Northern Ireland demonstrated that it took more than policy to influence US locational decisions. For technical reasons, Northern Ireland was not designated a development area because of its special constitutional position within the UK, but as it had the highest rate of unemployment in the whole country – which during the 1950s reached over 9 percent – the UK government was extremely anxious to attract US investment. It not only built factories to rent, but offered a program of grants or loans for plant and machinery, together with training grants. In 1956, British officials noted that though they wanted US investment in the country as a whole, they wanted "it most in Northern Ireland and are doing most to get it there."[92] Camco, which began manufacturing oil well equipment for export in Northern Ireland in 1958, cited "very good assistance towards capital outlay and newly built factory supplied at nominal rent" as the primary reason behind its location decision.[93] But, as Table 4.13 demonstrates, only a small number of US-owned factories had opened in Northern Ireland by 1962.

CONCLUSION

This chapter has employed an original database to describe the distribution and form of US manufacturing MNEs in Britain before 1962. Already established by the early twentieth century, US MNEs expanded rapidly in numbers in the 1920s. They continued to invest in the 1930s. War and its consequences slowed the growth, but it resumed on an unprecedented scale in the 1950s. US FDI was concentrated in a relatively narrow range of products; between 1908 and 1962 18 product lines accounted for over half of all new entries – in many of which they secured a large market share in Britain. These were industries in which the United States had become the world leader through innovation in technology and organization. MNEs became the vehicles for the diffusion of these innovations to other developed economies such as Britain.

US companies used both acquisitions and greenfield investment to enter Britain. There were fluctuations over time in choice of entry mode. The proportion of new entries through acquisitions rose in the first two decades of the study, then fell sharply in the 1930s before rising again. This chapter has examined a number of possible explanations about these shifts in the economic environment, protectionism, the exchange rate regime, and industry-specific factors.

A focus on firms, rather than FDI, enables MNEs to be seen as evolving business organizations rather than conduits for financial flows. Although US firms entered Britain through either an acquisition or a greenfield investment, both modes were employed in their future growth. In some periods at least, US firms first developed licensing, subcontractor, or supplier relationships with British firms before acquiring them. Once established, the operations of US firms became more complex over time as multi-plant and multi-product operations developed. The database also demonstrates quite high rates of divestment, and reveals that a significant proportion of US investments in Britain were short-lived. Although there were common influences on divestments such as the Depression in the 1930s, the multiple and idiosyncratic factors at work in individual cases make general explanations difficult. What does emerge is a sense of the fragility and riskiness of MNE investment. Whatever the size of any initial US advantage in the British market, it was difficult to sustain it over time. Moreover, although acquisitions have been often treated as a less risky means of entering a foreign market than greenfield investment, a significant percentage of US firms exiting from Britain originated as acquisitions.

The question arises of what was distinctive about US MNE activity in Britain compared with other host economies for US investment. The most striking characteristic was its size. US FDI in manufacturing in this period was concentrated in the developed market economies of Canada and Western Europe, and although Canada was always the most important host, throughout this period Britain came second. In 1929 it accounted for 43 percent of total US manufacturing FDI in Europe. In 1962 it accounted for 51 percent.[94] That year the sales of US manufacturing affiliates in Europe were equivalent to 19 percent of US affiliates worldwide, and 44 percent of US affiliates in Europe.[95] Britain's attractiveness as a host can be explained by cultural and linguistic similarities and their effect on reducing uncertainty and information costs, a large high-income market, the ease of making acquisitions, political stability, and liberal inward investment policies.

The database evidence points to some other differences of US MNEs in Britain compared, especially, with other European countries. There seems to have been a greater preference for wholly owned subsidiaries than elsewhere in Europe, though not Canada. Britain seems to have attracted considerable US R&D, and was at least in several cases the location chosen by US companies to begin the internationalization of their research activity. The database has also shown the extensive exporting activity of US affiliates in Britain, even in the interwar years. Britain was regarded over the long term as an attractive "export platform" to penetrate other markets, beginning with sterling area markets, then, later, the European market. Overall, US companies found Britain an attractive place to do business. As a group, they often seemed able to perform their business more efficiently than the local firms.

Although the chapter has sought to cover a wide range of issues related to US MNEs in Britain before 1962, a major limitation is that the significance of many of the issues raised here need comparative evidence to fully understand their significance. In 2013, there remain no comparable databases for other countries.

NOTES

1. This chapter is a revised version of an article originally published as Geoffrey Jones and Frances Bostock, *Business History Review*, **70** (2) (1996), pp. 207–56. The final section of the original article on public policy has been omitted. The dataset which it employed is now stored at the UK Data Archive. http://www.data-archive.ac.uk as SN 3142: Impact of Foreign Multi-National Investment in Britain Since 1850. PIs Jones and Bostock (1994). Subsequently Andrew Godley and Scott Fletcher compiled extensive data on foreign retailer investment in Britain. This is stored at the UK Data Archive as SN 4240: Foreign Multinational Retailers in Britain, 1850–1962 database. (2000) PIs Godley and Fletcher.

This database provides access to the Godley/ Fletcher revised and augmented version of the original database, including the retailing data, and accessible in a more user-friendly format. Among the most important publications from this new database, see Andrew Godley, "Foreign multinationals and innovation in British retailing: 1850–1962", *Business History*, **45** (1) (2003), pp. 80–100; idem and Scott Fletcher, "Foreign direct investment in British retailing, 1850–1962," *Business History*, **42** (2) (2000), pp. 43–62.

2. Derek F. Channon, *The Strategy and Structure of British Enterprise*, London: Macmillan, 1973, p. 28.

3. Report of the Committee of Enquiry into the Relationship of the Pharmaceutical Industry with the NHS, 1965–67, Cmnd 3410.

4. Unpublished paper by Economist Advisory Group, "The growth of foreign investment in the United Kingdom and the attitudes and policies which have resulted", 1967.

5. John H. Dunning, *American Investment in British Manufacturing Industry*, London: Routledge, 1958, p. 181.

6. Mira Wilkins, *The Maturing of Multinational Enterprise*, Cambridge, MA: Harvard University Press, 1974, pp. 56,182–5.

7. Ibid., p. 331.

8. William H. Davidson, "The location of foreign direct investment activity: country characteristics and experience effects," *Journal of International Business Studies* **11** (2) (1980), pp. 9–22.

9. Mira Wilkins, *The Emergence of Multinational Enterprise*, Cambridge, MA: Harvard University Press, 1970, p. 113; idem, "European and North American multinationals, 1870–1914: comparisons and contrasts," *Business History*, **30** (1) (1988), p. 24; Harm G. Schröter, *Aufstieg der Kleinen*, Berlin: Duncker & Humblot, 1993, pp. 59ff.

10. Frank A. Southard, *American Industry in Europe*, Boston, MA: Houghton, Mifflin, 1931; Wilkins, *Emergence* and *Maturing*; Chandler, *Scale*; Dunning, *American*.

11. Mira Wilkins, "Comparative hosts," *Business History*, **36** (1) (1994), pp. 18–50.

12. For a recent criticism of the use of FDI data, see Sjoerd Beugelsdijk, Jean-François Hennart, Arjen Slangen and Roger Smeets, "Why and how FDI stocks are a biased measure of MNE affiliate activity," *Journal of International Business Studies*, **41** (9) (2010), pp. 1444–59.

13. Wilkins, *Maturing*, p. 184.

14. See Max D. Steuer et al., *The Impact of Foreign Direct Investment on the United Kingdom*, London: HMSO, 1973.

15. James W. Vaupel and Joan P. Curhan, *The Making of Multinational Enterprise*, Boston, MA: Division of Research, Graduate School of Business Administration, 1969); idem, *The World's Multinational Enterprise*, Boston, MA: Division of Research, Graduate School of Business Administration, 1973.

16. Joan P. Curhan, William H. Davidson and Rajan Suri, *Tracing the Multinationals*, Cambridge, MA: Ballinger, 1977.

17. Chandler, *Scale*, 158–9; Benjamin Gomes-Casseres, "Ownership structure of foreign subsidiaries," *Journal of Economic Behavior and Organization*, **11** (1) (1989), pp. 1–25.

18. Frances Bostock and Geoffrey Jones, "Foreign multinationals in British manufacturing, 1850–1962," *Business History*, **36** (1) (1994), pp. 89–126. An earlier study based on a smaller sample of firms is Jones, "Foreign multinationals and British industry before 1945," *Economic History Review*, **41** (3) (1988), pp. 429–53.

19. In addition, the Standard Industrial Classification (SIC) coding used in the original database has been changed from the British to the US system to facilitate comparisons with work using the Vernon database.

20. US Department of Commerce, *American Direct Investments in Foreign Countries, 1940*, 1942. Dunning, *American*, found 205 companies manufacturing in Britain in 1953.

21. *Board of Trade Journal*, 26 January, 1968.

22. Chandler, *Scale*, pp. 158–9.

23. Dunning, *American*, p. 93.

24. Bostock and Jones, "Foreign multinationals," pp. 97.

25. Andrew Godley, "Pioneering foreign direct investment in British manufacturing," *Business*

History Review, **73** (3) (1999), pp. 394–429. Dunning, *American*, p. 36, estimates total British employment in all US manufacturing affiliates at 12 000–15 000 people, but this is clearly a considerable underestimate.

26. Dunning, *American*, ch. 1; Wilkins, *Emergence*, pp. 29–30, 37–45 and passim; Bostock and Jones, "Foreign multinationals".
27. Wilkins, *Maturing*, pp. 60–91.
28. Ibid., p. 191.
29. Raymond Vernon, "International investment and international trade in the product cycle," *Quarterly Journal of Economics*, **80** (2) (1966), pp. 190–207.
30. Chandler, *Scale*, pp. 158–9.
31. Chandler, *Scale*.
32. Geoffrey Jones, "Big business, management and competitiveness in twentieth century Britain," in Alfred D. Chandler Jr., Franco Amatori and Takashi Hikino (eds), *Big Business and the Wealth of Nations*, New York: Cambridge University Press, 1999.
33. Geoffrey Jones, "British multinationals and British business since 1850," in Maurice W. Kirby and Mary B. Rose (eds), *Business Enterprise in Modern Britain from the Eighteenth to the Twentieth Centuries*, London: Routledge, 1994.
34. John H. Dunning, *US Industry in Britain*, London: Wilton House, 1976, p. 28.
35. Stephen Nicholas, "Agency contracts, institutional modes, and the transition to foreign direct investment by British manufacturing multinationals before 1939," *Journal of Economic History*, **43** (3) (1983), pp. 675–86; idem, "The theory of multinational enterprise as a transactional mode," in Peter Hertner and Geoffrey Jones (eds), *Multinationals: Theory and History*, Aldershot: Gower, 1986.
36. Wilkins, *Emergence*, pp. 207–13; Wilkins, *Maturing*, pp. 417–22, 432–7.
37. Coro Inc., Annual Reports.
38. Curhan et al., *Tracing*, p. 38.
39. Michael Dubin, "Foreign acquisitions and the growth of the multinational firm," DBA thesis, Graduate School of Business Administration, Harvard University, 1976; Frederick T. Knickerbocker, *Oligopolistic Reaction and Multinational Enterprise*, Boston, MA: Harvard University School of Business Administration, 1973. There have been many contributions to the theory since the first version of Chapter 4, this volume, was published. See Peter J. Buckley and Mark C. Casson "Analyzing foreign market entry strategies: extending the internalization approach," *Journal of International Business Studies*, **29** (3) (1998), pp. 539–61, and for a brief survey of recent literature, Keith D. Brouthers, "A retrospective on: institutional, cultural and transaction cost influences on entry mode choice and performance," *Journal of International Business Studies*, **44** (1) (2013) pp. 14–22.
40. Annual reports and Moody's.
41. Edward J.T. Collins, "Brands and breakfast cereals in Britain," in Geoffrey Jones and Nicholas J. Morgan (eds), *Adding Value: Brands and Marketing in Food and Drink*, London: Routledge, 1994.
42. Michael S. Moss and John R. Hume, *The Making of Scotch Whisky*, Edinburgh, 1981.
43. This typology is based on Michael Bordo, "The gold standard, Bretton Woods and other monetary regimes: a historical approach," *Federal Reserve Bank of St. Louis Economic Review*, **75** (2) (1993), pp. 123–87. It is possible to describe the currency regimes in different ways, and certainly borderline years such as 1925/6 and 1931/2 can be reallocated.
44. Robert Z. Aliber, "A theory of foreign investment," in Charles P. Kindleberger (ed.), *The International Corporation*, Cambridge, MA: MIT Press, 1970.
45. Barry Eichengreen, "The corporate performance of fixed and flexible exchange rate regimes: interwar evidence," in Niels Thygesen, Kumaraswamy Velupillai and Stefano Zambelli (eds), *Business Cycles: Theories, Evidence and Analysis*, New York; Macmillan, 1991, pp. 243–7.
46. Vittorio Grilli and Graciela Kaminsky, "Nominal exchange rate regimes and the real exchange rate," *Journal of Monetary Economics*, **27** (2) (1991), 197.
47. Leslie Hannah, *The Rise of the Corporate Economy*, London: Metheun, 1983, pp. 91–7.
48. Jean-François Hennart and Young-Ryeol Park, "Greenfield vs. acquisition: the strategy of Japanese investors in the United States," *Management Science*, **39** (9) (1993), pp. 1054–70.

49. Chandler, *Scale*, pp. 385, 388; Charles Wilson, *The History of Unilever*, vol. 2, London: Cassell, 1954, pp. 344–50.
50. Pfizer Annual Reports 1950–62; Focus on *Pfizer*, 1961.
51. Robert Bruce Davies, *Peacefully Working to Conquer the World: Singer Sewing Machines in Foreign Markets, 1854–1920*, New York: Arno Press, 1976, p. 197; David Hounshell, *From the American System to MA Production, 1800–1932*, Baltimore, MD: Johns Hopkins University Press, 1984, p. 95; Andrew Godley, "Singer in Britain: the diffusion of sewing machine technology and its impact on the clothing industry in the United Kingdom, 1860–1905," *Textile History*, **27** (1) (1996), pp. 61–3.
52. Daniel Green, *CPC (United Kingdom): A History*, Stevenage: The Company, 1979.
53. Bostock and Jones, "Foreign multinationals," p. 109.
54. William Henry Beable, *The Romance of Great Business*, vol. 2, London: Heath Cranton, 1926; *Red Book of Commerce*, various dates.
55. Dunning, *American*, p. 96.
56. Wilkins, *Maturing*, p. 415.
57. Ibid., pp. 184–91.
58. Curhan, et al., *Tracing*, p. 168.
59. The origins of two firms which exited in 1950–62 cannot be established.
60. Annual reports; *Red Book of Commerce*, various dates.
61. George Tilghman Richards, *The History and Development of Typewriters*, London: HMSO, 1964; *Anglo-American News*, February, 1928; *Red Book of Commerce*, 1933, 1935.
62. Howard Cox, "Growth and ownership in the international tobacco industry: BAT 1902–1927," *Business History*, **31** (1) (1989), pp. 44–67; Chandler, *Scale*, p. 247.
63. Bostock and Jones, "Foreign multinationals," p. 107.
64. Peter Martland, "A business history of the Gramophone Company Ltd, 1897–1918," unpublished PhD dissertation, Cambridge University, 1993, pp. 298–9. See also the expanded version of this doctoral thesis, Peter Martland, *Recording History: The British Record Industry, 1888–1931*, Lanham, MD: Scarecrow Press, 2013.
65. William J. Reader, *Metal Box: A History*, London: Heinemann, 1976, p. 52–4; Chandler, *Scale*, pp. 318–20.
66. Roy Church, *The Rise and Decline of the British Motor Industry*, Basingstoke: Macmillan 1994, pp. 36–7; Steven Tolliday, "The rise of Ford in Britain: from sales agency to market leader, 1904–1980," in Hubert Bonin, Yannick Lung, and Steven Tolliday (eds), *Ford, 1903–2003: The European History*, vol. 2, Paris: P.L.A.G.E., 2003, pp. 7–57.
67. Curhan, et al., *Tracing*, p. 24.
68. Idem, p. 24.
69. Dunning, *US Industry*, p. 13.
70. Richard E. Caves, *Multinational Enterprise and Economic Analysis*, Cambridge: Cambridge University Press, 1982, p. 87.
71. Andrew Godley kindly provided this information from his research on the Singer archives deposited at the State Historical Society in Madison, WI.
72. John A. Cantwell, "The globalisation of technology: what remains of the product cycle model?" *Cambridge Journal of Economics*, **19** (1) (1995), pp. 155–74.
73. Wilkins, *Maturing*, p. 84; David Edgerton, "Industrial research in the British photographic industry, 1879–1939," in Jonathan Liebenau (ed.), *The Challenge of New Technology*, Aldershot: Gower, 1988.
74. Mira Wilkins and Frank Ernest Hill, *American Business Abroad: Ford on Six Continents*, Detroit, MI: Wayne State University Press, 1964, pp. 291–2, 303, 384, updated edition, Cambridge: Cambridge University Press, 2011.
75. Peter Young, *Power of Speech: a History of Standard Telephones and Cables, 1883–1983*, London: Allen & Unwin, 1983.
76. Michael Brech and Margaret Sharp, *Inward Investment*, Chatham House papers no. 21, 1984, pp. 41–62; Jones, "Big business".
77. Dunning, *US Industry*, p. 20. Dunning's data are derived from *US Direct Investment Abroad, Part 1: Investment Position, Financial and Operating Data*, Group 2, preliminary report 1971, p. 123.

78. Dunning, *US Industry*, pp. 26, 100.
79. The current study is no exception. Only limited and fragmentary data were located on importing activities.
80. United Nations, *World Investment Report 1994*, New York: United Nations, 1994, p. 122.
81. P.J. Cain and A.G. Hopkins, *British Imperialism: Crisis and Reconstruction 1914–1990*, London: Longman, 1993, ch. 5, 11.
82. Godley, "Early foreign direct investment".
83. Wilkins and Hill, *American*, pp. 247, 304.
84. For example, annual reports of Polymer Corporation and Avon Products.
85. Dunning, *American*, pp. 281–9.
86. Replies to questionnaires on American enterprises in Britain, 1963 and 1965, Dunning database, University of Reading.
87. See also Christopher M. Law, *British Regional Development since World* War I, Newton Abbot: David and Charles, 1980.
88. Dunning, *American*, pp. 84–90.
89. Geoffrey Jones, "The British government and foreign multinationals before 1970," in Martin Chick (ed.), *Governments, Industries and Markets*, Aldershot: Edward Elgar, 1990. On British public policy, see also subsequent research, especially Tim Rooth and Peter Scott, "British public policy and multinationals during the "dollar gap" era, 1945–1960," *Enterprise & Society*, **3** (1) (2002), pp. 124–61.
90. Peter Dicken and Peter E. Lloyd, "Geographical perspectives on United States investment in the United Kingdom," *Environment and Planning* (1976), pp. 696–7.
91. Dunning, *US Industry*, p. 12.
92. Secret directive to British Information Services about publicity regarding development areas and American industrial investment, 11 September, 1956, T 2341616, National Archives, UK.
93. Replies to questionnaires on American enterprises in Britain, 1965, Dunning database, University of Reading. See also Camco Inc. *Annual Report*, 1959.
94. Wilkins, *Maturing*, pp. 185, 331.
95. Dunning, *US Industry*, p. 31, citing *Survey of Current Business*.

5. The Imperial Bank of Iran and Iranian economic development, 1890–1952[1]

OVERVIEW

Between 1889 and 1928 a British bank served as the state bank and bank of issue of Iran (usually known as Persia until the 1930s), and held a virtual monopoly of the modern banking sector of that country. The Imperial Bank of Persia was one of a group of British "overseas banks" founded in the nineteenth century which pioneered banking and established branches in Asia, Australasia, Africa, and South America. A number of these banks built widespread branch networks: the branches of the Oriental Bank Corporation in the 1880s, for instance, spanned Africa, Australasia, and Asia.[2] The geographical spread of operations of these banks was far wider than those of British manufacturing MNEs until after 1945, and they represent a fascinating, and much neglected, manifestation of British international business. The British overseas banks were "free-standing companies."[3] They did not grow out of the domestic operations of any existing bank headquartered in Britain and conducted no domestic banking, although they sometimes collected British deposits, at least before World War I.

THE HISTORY OF THE IMPERIAL BANK

The Imperial Bank was founded in London in 1889 on the basis of a concession from the Iranian government which made it the state bank, with the exclusive right to issue notes and tax-free status, for 60 years. Nineteenth-century Iran has been described as "one of the most backward countries in the world."[4] It attracted little FDI. There was a modest road construction company.[5] A British oil syndicate was also formed in 1901, which, after a lot of trouble, finally discovered a huge oil field in 1908 which represented the birth of the Middle East oil industry, and of one of the world's largest oil companies, the Anglo-Persian Oil Company, which became the Anglo-Iranian Oil Company in 1935 and eventually took the name BP in 1954. It was not until the 1930s that Iran acquired any railroads or modern industry. Iran was also subject, especially before 1914, to foreign interference because of its geopolitical situation between the Russian Empire and British India.[6]

An immediate question is why British investors should want to found a bank in such a country. The peculiar answer is that the bank was founded by mistake. The story went back to a concession given in 1872 to Baron Julius de Reuter, naturalized Briton and founder of Reuters News Agency, which granted him control over most of Iran's natural resources. Long regarded as a deplorable example of the corrupt ruling Qajar Shahs selling their country to Western capitalists, the Reuter Concession can also be seen as an attempt by the government to promote economic growth. The core of the concession was a plan to build railroads, which the government recognized it had neither the capital nor the technology to construct itself.[7]

The Reuter Concession was opposed within Iran and by Russia, forcing the Shah to cancel it, and it was not until 1889 that Reuter was able to get compensation. In 1887 the Russians forced the Shah to agree not to give railroad concessions to any foreign company without their permission. Reuter had a brilliant idea. An obscure article in the 1872 concession had given him the right to establish a national bank. Reuter argued that such an institution would be an Iranian rather than a foreign company, and therefore free from the Russian veto on building railroads. The Shah liked the idea, and almost to the last moment of the negotiations for the Imperial Bank's concession (signed 30 January 1889), the Iranians and the British were preoccupied by railroads. However, Russian pressure forced the omission of the magic word "railroad" from the concession, and in March the Tsar forced the Shah into a five-year moratorium on the construction of all railroads. Reuter and the Shah were left with a bank instead of a railroad.[8]

The Imperial Bank was publicly floated in London. The Eastern trading house of David Sassoon took around 30 percent of the share issue and had a seat on the board. Other directors illustrated the original purpose behind the Bank. There was a representative of Glyn Mills, a domestic British bank active in the finance of foreign railroads.[9] Sir William Keswick, the Bank's chairman, was a former chairman of the Hongkong Bank, which was active in multiple "development" projects in China. The Board sat in London, supported by a tiny London Office, and with the chief executive in Tehran. The staff sent out to manage the Bank in Iran, as well as Iraq and India where the Bank established branches in the 1890s, were almost entirely British.

The Imperial Bank's history can be split into pre- and post-1928 periods. Before 1928 it was effectively the only modern bank in the country, with the exception of a Russian bank founded in 1890, which made a lot of "political" loans and ended life in disarray.[10] The Imperial Bank had 24 branches in all major Iranian cities by 1928, which served retail and service markets – taking deposits, making advances, financing trade, and dealing in foreign exchange.

It also functioned as the state bank – issuing bank notes; importing silver for mintage into currency; keeping the government's accounts and acting as a recipient of its revenues; and making advances to the government. In addition, the Bank also floated Iran's two foreign loans in London (1892 and 1911), and British government loans were on-lent through the Bank to the Iranian government between 1903 and 1919. The British government loans were used as an instrument of diplomacy, and on occasion the Foreign Office obliged the Bank to cease lending to Iranian governments it did not like.[11]

The Imperial Bank's wide range of functions was matched by a wide range of obligations. The British shareholders expected dividends. The Shah wanted a state bank. The Foreign Office wanted an agent of Empire. The Bank's policies fluctuated according to which "interest group" exerted the most influence. When crunches came, as in the two world wars, the Bank put the interests of the British government first, those of the shareholders second, and the Iranian government's last.[12]

This order of priority helps to explain the second stage of the Bank's history from 1928 to 1952, when it was attacked by nationalist governments and eventually withdrew from Iran. A striking feature of this period was the violent reaction against British business as a whole in Iran, especially the two enterprises which dominated the modern sectors of the economy: the Anglo-Iranian Oil Company and the Imperial Bank. By the early 1950s there was nothing left of British business in Iran except a single firm of contractors.[13] The foundation of the new Pahlavi dynasty by Reza Shah in the mid-1920s was followed by a campaign to modernize Iran, and to challenge foreign business. A central bank, Bank Melli, was founded in 1928. The Imperial Bank lost its role as the state bank, and in 1933 had to relinquish its note-issuing powers. In the 1930s exchange controls and barter agreements destroyed the Bank's business in financing foreign trade. Foreign exchange business became increasingly centralized on Tehran, leaving the Bank's extensive provincial branch network to waste away.

Opportunities to participate in Iranian industrialization were spurned as the Bank went into a corporate sulk. In 1936 the seven Board members had an average age of 71, with an 83-year-old chairman, who had become a director in 1913 after retiring from the Indian Civil Service. The directors resembled a collection of Old Testament prophets: they certainly had no sympathy for the new Iran. The Imperial Bank lost market share rapidly to Bank Melli – by 1939 it held only 9 percent of Iranian bank deposits – and closed half its branches in the 1930s. After a respite during World War II, when Britain and Russia deposed Reza Shah and occupied Iran, the Bank was subjected to growing government regulation. The Bank decided to pull out, and it concentrated on opening new branches in the Arabian Gulf in the 1940s.[14] In September 1951 the Bank was banned from dealing in foreign exchange during the dispute about the nationalization of the Anglo-Iranian Oil Company, and left Iran in the following year.[15]

IMPACT OF THE IMPERIAL BANK ON THE IRANIAN ECONOMY

Few could disagree with Rondo Cameron's view that in a developing economy "financial innovation . . . may assume an importance commensurate with technical innovation in industry."[16] However, British overseas banks were rarely cast as positive economic forces. This section argues that, at least with regard to Iran, there were more positive gains, as well as some serious negatives.

Did the Bank extract "large" profits from Iran for its British shareholders? British banks in this period were allowed to disguise their profits by making transfers to or from "inner" or "secret" reserves before reaching their published profit figure. The Imperial Bank's "real" profits were on average about twice as high as its published profits between 1890 and 1952.[17] A comparative study of the ratio of such "real" profits to shareholder funds between the Imperial Bank and other British overseas banks for which such data are known showed that the Imperial Bank was less profitable by this measure than all the other banks between 1896 and 1913. However, it had by far the highest ratio between 1921 and 1929, and even a much weakened performance during the following decade left it more profitable than both the Chartered Bank, which had a large branch network in Asia, and Bolsa, which had a large branch network in Latin America. A comparative study of NPV returns shows that the Imperial Bank's shareholders received average returns compared with those of other overseas banks between 1896 and 1913, although returns were smaller compared with two leading domestic banks. However, the Imperial Bank shareholders did very well during the 1920s, with their returns only being exceeded by two British overseas banks active in Australia and New Zealand, and even did well during the following decade, earning positive returns when the shareholders of almost all other banks had negative returns.[18]

It is not straightforward to interpret these profitability data. The strong profitability and dividend performance during the 1920s was due largely to the profits made by the Imperial Bank during World War I, especially from servicing the British Army. During the 1930s the Iran banking operations contributed little to the Bank's overall profits. Between 1931 and 1939 the profits from the Bank's London office exceeded by a large margin those from Iran: indeed, in 1931, 1933, 1934, and 1935 the Bank made losses in Iran. The profits made in London were derived from investment income, and, in 1933 and 1934, from the sale of investments. The Bank's profitability in Iran increased sharply after the Allied occupation of the country in 1941, but fell away once more when the British military left.

Iran, then, was no El Dorado for the Imperial Bank. It made relatively small profits as it pioneered modern banking before World War I, and subsequently it was most profitable when Iran had a British military presence during the world wars. This is not surprising given the undeveloped nature of the economy. During the interwar years the Bank also made little attempt to adjust to the changing political circumstances of the country. This reflected a widespread failure in the British government as well as business to understand modern Iranian nationalism.[19] As pressures mounted, the Bank's management preferred to move to new virgin territories rather than confront the complex and evolving political situation. During the 1940s the Bank (known as the British Bank of the Middle East after 1952) established itself as the first and only bank in many of the small Arabian Gulf states, including Kuwait, Dubai, and Oman.[20]

With regard to the impact on the Iranian economy, the Bank pioneered modern banking in the country. It operated nationally, and when Iran was divided into British and Russian "spheres of influence" in 1907, the Bank's branches spanned both sides. The Bank, unlike the oil company,[21] was not "enclavist." It was arguably the only truly "national" institution in Iran before the 1920s.

Iran was not without financial institutions before the arrival of the Imperial Bank, and any consideration of its impact needs to assess its effects on the traditional moneylenders (*sarrafs*). The impact was remarkably little. In 1908 the Bank estimated that it handled only 6.5 percent of Iran's foreign trade finance, with the remainder mainly in the hands of sarrafs. The flexibility of their loan terms and cultural ties were among the factors which preserved the sarrafs from Imperial Bank competition. The Imperial Bank's "advantages" over local financiers were limited to certain sectors of the banking market. The Imperial Bank did not retard the development of indigenous modern banking. It was obstructive when the Bank Melli was being formed in 1928, but to little effect, as the political situation in Iran had moved beyond its control.[22]

An MNE can make an important contribution to a host economy by supplying foreign capital, and thus filling a resource gap in that economy between desired investment and domestic savings. The Iranian economy can be categorized as "capital-short" in this era, but the Imperial Bank did little directly to improve the situation. The convention of British banking was to transfer as little as possible of shareholders' funds to a foreign country, because of exchange and political risks. Around £500 000 of capital (equivalent to $62 million in 2013 US dollars) was transferred to Iran by the Bank by 1891, but some of this was subsequently remitted back again, and at the end of the 1920s all capital not in fixed assets was remitted to Britain. The Imperial Bank was not a significant source of funds to supplement domestic savings.

The Bank raised most of its funds from within Iran. The strategy was to use a branch network to build up a local deposit base, which then financed lending. Reverting to theory, the Imperial Bank's "advantage" lay not so much in supplies of capital, but in superior skill and enterprise, together with access to British political and military influence. The bank's unwillingness to use its own funds attracted growing criticism in Iran, and became a major bone of contention in the 1930s. On several occasions between 1933 and 1936 the government asked the Bank to provide funds, on commercial terms, to help finance the industrialization program, only to be turned down (against the advice of the Bank's Tehran management) by the Board in London. The Bank was eventually forced into lending in 1936 under extreme coercion.[23]

The Bank did, however, make a contribution to the Iranian economy by mobilizing domestic savings. Arguably, much of this money would have remained hoarded, or locked into traditional money lending, at least until the creation of the Bank Melli. Nevertheless considerable doubts have been expressed about the uses to which the mobilized savings were put. It has been claimed that the Bank "discriminated against Persians in giving credit."[24] British banks in India, Egypt, and Africa, especially before 1914, largely lent to British firms and trading companies, usually to finance foreign trade, but in Iran the Imperial Bank always lent to local merchants: the few expatriate firms offered too little business. Moreover, the Bank's managers in Iran, despite the concerns of the Board in London, were prepared to abandon British banking orthodoxy and made unsecured loans on the basis of a customer's "name." However, it does seem that expatriate firms were often granted larger credit facilities than Iranian merchants. In the early 1920s, for example, an expatriate firm in the carpet industry was allowed unsecured overdrafts up to £35 000, a level of credit higher than that allowed to "local" enterprises.

A greater criticism of the Bank's lending policies was that it primarily provided Iranian merchants and expatriate firms alike with short-term credit for working capital. The provision of long-term capital for industrial investment on the lines of German-style investment banking might have had a more beneficial developmental function. However, short-term credit freed the resources of merchants for fixed investment, especially as credit facilities were frequently rolled over beyond the conventional six-month period. By these means the Bank played an important role in the finance of the expanding carpet industry (largely run by expatriate European firms) in pre-1914 Iran. There were many and varied obstacles to industrialization in Iran before the late 1920s – political instability, absence of tariffs, poor labor supplies – and it is doubtful if the Bank could have overcome such constraints by longer-term advances, especially as there is no evidence of an unfilled demand. It is perhaps noteworthy that the Bank Melli, after its formation in 1928, did not embark on any industrial promotion role on the lines of Bank Misr in interwar Egypt, although the government did establish an Agricultural and Industrial Bank which provided cheap credit to the burgeoning industrial sector in the 1930s.[25]

Whether the Imperial Bank's preoccupation with the finance of the foreign trade sector was beneficial to Iran is also debatable. The Bank served before 1914 to strengthen the links between Iran and the international economy. Iran's growing dependence on primary commodity exports, such as opium, and the importation of manufactured cotton textiles, both activities with whose finance the Bank was largely concerned, may not have been the ideal development pattern, although in the political and economic circumstances before 1914 it is hard to envisage viable alternative scenarios for Iran, and there were significant income gains from the trade sector. The Bank should not be seen as an instrument drawing Iran into an exclusive trading relationship with Britain's Asian empire. Certainly, before 1914, the Bank's southern branches in Iran were primarily concerned with financing trade and arranging exchange between Iran, Britain and British India. In 1927, 80 percent of the lending of the Bushire, Shiraz, and Esfahan branches was to finance Iranian exports of opium to the East, especially the British colony of Singapore and China. However, the Bank's northern branches, such as Tabriz, Mashad, and Rasht, were largely engaged before 1914 in financing Russo-Iranian trade, such as the large Iranian exports of rice and cotton to its northern neighbor. During the 1920s the Mashad branch financed exports of cotton and wool to the Soviet Union, and Rasht financed trade in rice, cotton, and dried fruits, while all the northern branches worked closely with the Soviet trade monopolies established after the 1917 Revolution.

The Imperial Bank performed only a marginal entrepreneurial role in Iran, although it did more in this direction than domestic banks in Britain. As befitted an institution founded by people who wanted to build railroads, the Bank became involved in road construction and mines in the 1890s, with disastrous results. Again, just before 1914 the Bank was involved in an attempt to build railroads – the Persian Railroads Syndicate – but this too was unsuccessful.[26] Iran's first railroads were built by the Iranian government in the 1930s. The Imperial Bank probably made a more important contribution to business enterprise in Iran before 1914 by encouraging a fall in the high interest rates prevailing in the traditional economy.

The Bank did stimulate the Iranian economy by contributing to its monetization. It constructed a nationwide branch network in a country which previously lacked a national financial market. It introduced a paper currency, and reformed the metallic coinage before 1914. However, the economic benefits of these measures were to some extent muted. The note issue grew slowly and spasmodically (nil in 1890; £500 000 in 1905; £180 000 in 1916; £2.5 million in 1928). The Bank's charter obliged it to maintain high cash reserves against the note issue, limiting its enthusiasm for expanding the issue. Moreover, the acceptance of notes was reduced because they were only payable at par at the branch of issue: a Tabriz note would only be encashed in Tehran at a discount.[27] Despite complaints from the Imperial Bank's own managers in the 1920s this policy was not changed until 1929, when the Bank Melli forced the matter by encashing Imperial Bank notes at par all over the country.[28]

Arguably, one of the Imperial Bank's most clear-cut contributions to Iranian economic development was its educational role. This may seem paradoxical. The Bank had little interest in education and offered no formal training to its staff. The Bank's British staff were recruited for their "character" and sporting abilities, and offered only on-the-job training.[29] Yet in Iran before the 1920s the Bank provided one of the few stable sources of employment where basic office and banking skills could be acquired, and the English language studied. The numbers employed were small – never more than 400 at any one time. In contrast the oil company employed 20 000 Iranians in 1930. Nevertheless, the Bank's role in training a modern business elite was noteworthy, as it was to be again in the Arabian Gulf in the 1940s and 1950s.

There were flaws here too. Like all British overseas banks until the 1950s, the Imperial Bank would not employ locals as managers. In contrast, the Imperial Ottoman Bank, which had mixed British, French and Turkish ownership, employed Middle East nationals in managerial positions from an early date.[30] Attitudes within the Imperial Bank would now be regarded as grotesquely racist. The Bank's first chief executive, Joseph Rabino, was born in London but with an Italian father, and he was always regarded with great suspicion by his Board. When he resigned in 1908 one director cited with approval a view that the Bank would henceforth be a "white man's bank."[31] In the interwar years, there was a steady flow of Iranian staff from the Imperial Bank to national institutions, especially the Bank Melli. The Bank came to perform a valuable role as an involuntary training school for the modern economic sector. Needless to say the Imperial Bank did not welcome this role, and in one case it was positively ruinous. In 1936 the Bank's most prominent local employee, Abol Hassan Ebtehaj, resigned after having his requests for promotion rejected. By 1942 he had become the governor of the Bank Melli, and proceeded over the following eight years to wage a relentless war of attrition against his former employer.[32]

Ebtehaj's policies were driven by a deep resentment of how his country had been treated by foreign powers, especially Britain. For many Iranians any positive economic gains from British enterprise in Iran were outweighed by the effect on the country's sovereignty. The Bank was widely seen as an agent of British imperialism, and with reason. During the two world wars, and in the early 1920s, the Imperial Bank put British diplomatic interests before those of Iran. Reza Shah referred bitterly to "Lord Curzon's Bank of Persia," in view of the Bank's apparent subservience to the British foreign secretary.[33] In fact, matters were not so simple. The Bank was never entirely the tool of the British government: it had to make profits for its shareholders. Conversely, the Foreign Office distrusted the Bank before 1914, as it did most British business interests. During the interwar years Foreign Office officials were often dismissive of the Bank's reactionary policies. However, the relationship between the Bank and the British government was sufficiently close for it to be no surprise that Iranians missed the peculiarly British nuances of the situation.

Paradoxically the Bank may have assisted Iran to retain independence before World War I. The Bank helped to reform the ramshackle financial administration of the government. More importantly, lending to the government helped to prevent Iran from falling under the direct dominion of Britain and/or Russia. True, the Bank acted as a channel for British government loans and issued Iran's loans on the London Stock Exchange. It can thus be cast as an instrument in an imperialist "strangling" of Iran. However, the Bank's own large advances to the government before 1914 kept the army paid, and thereby ensured that some central-government presence was maintained in parts of the country. They also enabled Iran to meet sufficient of its debt repayments to the British and Russian governments for them never to be given an excuse to end Iran's independence. The British government trusted the Imperial Bank as it did no other "Iranian" institution, and the British authorities were prepared to work through it rather than directly. Certainly, Iranian governments preferred borrowing from the Bank to borrowing from foreign governments, whose loans carried political conditions.[34]

Yet it was appearances which shaped perceptions, and those appearances were of the Imperial Bank as part of a British ecosystem to subjugate and denigrate a country with a proud and rich traditional culture. The bank also owed its initial position to a geopolitical situation which saw Britain and Russia divide the country into "spheres of influence." Iranians had not been considered fit to be appointed to managerial positions even in their own state bank. These and similar policies by other expatriate firms inevitably fostered the growing nationalism which ultimately resulted in not only the exit of the Imperial Bank, but also the nationalization of the Anglo-Iranian Oil Company in the early 1950s. The subsequent overthrow of the Iranian government by the British and US intelligence services in 1954, and their subsequent support for the increasingly corrupt regime of the Shah, set in motion resentments and imbalances which would result in the Islamic Revolution in 1978.[35]

CONCLUSION

In nationalist literature in Iran, the Imperial Bank, like the Anglo-Persian Oil Company, has often featured as a rapacious capitalist and imperialist agent. While serious criticisms can be leveled at the Bank's policies, such a view exaggerates the capacity of the Imperial Bank to be rapacious. Established by people who wanted to build a railroad rather than run a bank, the Imperial Bank had a struggle to make profits even when it held a banking monopoly. It made most money when the British Army occupied or fought in Iran during the two world wars. During the interwar years, the Bank's political judgment was jejune, while in the 1940s it was crippled by the actions of an aggrieved former employee now heading its national rival.

From a long-term perspective, the impact of the Bank on the Iranian economy can be seen as a mixture of costs and benefits. It does seem that the benefits outweighed the costs before the 1920s, even though the Bank could have improved on its developmental impact. During the 1930s the Bank's hostility to Iranian government policies, especially industrialization, only added to the many obstacles in the way of the country's economic development. A final reflection takes an Iranian government perspective. The nineteenth-century Shahs had originally sought the assistance of foreign businessmen such as Reuter to modernize their very backward economy. Although they preferred a railroad to a bank, they had persuaded a group of British capitalists to establish a bank, and transfer sufficient skills and resources to Iran to ensure its survival. This institution had given Iran a modern banking system; facilitated trade; issued a paper currency; financed the government; mobilized savings; and provided a cadre of skilled Iranian bankers. When, during and after the 1920s, Iran had developed sufficient resources to have its own bank, the services of the Imperial Bank were unceremoniously disposed of.

From another perspective, however, the Bank formed part of a quasi-colonial system which treated Iranians as second-rate people in their own country. The policies of Iranian governments, like their Chinese counterparts, during the second global economy can only be understood within the context of the humiliations suffered during the first global economy.

NOTES

1. This chapter is a revised version of an article first published in *Business and Economic History*, vol. 16, 1987.
2. Geoffrey Jones, *British Multinational Banking 1830–1990*, Oxford: Clarendon Press, 1993, pp. 20–21, 23, 25, 27; Albert S.J. Baster, *The International Banks*, London: P. S. King, 1935; reprinted New York: Arno Press, 1977, p. 164.
3. Mira Wilkins, "Defining a firm: history and theory," in Peter Hertner and Geoffrey Jones

(eds), *Multinationals: Theory and History*, Aldershot: Gower, 1986, pp. 84–7; Mira Wilkins, "The free-standing company, 1870–1914: an important type of British foreign direct invest-ment", *Economic History Review*, **41** (2) (1988), pp. 259–82. This argument is developed further in Geoffrey Jones, "British overseas banks as free-standing companies," in Mira Wilkins and Harm Schröter (eds), *The Free-Standing Company in the World Economy 1830–1990*, Oxford: Oxford University Press, 1998, pp. 344–60.

4. Julian Bharier, *Economic Development in Iran 1900–1970*, London: Oxford University Press, 1971, p. 20.

5. David McLean, "Constructors in a foreign land: Messrs Lynch & Co on the Bakhtiari road 1897–1913," *Business History*, **54** (4) (2012), pp. 487–509.

6. Firuz Kazemzadeh, *Russia and Britain in Persia*, New Haven, CT: Yale University Press, 1968.

7. Guity Nashat, *The Origins of Modern Reform in Iran, 1870–1980*, Urbana, IL: University of Illinois Press, 1981, p. 21.

8. Geoffrey Jones, *Banking and Empire in Iran*, Cambridge: Cambridge University Press, 1986, ch. 1.

9. Roger Fulford, *Glyn's 1753–1953*, London: Macmillan, 1953, p. 133.

10. B.V. Ananich, *Rossikoe Samoderzhavi i Vyvoz Kapitalov*, Leningrad: Nauka, 1975.

11. Jones, *Banking*, pp. 87, 92, 116–7, 128, 192–3.

12. Ibid., ch. 6, 11.

13. Frances Bostock and Geoffrey Jones, "British business in Iran 1860s–1960s," in Richard Davenport-Hines and Geoffrey Jones (eds), *British Business in Asia since 1860*, Cambridge: Cambridge University Press, 1988.

14. Kazemzadeh, *Russia*.

15. Jones, *Banking*.

16. Rondo Cameron, et al., *Banking in the Early Stages of Industrialization*, New York: Oxford University Press, 1967, p. 8.

17. Geoffrey Jones, *Banking and Oil*, Cambridge: Cambridge University Press, 1987, pp. 276–9.

18. Jones, *British*, Appendix 5.

19. William R. Louis, *The British Empire in the Middle East 1945–1951*, Oxford: Clarendon Press, 1984, pp. 638–40; 651–3.

20. Jones, *Banking and Oil*, ch. 10.

21. Ronald W. Ferrier, *The History of the British Petroleum Company*, Cambridge: Cambridge University Press, 1982, p. 398.

22. Jones, *Banking*, pp. 207–8.

23. Ibid., pp. 227–33.

24. Julian Bharier, "Banking and economic development in Iran," *Banker's Magazine*, 204, (1967), p. 295.

25. On Bank Misr, see Eric Davis, *Challenging Colonialism: Bank Misr and Egyptian Industrialization, 1920–1941*, Princeton, NJ: Princeton University Press, 1983; Robert L. Tignor, *State, Private Enterprise, and Economic Change in Egypt, 1918–1952*, Princeton, NJ: Princeton University Press, 1984.

26. Jones, *Banking*, pp. 56–64, 92–4, 129–31.

27. Ibid., p. 126.

28. Ibid., p. 219.

29. Jones, *Banking*, ch. 5, 10.

30. André Autheman, *La Banque impériale ottomane*, Paris: Comité pour l'Histoire économique et financière de la France, 1996.

31. Ibid., p. 108.

32. Ibid., pp. 305–9, 315–31; Frances Bostock and Geoffrey Jones, *Planning and Power in Iran: Ebtehaj and Economic Development under the Shah*, London: Frank Cass, 1989.

33. Jones, *Banking*, pp. 195.

34. Ibid., pp. 115–24.

35. Bostock and Jones, *Planning*, ch. 9.

6. MNEs, economic development, and social change in Asia[1]

OVERVIEW

This chapter offers a historical perspective on the role of MNEs in the economic development and the process of social change in Asia. Since the nineteenth century MNEs have been important in transferring across borders knowledge, technology, and organizational skills, and in facilitating trade flows. However, as the previous chapter on Iran explored, this impact has typically involved costs as well as benefits. Outcomes were shaped not only by MNE strategies, but also by the economic, social, and political characteristics of the host economy. This chapter explores this issue further by looking broadly at Asia.

The chapter has three sections. First, it surveys long-term patterns of MNE investment in Asia. Second, it examines the developmental impact of this investment, again providing a long-term perspective. Finally, it explores the role of MNEs on aspects of social change and environmental sustainability in Asia.

MNEs, ASIA, AND GLOBALIZATION WAVES

Asia's role in the waves of globalization since the nineteenth century have varied greatly over time. During the first global economy, Asia was on the wrong side of the Great Divergence. Its formerly huge handicraft industry faced the challenge of cheap manufactured textiles, large regions in South and Southeast Asia fell under Western imperial control, and the states which stayed sovereign, such as China, Japan, and Thailand, faced a precarious struggle to survive.

The structure of MNE investment in Asia broadly reflected this wider political and economic context. As discussed further in the following section, Western firms sought Asian markets for manufactured staples, and more importantly they sought raw materials and food for their industries and urban populations. Asia received 21 percent of total world inward FDI in 1914 and 25 percent in 1938. India and China were the two largest Asian hosts.[2]

Asia's position as a home region for MNEs rested primarily on Japan where, as shown in Chapter 2, institutional reforms associated with the Meiji Restoration had facilitated the emergence of modern business enterprises. Although Japan as an economy was a net capital importer before 1914, Japanese cotton textile firms and trading companies had made significant direct investments, especially in Asia. Although the stock of Japanese FDI never reached 3 percent of the world total, in 1930 it may have counted for between 11.5 and 13.6 percent of Japan's gross national income. As a point of comparison, even in the mid-1980s the ratio of Japanese outward FDI to its national income was only 5.9 percent. Certainly by the interwar years, Japanese textile, trading and mining firms had made extensive investments in the markets and resources of Asia.[3]

Japanese firms were not entirely alone crossing borders. Cochran has also shown the vitality of Chinese trading networks in Southeast Asia during the interwar years.[4] European empires provided a political and security umbrella for Chinese and Indian commercial diaspora, which created businesses which were linked across national borders by ties of family, clan, and ethnicity.[5] South Asians who migrated to East Africa during the nineteenth century created substantial trading businesses which connected Asia and Africa.[6] These business networks were major forces of regional and international integration, and highly fluid, as they involved both permanent and temporary flows of people who moved money and goods within and across regions.[7] The extent and impact of these networks are simply not captured by FDI estimates. It is a huge gap.

During the era of constrained globalization Asia's significance in global capitalism declined. After 1949 Communist China blocked inward FDI. Postcolonial countries took national ownership of many natural resources. In Malaysia, the New Economic Policy launched in 1971 led to the localization of the extensive plantation businesses owned by British business groups.[8] During the 1970s, Indian government policies, especially price and exchange controls, and demands for local equity participation, resulted in many MNEs divesting from that country. For multiple reasons, and especially government restrictions on wholly owned subsidiaries, there was little inward FDI in Japan. In 1980 the stock of inward FDI of Britain alone was virtually double that of South, Southeast, and East Asia including Japan combined, which had shrunk to 7 percent of the world total.

Asian outward FDI was also limited. The first wave of Japanese MNE investment was swept away by World War II, whose aftermath saw all the country's overseas assets expropriated. Subsequently Japanese outward FDI remained at low levels until its resumption of growth from the 1970s. Japan's general trading companies, or *sogo shosha*, survived their dismantling by the Allied occupation after World War II, and emerged as central players in both Japan's foreign trade and FDI before the 1970s.[9]

Asia returned to a central place during the second global economy. By 1990 the continent, including Japan, accounted for around 17 percent of world inward FDI stock. By 2011 it held 21 percent. The most dramatic change was in China, where inward FDI began to increase after the gradual opening of the domestic market to FDI in the 1980s, and the extension of the liberalization program to services during the following decade. From 1979 until 2000 China absorbed, on a cumulative basis, over $346 billion of inward FDI. Although inward FDI only represented around 5 percent of Chinese GDP during the second half of the 1990s, and amounted to less than one-seventh of total investment, foreign MNEs accounted for one-half of gross exports.[10] As elsewhere, FDI flows were clustered. China, Hong Kong, and Singapore were the largest host economies, accounting for over half of the total inward investment in Asia. Within China, the coastal regions attracted the lion's share of inward FDI.[11] India, like Japan, remained a modest host for inward FDI until recently, although this did not capture the importance of the Indian IT services industry in the global economy from the 1980s through outsourcing and offshoring contracts with foreign firms.[12]

The really big change was the growing importance of Asia as a home region for MNEs, despite the diminishing importance of Japan. Between 1990 and 2011 Japan's share of world outward FDI fell from 10 to 5 percent. However while the rest of Asia accounted for less than 3 percent of world outward investment in 1990, by 2011 it accounted for 12 percent.[13]

During the 1960s manufacturers from South Korea and Taiwan had begun to invest abroad, typically in other Asian or other emerging markets. They were usually small-scale and used labor-intensive technology.[14] A second wave of firms began to expand globally from the 1980s, often after they had built scale and corporate competences in their protected domestic markets. They were prominent in assembly-based and knowledge-based industries including electronics, automobiles, and telecommunications.[15] These investments often originated from firms embedded in the business groups including the Korean chaebol.[16] During the 1990s China also emerged as a large outward investor. Access to foreign markets and a search for a stable supply of resources drove this initial wave of investment. China accounted for around 1.7 percent of world outward FDI in 2011, and Hong Kong a further 5 percent.[17]

By the second decade of the twenty-first century, non-Japanese Asian firms were rapidly growing among the ranks of major MNEs. Firms such as Huawei, Lenovo, and Haier from China, Tata and Birla from India, Samsung from South Korea and HTC from Taiwan grew businesses which were globally competitive, despite the challenges of building brands and innovatory capacity. Over the space of two decades from the 1990s, to give one example, the Chinese white goods manufacturer Haier transitioned from a contract manufacturer in China to a leading branded-consumer-goods MNE with large market shares in both developed and emerging country markets.[18] In contrast to the first global economy, these "emerging giants" were sometimes on the frontiers of advanced technologies. Huawei's 20 percent of the global internet router market was a striking example, but it was not alone. Suzlon, an Indian company established in 1995, had become the world's third largest wind turbine manufacture by 2013.[19]

MNEs AND ASIAN ECONOMIC DEVELOPMENT

The links between MNE investments and developmental outcomes are complex. MNEs impact economies in multiple ways. There are benefits and costs, as well as differences over time in both. The use of FDI as a proxy for MNE activity adds further complexities, as the quantity of FDI is a poor indicator of nature of the impact that MNEs have on a host economy. Even in cases where a positive relationship between the quantity of FDI and growth can be identified, the direction of causality is not necessarily from the former to the latter. A final challenge is the vexed question of defining the "counterfactual" position – what would have happened if the MNE investment had not been made?

These problems are well illustrated in the case of Asia, where the existence of a robust and generalizable correlation between MNE activity and economic development is unclear. In the second half of the nineteenth century, the leading host economies were India and China, but it was Japan which achieved the real breakthrough to modern economic growth. Subsequently, the link between MNEs and the East Asian "economic miracle" has been far from clear. Singapore's growth rested on foreign MNEs, but South Korea and Taiwan followed the Japanese example of restricting wholly owned FDI while seeking externalized forms of technology transfer. The Asian economies which developed the most diverse, complex, and technologically dynamic industrial sectors – Japan, Republic of Korea, and Taiwan – were precisely those with the least reliance on inward FDI. Yet other Asian countries with low levels of inward FDI, like Pakistan, Myanmar, Cambodia, and North Korea, did not flourish.

Analysis at this level of generalization is excessively broad-brush, however, and it may be more helpful to consider the multiple impacts of MNEs on Asian development. In a long-term perspective, the generation of trade was one of the most important consequences of MNE activity. While the gains from trade are well understood, history also shows that what is being traded matters also. The opium trade with nineteenth-century China is a case in point. As the affluent middle class in Britain and the West sought to consume increasing amounts of tea, formerly a luxury product for aristocrats, Western trading houses such as the English East India Company and, later, merchant houses such as Jardine Matheson sought supplies of tea from China, where almost all of the crop was grown. Yet China's own handicraft industry meant it had little need for the textiles produced in Britain, and only wanted silver bullion. The Western merchants found the solution in the narcotic opium, whose growth they encouraged in India, where the East India Company had acquired a territorial presence during the second half of the eighteenth century. They transported the opium to China against the wishes of the Chinese government, but supported by Western governments in two infamous Opium Wars. Although the opium trade sparked the growth of Hong Kong as a commercial entrepot, the social consequences for Chinese society were dire.[20] It seems moot in such circumstances to talk of gains from trade.

Between the late nineteenth century and the 1930s, Western firms built an infrastructure in Asia to exploit and export primary commodities. Western trading companies were especially crucial, not simply in promoting trade flows but also in creating these resource industries in the first place. They established, and then managed, India's tea and Malaysia's rubber plantation industries. The developmental consequences of reliance on commodity exports, however, were at best mixed. In the case of India, the MNE investment in tea and other commodities was part of the story of the country's transition over the course of the nineteenth century from being a world hub of handicraft textile manufacturing to being a primary commodity producing economy. Yet the Western trading companies were sometimes also first movers in establishing manufacturing operations. In India, they established jute mills from the late nineteenth century, and subsequently engaged in cotton textile, sugar, and other consumer goods manufacture. Later, the Western trading companies in Malaysia began that country's modern manufacturing industries in the 1950s and 1960s.[21] Japanese *sogo shosha* were also important in trade promotion throughout the region. Before the 1930s the fastest growth in trade in Asia was not between Asia and the developed world, but intra-Asian trade, and here the Japanese trading companies were major facilitators.[22]

The building of physical infrastructure by foreign MNEs made a significant contribution to development. This process began with the companies which built and managed the sea and land cables which connected Europe and Asia by electric telegraph during the nineteenth century. Western shipping and trading companies built ports and regional and international shipping lines which facilitated the growth of a regional economy.[23] During the 1930s Western MNEs were instrumental in building electricity power facilities in the major Asian cities.[24]

Western manufacturing MNEs had limited investments in Asia in the first global economy, but some were significant. This was especially true in Japan, where firms such as ITT, General Electric, Siemens, Dunlop, and J. & P. Coats built pioneering industrial plants.[25] Singer Sewing Machines, which entered Japan in 1900 and 10 years later accounted for four-fifths of the local sewing machine market, introduced its global selling and marketing system to Japan, and with US-style salesmanship.[26] Swiss MNEs such as Brown Boveri, Nestlé, Sandoz, and Sulzer were early investors in Japan, strengthening sectors where domestic enterprise was weak such as chemicals, and contributing substantially to the growth of the local machinery industry.[27]

In China, although the number of foreign manufacturing businesses was not great, some, such as Japanese textile manufacturing companies and Western firms such as British American Tobacco (BAT), were substantial in both size and impact. They built large corporate hierarchies, and also developed distinctive relationships with Chinese business and social networks. The case of BAT was striking in this regard. BAT's US predecessor began exporting to China in the 1890s, and the country became the largest single market for the first 25 years after BAT was founded. An initial factory in Shanghai was followed by others after 1905. By 1914 BAT was manufacturing in China between one-half and two-thirds of the 12 billion cigarettes it sold in that market.

BAT was fully integrated from control over the growing of tobacco through all stages of production and forward to distribution and marketing in China. The company developed accounting and control systems that both monitored its cigarettes and minimized the risk of bad debts. It fostered competition within its own sales teams by creating parallel distribution mechanisms, in particular through the creation of a joint venture with a local Chinese firm, which accounted for one-third of all BAT sales during the interwar years, and enabled it to market its goods and generate sales even in the remotest parts of the country. By 1937 BAT's annual sales had reached 55 billion cigarettes in China. As with other Western investments, the Japanese invasion in 1937, and the Communist Revolution in 1949, ended the business.[28]

During the second global economy the dynamic role of MNEs in the trade expansion of Asian countries has been evident. Singapore provided an extreme case where over 80 percent of total manufacturing exports in the 1980s were accounted for by foreign affiliates, but the percentages have also been high for a number of countries. In the same period foreign affiliates accounted for 37 percent of Thailand's manufactured exports and 41 percent of Malaysia's.

The gains from this trade were, however, sometimes less than appeared at first sight. The foreign-exchange benefits were often limited because of the low value added locally in products such as electronic components. Foreign firms often limited export opportunities for subsidiaries, while MNE affiliates were typically more import-intensive than domestic firms. In two of the most important East Asian economies, Korea and Hong Kong, local firms accounted for the bulk of export promotion during the 1980s and 1990s, although Japan's *sogo shosha* were sometimes important. This was the case in Taiwan, where the *sogo shosha* handled over 50 percent of that country's total exports in the early 1980s. The *sogo shosha* performed a strategic role in finding markets for products of Taiwan's small and medium-sized firms. Elsewhere in Malaysia, Indonesia, and more recently China, the *sogo shosha* were also important as promoters of exports both to Japan and to third countries.[29]

The emergence of integrated international production systems within MNEs during the second global economy had important implications for Asian economies. By the 1990s Japan's Toyota, for example, had established an integrated manufacturing system in the Asia region. In 1995 one-third of that company's overseas production – some 371 000 vehicles – was accounted for by its plants in China, Indonesia, Malaysia, Philippines, Taiwan, and Thailand. This network of affiliates supplied parts to local and regional networks including Japan. Toyota also exported diesel engines from Thailand, transmissions from the Philippines, steering gears from Malaysia, and engines from Indonesia. The growth of integrated international production in services also had important implications for Asian economies. The integrated trading networks of MNEs are increasingly accounting for the trade behavior of host economies. A study of the affiliates of US MNEs in seven Southeast and East Asian economies showed a strong tendency to export to markets in which there are other affiliates of the same parent firms.[30]

A second area of impact of MNEs was the transfer of technology, innovation and organizational skills. Before World War II Western trading companies, mining and plantation companies, and banks provided major channels of mining, engineering, transportation, commercial, and financial technologies into Asian host economies which – at that time – lacked alternative means of acquiring such technologies.[31] Technological diffusion was constrained, however, by the nature of the host economy. High illiteracy rates, underdeveloped infrastructures and alien business cultures were formidable obstacles to diffusion.

During the second global economy, the manufacturing affiliates of MNEs are more readily identifiable in transferring technological and organizational skills to Asian economies. Japanese automobile and electronics affiliates transferred team-based organizational, just-in-time inventory procedures and quality control production methods to their Asian affiliates.[32] The R&D activities of MNEs in Asian countries were sometimes quite significant. In India and Singapore, the share of aggregate R&D expenditure attributable to foreign firms exceeded 15 percent as early as the 1970s. Much of this was related to the adaptation of technology transferred from the parent firm to local needs, but from the 1990s large Western MNEs began transferring significant R&D capabilities to both India and China. For example, since the 1970s Malaysia has developed a wide range of high-technology exports driven almost entirely by MNEs, but that country's technological base has remained undeveloped. However from the 1990s large Western MNEs established substantial R&D facilities in both India and China, which became hubs for the offshoring of innovation, despite concerns, especially in China, about IP protection.[33]

A third area where MNEs can impact development is in influencing the structure of markets in host economies, and they can also impact the competitive environment through their linkages with local enterprises. In the first global economy, the extensive MNE natural-resource investments often appear enclavist, but tin, rubber, and tea production in Asian economies has been found to have stimulated transport facilities and engineering capacity, which could be turned to other uses.[34] It is increasingly evident too that Western firms typically interacted with local business networks rather than existing in splendid isolation.

The enclave issue arose in a new guise through the location of much manufacturing FDI in export-processing zones (EPZ). EPZs had a long history stretching back probably to the creation of such a zone in the US territory of Puerto Rico in 1947. In 1965 the first Asian zone was opened in Kandla, near Mumbai in India. Taiwan opened such a zone in the following year, and in South Korea in 1970. In 1979 China opened its first Special Economic Zone. In countries where export-oriented FDI has been concentrated into such zones, linkages with local firms have sometimes been weak. In such situations, MNEs had to cross the "border" in order to source locally, and they preferred to source in neighboring countries.

Host government policies have impacted outcomes considerably. The low linkage effects derived from Malaysia's electronics industry, concentrated in EPZs in Penang and elsewhere, has been extensively studied. The government's concern that foreign MNEs should not strengthen local ethnic Chinese business interests led to policies that did not encourage local linkages such as permitting foreign companies to have 100 percent ownership of their subsidiaries provided they exported their entire output.[35] In contrast, in Taiwan there were stronger linkage effects between MNEs and local firms during the formative stage of the electronics industry during the 1960s and 1970s. Government negotiated much of the entry term requirements with MNEs, requiring them to locally procure a fixed amount annually. Backward linkages resulted from the strengthening of supplier relationships with local Taiwanese firms. Forward linkages were created because, after receiving the technology and managerial know-how, many local firms began to develop their own product lines.[36]

More generally, the growing use of subcontracting and outsourcing strategies by MNEs during the second global economy had a significant impact on the linkages issues. In electronics, networks of subcontractors developed throughout Asia. This outsourcing of production required close cooperation between different participants in the value-added chain, and provided small and medium-sized firms with new opportunities for skills upgrading and access to new technology and advances in production methods.

In broader terms, MNEs have sometimes been seen as playing an important historical role in an interactive industrial restructuring in Asia that has been described as the "flying-geese paradigm". Ozawa and others have suggested that their contribution was especially important in providing a transmission mechanism for flows of knowledge and technology, and as facilitators of trade.[37] The role of MNEs in Asian industrial restructuring evolved over time. As Japanese labor costs rose, Japanese manufacturers of labor-intensive goods began to relocate production in neighboring cheap-labor countries, especially Taiwan, Korea, Hong Kong, and Singapore. This set a pattern whereby the Japanese economy was continuously restructured in each generation by shifting lower-value-added activities abroad, especially to Asia. In the countries in which Japanese (and also US) MNEs went, they helped to create export-oriented electronics, textile, and other industries. As South Korea, Taiwan, and other industrializing countries in turn absorbed the new technologies and organizational structures, their own MNEs invested in neighboring countries. The cycle has continued to the present day. As labor costs rise in China, so Chinese firms have sought lower production costs in Vietnam and Cambodia. Inward and outward FDIs have thus interacted in a dynamic process of restructuring.

The flying-geese model offers an attractive evolutionary model to understand the dynamic impact of MNEs on regional development. However it is misleading in so far as it suggests a linear, inevitable, and positive outcome. The historical evidence suggests instead that outcomes are highly contingent on factors quite exogenous to MNEs, including the policies of host governments, and the social and educational levels of host societies. Consequently, MNEs may create a highly successful export-oriented industry in an economy, but one with weak linkages to local firms and a low-value-added content in a neighboring economy. Moreover situations are always changing. As one study of MNEs in China since 1978 has emphasized, Chinese government policies, the Chinese business system, and MNE strategies have all evolved in significant ways over the last three decades.[38] From a broad perspective, there is the question of the impact of MNE activities on countries to which little FDI has flowed. If MNEs create a regionally and globally integrated economy, what are the consequences for those countries and regions left out of the process?

MNEs AND SOCIAL CHANGE IN ASIA

MNEs have impacted lifestyles, income distribution, and social structure in

Asia. By transferring alien technologies and organizational forms across borders, they have also disturbed preexisting social and economic arrangements. New technologies have been embedded in foreign cultural assumptions and values. This section explores the nature of this impact on Asia over time.

The most direct social impact of MNEs has come from the creation of employment. It seems likely that the importance of MNEs in creating employment in Asia may have been relatively greater historically than today, primarily because of the vast numbers of workers who were employed in the labor-intensive service and natural-resource sectors. The random data which has survived suggests that the scale of employment provided by foreign enterprise was considerable before the 1940s. The highly diversified Western trading companies were huge employers of labor. James Finlay, the British-owned trading company whose business included vast tea estates, employed at least 140 000 people, largely in India, in the 1940s. Jardine Matheson employed 250 000 people in China before 1949.[39] The large numbers of jobs in menial and low-skilled occupations in these early MNE agricultural, mines, service, and manufacturing activities provided opportunities and incomes which were higher at the margin than those available in the indigenous sector, but the skill mix offered limited opportunities for the upgrading of human skills and competences.

Yet the social consequences of these jobs should not be underestimated. An example can be taken from the Indian tea investments of James Finlay. During the 1890s this company cleared the jungle valleys and planted tea in an area known as the High Range in Travancore, South India. At this time the area was lightly populated by about 2000 indigenous inhabitants. The tea estates attracted a large number of Tamils from the drought areas of Madras State. Between the 1890s and 1950s the population rose from 2000 to 60 000. Finlay built a social infrastructure around their tea estates, constructing roads, generating electricity, operating a private telephone system, and providing medical and primary education facilities. This kind of regime, which was by no means atypical, was "paternalistic", but it also involved the transfer of social technologies and cultural values with considerable consequences.[40]

At least until the 1950s, it was rare to find local Asians employed in senior managerial positions in the region, at least outside Japan, where foreign MNEs such as Singer Sewing Machines rarely employed many expatriates.[41] This was explicable by a shortage of suitably qualified Asians, but it is obvious also that racial prejudices were major influences. US MNEs, as a study of American companies in Malaysia before Independence in 1957 has shown, were as guilty in this regard as their European counterparts.[42] Western racial attitudes towards Asians changed slowly, but harsh economic realities tended to impact employment practices over time. From the 1930s, cost-saving began to provide an important incentive to employ locally recruited staff. The events

of the World War II, the end of colonialism, and assertive new local governments soon resulted in widening job opportunities for Asians.[43]

Although during the second global economy MNEs have been significant
job creators in Asia, their relative importance in this respect is probably less
than earlier. By the mid-1990s, according to one estimate, MNE affiliates
accounted for around 12 million jobs in developing countries in the world. In
Asia, most of the employment was in labor-intensive jobs in China and a handful of other countries. Only in a number of the dynamic economies was the
MNE affiliate share of the economically active population significant. In the
1990s it was 21 percent in Singapore, and 4 percent in Malaysia, but no other
country approached even the Malaysian level. However, the role of MNE
employment in the modern manufacturing sector was more substantial. While
Singapore's figure of almost 60 percent during the 1990s was exceptional, the
MNE affiliate share of paid employment in manufacturing was 40 percent Sri
Lanka, 20 percent in Philippines and Indonesia, and over 15 percent in
Thailand during that decade.

MNEs have also created a considerable amount of indirect employment in
Asian countries through linkages with subcontractors and suppliers.
Historically, it is hard to suggest even a meaningful guestimate of such job
creation. However, the employment impact outsourcing to Asia as the second
global economy took hold is evident. Estimates for the 1980s suggested that
one or two jobs were generated indirectly for each job directly created by
foreign affiliates in ASEAN countries.[44] Cisco, the Silicon-Valley-based
networking company which outsourced most of its manufacturing, estimated
in 2007 that it supported some 50 000 jobs in China through its manufacturing
purchasing in the country.[45]

The quality rather than the quantity of employment provided by MNEs is a
key issue. A great deal of job creation in the EPZs was in the form of low-cost
labor. Both the kinds of jobs generated and the long-term sustainability of
these jobs are problematic issues. The predominance of assembly-type operations created in the electronics, textiles, and garments industries meant that
the type of employment created consisted primarily of unskilled and semiskilled jobs. The working conditions in these zones typically included long
hours, with limited job security.

There is limited evidence on the gender impact of Western MNEs on Asian
societies. The first global economy coincided with a sharper definition of
gender roles in Western countries, with Victorian women withdrawing to what
was called the private sphere. However, women often provided large supplies
of low-cost labor needed in basic manufacturing processes. In Meiji Japan the
modern textile industry, for example, had a huge female labor force. In
contrast, in India globalization saw a sharp drop in female work opportunities.
The disruption of traditional handicrafts resulted in a huge fall in female

employment. Meanwhile employment in new activities, such as tea plantations, was primarily male-dominated, reflecting a number of cultural factors
including the very early age of marriage of women and a lack of social acceptance of genders working together at the same sites.[46]

However sometimes new technologies introduced by MNEs in Asia could
have a significant impact on gender relations. Singer's worldwide diffusion of
the sewing machine from the late nineteenth century provides a compelling
example. In the Ottoman Empire, which included at that time states such as
modern-day Lebanon and Syria, the sewing machine provided a stimulus for
a revival of manufacturing industry through providing a machine which could
make clothes, shoes, and even umbrellas. It held a particular significance for
women who faced societal restrictions on working or trading outside the
home. The sewing machine was a relatively cheap piece of equipment, which
Singer made more accessible through its installment payment system, which
enabled women to work from home to increase family income. In this region,
it has also been shown to have generated a rise in away-from-home formal
employment for women, as the new textile industry often employed some
women. In the new shoemaking industry which the machine helped create in
Istanbul, women were employed completing the work done on machines by
men.[47] Meanwhile in Japan in the early twentieth century, Singer established
a cadre of women who worked with the firm's direct-selling male staff to
educate potential consumers and grow the market for the machine. They were
trained at a Singer Sewing Machine Academy established in Tokyo, and would
offer instruction at smaller Singer sewing schools located in retail stores
around the country. These female Singer workers emphasized the importance
of female self-reliance and economic independence.[48]

A large proportion of the labor force employed by MNEs in the EPZs
developed from the 1960s were young females. Firms regarded women as
cheaper to employ, less likely to unionize, and having greater patience for
monotonous work in assembly operations. This provided employment opportunities for women who had previously had low levels of participation in paid
economic activities because of socio-cultural traditions and overt discrimination. It has also improved women's access to education, and gave them a
higher measure of independence. But since these jobs were overwhelmingly
low-paid and low-skill, they can also be regarded as confirming rather than
challenging the lowly status of women in certain countries. The young female
workers employed by MNEs faced particular problems. In data-processing
activities in Southeast Asian countries, women workers have tended to suffer
frequently from exhaustion and stress. A high rate of abnormalities in preg-
nancies has been observed. From another perspective, the greater employment
opportunities for women than men has disrupted traditional gender roles,
sometimes causing acute social dislocation in communities.[49] A study of EPZs

in Sri Lanka, published in 2011, identified a highly complex impact on their female employees, which was simultaneously empowering and disempowering.[50]

During the second global economy MNEs from a number of Western countries, notably the United States, have increasingly employed women in senior managerial positions. Exposure to women in senior managerial positions in MNEs might have been expected to break down stereotypes and social restrictions in the employment of women in senior positions in Asian economies where female emancipation was less advanced. In practice, it is not evident that MNEs have had a strong impact on lessening gender discrimination. Western MNEs have sometimes not sent female managers to work in Asia on the grounds that local cultural assumptions would render them ineffective. This is a debatable proposition. As Adler argued in a study of North American women managers assigned to Asia during the 1980s, such expatriates were first and foremost seen as foreigners. Therefore the rules governing the behavior of local women which limited their access to managerial responsibility did not apply. Indeed, it turned out that in Adler's study most female expatriates had more problems with their own organizations than with Asian customers and employers.[51]

There has been a more positive trend more recently as Western MNEs in South Korea and Japan discovered that undervalued women in their own countries provided a welcome source of female managerial talent which few local firms used. A study of MNEs with Korean subsidiaries showed that they were far more likely to hire women into management roles than local Korean firms, which were unlikely to hire woman managers at all, and that this was associated with a significant improvement in corporate performance. However foreign firms still felt constrained from publically emphasizing their use of female managers at a high level, out of concerns of offending the conventions of Korean society and male elite networks.[52]

Potentially, the provision of training to their employees, both male and female, by MNEs can be one of the most significant contributions to social change. This is a difficult area on which to offer generalizations because there are so many variables influencing the training programs of MNEs, including the type of funding, the size of the investment, the mode of entry, the state of existing labor market, and the business culture of the investing firm. In general, it has frequently been the case that MNEs spent more on training in their foreign affiliates than do similar local firms in a host economy, but with wide variations depending on firm size and industry. In China, and elsewhere, public-policy pressures often resulted in large MNEs investing heavily in training. By 2007 Cisco, which had entered China on a small scale in 1994, had trained 90 000 Chinese students in networking technologies.[53]

The extent to which the highest position in an affiliate is open to local nationals remains an important issue in the employment creation function of MNEs. Generally speaking, all MNEs rely to some extent on small numbers of expatriates typically concentrated in senior management positions or key technical jobs. In general in Asia, there is a trend towards localization driven by a number of factors, including the relative cost of expatriate staff. This trend seems especially advanced in the case of US firms. There are greater problems for countries where personal networks and tacit rules rather than bureaucratic systems are important to the functions of companies. Thus European companies in Asia in the first half of the century, and Japanese companies today, experienced many more problems in incorporating nationals into their management systems.

Finally, the impact of MNEs on the Asian natural environment needs to be considered. During the 1970s the "pollution haven" hypothesis was formulated which predicted that increased capital mobility, combined with a tightening of environmental regulations, would lead to the relocation of pollution-intensive industries to pollution havens in less developed countries unless regulatory harmonization was undertaken to remove this incentive. The Bhopal disaster in 1984, when a gas plant in the Indian state of Madhya Pradesh owned by Union Carbide, then a leading US MNE, exploded, killing over 2000 people and exposing hundreds of thousands of others to toxic gas, provides a very obvious case in support of such an argument. In general, however, the empirical evidence in support of this hypothesis in its crudest form is not strong. A more sophisticated "neo-pollution haven" hypothesis, based on the notion of nations competing against each other for the wealth created by footloose MNEs, has seen some emerging Asian economies gaining unfair advantage, by ravaging their environment to gain competitive advantage in the world market.

Historically, MNEs played a significant role in tropical deforestation in Asia. Western trading companies stripped the teak forests of Burma and tropical forests of Southeast Asia with considerable negative environmental effects. More recently, Japanese firms played a considerable role in logging in Southeast Asia, with (again) negative environmental consequences. Even if not directly involved in logging, MNEs often participated in processing and distribution. However what remains unclear is the distinctive contribution of MNEs as such to tropical deforestation, and how far their strategies and standards differed from domestic firms and from the policy framework set by governments.

It is harder to find supporting evidence that MNEs have located pollution-intensive activities in Asia. Indeed it seems unlikely that environmental cost differences have been major determinants of MNE investments. As for the environmental standards used by MNEs, the literature suggests that MNEs adopted lower environmental standards in their operations in Asian developing countries than in developed ones, but that because of their visibility as well as their access to clean technology, MNEs often have better environmental records than local firms. Indeed more recent research has cast MNEs as setting environmental standards. The rapid increase of international production and globalization of markets has obliged firms to operate under different environmental regimes along with selling to cultures with differing levels of environmental consciousness. This may provide for firms to adapt their best practice technology internally – making possible proprietary gains from process innovations – and thus MNEs may contribute to improved rather than degraded production standards in both Asia and globally.[54]

CONCLUSION

This chapter has explored the impact of MNEs on development and social change in Asia over the long term. It has argued that they have promoted trade, transferred management and technologies, and performed a dynamic role in economic restructuring more generally. They have created employment, widened job opportunities, and developed human resources. MNEs have also exercised a considerable impact on the Asian environment which has been quite possibly negative in the past, but they may now be setting environmental standards.

However history also provides cautionary lessons, especially to policy-makers seeking to learn from it. First, the impact of MNEs has been neither continuous nor even. MNEs have never been evenly spread around Asia. They remain heavily clustered geographically. Second, while there is little support for the once-fashionable view that the effects of MNEs were uniformly bad, it is also evident that they are not a panacea for a country's economic problems. The economic and social effects are mixed, and depend on a range of variables. Third, the Asian experience demonstrates strongly that the economic and social effects of MNEs have been heavily shaped by host country public policy and by local institutional and cultural conditions. MNEs do not do things to countries and societies: they interact with them. For better or worse, they have not transformed national institutions or radically shifted societal norms.

NOTES

1. This chapter is a very substantially revised version of a paper originally published in *Institute of Asia-Pacific Studies*, **39** (1997), pp. 3–23.
2. John H. Dunning and Sarianna M. Lundan, *Multinational Enterprises and the Global Economy*, Cheltenham, UK and Northampton, MA, USA: Edward Elgar, 2008, pp. 172–6.

3. Tetsuya Kuwahara, "Trends in research on overseas expansion by Japanese enterprises prior to World War II," *Japanese Yearbook on Business History*, (7)(1990), pp. 61–81.
4. Sherman Cochran, *Chinese Medicine Men: Consumer Culture in China and Southeast Asia*, Cambridge, MA: Harvard University Press, 2006.
5. Rajeswary A. Brown, *Capital and Entrepreneurship in Southeast Asia*, London: Macmillan, 1994; idem, *Chinese Big Business and the Wealth of Asian Nations*, London: Palgrave, 2000.
6. Gijsbert Oonk, *Merchant Princes of East Africa, 1800–2000: The Karimjee Jivanjee Family*, Amsterdam: Pallas, 2009.
7. Claude Markovits, *The Global World of Indian Merchants, 1750–1947: Traders of Sind from Bukhara to Panama*, Cambridge: Cambridge University Press, 2000.
8. Shakila Yacob and Khadijah Md Khalid, "Adapt or divest? The new economic policy and foreign businesses in Malaysia (1970–2000)," *Journal of Imperial and Commonwealth History*, **40** (3) (2012), pp. 459–89.
9. Shinichi Yonekawa (ed.), *General Trading Companies*, Tokyo: United Nations University Press, 1990.
10. Yasheng Huang, *Selling China: Foreign Investment during the Reform Era*, Cambridge: Cambridge University Press, 2003.
11. United Nations, *World Investment Report 2012*, Geneva: UNCTAD, appendix table 1.2.
12. Kamlesh Gagyar, *Foreign Direct Investment in India 1947–2007*, New Delhi: New Century Publications, 2006; Amar Nayak, *Multinationals in India*, New York: Palgrave Macmillan, 2008; Peter J. Buckley, Adam R. Cross and Sierk A. Horn, "Japanese foreign direct investment in India: an institutional theory approach," *Business History*, **54** (5) (2012), pp. 657–88.
13. United Nations, *World Investment Report 2012*, Geneva: UNCTAD, 2012.
14. Sanjaya Lall, *The New Multinationals: The Spread of Third World Enterprises*, Chichester: Wiley, 1983.
15. Roger van Hoesel, *New Multinational Enterprises from Korea and Taiwan: Beyond Export-Led Growth*, London: Routledge, 1999; John A. Mathews, *Dragon Multinational: A New Model for Global Growth*, Oxford: Oxford University Press, 2002.
16. Alice H. Amsden, *The Rise of "the Rest": Challenges to the West from Late-Industrializing Countries*, Oxford: Oxford University Press, 2003.
17. United Nations, *World Investment Report 2012*, appendix table 1.2.
18. Tarun Khanna and Krishna G. Palepu, "Emerging giants: building world-class companies in developing countries," *Harvard Business Review*, **84** (10) (2006); Tarun Khanna and Krishna G. Palepu, *Winning in Emerging Markets: A Road Map for Strategy and Execution*, Boston, MA: Harvard Business Press, 2012. On China, see Robert Pearce (ed.), *China and the Multinationals: International Business and the Entry of China into the Global Economy*, Cheltenham, UK and Northampton, MA, USA: Edward Elgar, 2011.
19. Geoffrey Jones and Loubna Bouamane, "Historical trajectories and corporate competences in wind energy," Harvard Business School working paper 11–112, 2011.
20. Geoffrey Jones, Elisabeth Koll and Alexis Gendron, "Opium and entrepreneurship in the nineteenth century," Harvard Business School case no. 9805010, revised 11 June 2011.
21. Geoffrey Jones, *Merchants to Multinationals*, Oxford: Oxford University Press, 2000.
22. Kuwahara, "Trends"; Yonekawa, *General*.
23. Jones, *Merchants*; J. Forbes Munro, *Maritime Enterprise and Empire: Sir William Mackinnon and his Business Network, 1823–93*, Woodbridge: Boydell Press, 2003.
24. William J. Hausman, Peter Hertner and Mira Wilkins, *Global Electrification*, New York: Cambridge University Press, 2008, p. 216.
25. Mark Mason, *American Multinationals and Japan*, Cambridge, MA: Harvard University Press, 1992, ch. 1.
26. Andrew Gordon, *Fabricating Consumers: The Sewing Machine in Modern Japan*, Berkeley, CA: University of California Press, 2012, ch. 2.
27. Pierre-Yves Donzé, "Switzerland and the industrialization of Japan: Swiss direct investments and technology transfers to Japan during the twentieth century," *Business History*, **52** (5) (2010), pp. 713–36.

28. Howard Cox, *The Global Cigarette: Origins and Growth of British American Tobacco 1880–1945*, Oxford: Oxford University Press, 2000, ch. 6; Sherman Cochran, *Encountering Chinese Networks: Western, Japanese, and Chinese Corporations in China, 1880–1937*, Berkeley, CA: University of California Press, 2000, ch. 3.
29. Dong-Song Cho, *The General Trading Company*, Lexington, MA: Lexington Books, 1987.
30. United Nations, *World Investment Report 1996*, Geneva: UNCTAD.
31. Geoffrey Jones, *Multinationals and Global Capitalism*, Oxford: Oxford University Press, 2005, pp. 262–6; Shakila Yacob, *The United States and the Malaysian Economy*, London: Routledge, 2008, ch. 4, 5.
32. Shoichi Yamashita (ed.), *Transfer of Japanese Technology and Management to the ASEAN Countries*, Tokyo: University of Tokyo Press, 1991.
33. Arie Y. Lewin, Silvia Massini and Carine Peeters, "Why are companies offshoring innovation? The emerging global race for talent," *Journal of International Business Studies*, **40** (6) (2009), pp. 901–25.
34. John Thorburn, *Primary Commodity Exports and Economic Development*, London: Wiley, 1977.
35. James V. Jesudason, *Ethnicity and the Economy*, Singapore: Oxford University Press, 1989; Pasuk Phongpaichet, "Japan's investment and local capital in ASEAN since 1985," in Yamashita, *Transfer*.
36. Vincent Wei-chen Wang, "Developing the information industry in Taiwan: entrepreneurial state, guerrilla capitalists, and accommodative technologies," *Pacific Affairs*, **68** (4), 1996.
37. Kiyoshi Kojima, "International trade and foreign investment: substitutes or complements," *Hitotsubashi Journal of Economics*, **16** (1) (1975); Terutomo Ozawa, "Foreign direct investment and economic development," *Transnational Corporations*, **1** (1) (1992); Terutomo Ozawa, *The Rise of Asia : The "Flying-Geese" Theory of Tandem Growth and Regional Agglomeration*, Cheltenham, UK and Northampton, MA, USA: Edward Elgar, 2009.
38. Jonathan Story, "China and the multinational experience," in David Coen, Wyn Grant and Graham Wilson (eds), *The Oxford Handbook of Business and Government*, Oxford: Oxford University Press, 2010, pp. 346–80.
39. Jones, *Merchants*.
40. Ibid; Geoffrey Jones and Judith Wale, "Merchants as business groups: British trading companies in Asia before 1945," *Business History Review*, **72** (3) (1998), pp. 367–408.
41. Gordon, *Fabricating*, p. 31.
42. Yacob, *United States*, p. 151.
43. Geoffrey Jones, *British Multinational Banking 1830–1990*, Oxford: Clarendon Press, 1993.
44. Paul Bailey et al. (eds), *Multinationals and Employment*, Geneva: ILO, 1993.
45. Geoffrey Jones and David Kiron, "Cisco goes to China: routing an emerging market," Harvard Business School case no. 805020, June 2012.
46. Tirthankar Roy, "Beyond divergence: rethinking the economic history of India," *Economic History of Developing Regions*, **27** (1) (2012), S57–S65.
47. Uri M. Kupferschmidt, "The social history of the sewing machine in the Middle East," *Die Welt des Islams*, **44** (2) (2004), pp. 205–9.
48. Gordon, *Fabricating*, pp. 40–42.
49. Jones, *Multinationals*, pp. 268–9; Jane L. Collins, *Threads, Gender, Labor and Power in the Global Apparel Industry*, Chicago, IL: University of Chicago Press, 2003.
50. Peter Hancock, Sharon Middleton, Jamie Moore, and Indika Edirisinghe, "Gender, status and empowerment: a study among women who work in Sri Lanka's export processing zones (EPZs)," Social Justice Research Centre, Edith Cowan University Australia, October, 2011, accessed at www.ausaid.gov.au/Publications/Pages/sri-lanka-research-gender-report.aspx, 8 July 2012.
51. Nancy J. Adler, "Pacific Basin managers: a gaijin, not a woman," *Human Resource Management*, **26** (2) (1987), pp. 169–91.

52. Jordan I. Siegel, Lynn Pyun, and B.Y. Cheon, "Multinational firms, labor market discrimination, and the capture of competitive advantage by exploiting the social divide," *Harvard Business School* working paper no. 11–011, revised January 2011.
53. Jones and Kiron, "Cisco".
54. Sarianna M. Lundan, "Internationalization and environmental strategy in the pulp and paper industry," unpublished Rutgers PhD, 1996; Sarianna M. Lundan (ed.), *Multinationals, Environment and Global Competition*, Oxford: JAI, 2004.

7. Managing political risk in global business: Beiersdorf 1914–90[1]

THE MANAGEMENT OF POLITICAL UNCERTAINTY

As MNEs crossed borders during the first global economy, the greatest challenge was to create managerial structures which operated effectively over substantial geographical distances. Although exporting strategies were disrupted by rising tariffs during the second half of the nineteenth century, governments only rarely imposed restrictions on firms simply because of their nationality. The era of high receptivity to foreign business changed dramatically after the outbreak of World War I. The management of distance was replaced by the management of governments as a central challenge faced by firms. Corporate strategies ranged from building strong local identities to divert nationalistic pressure, to participating in coups to overthrow foreign governments perceived as hostile.[2]

The peculiarities of twentieth-century German history meant that German-owned firms were especially vulnerable to political risk.[3] Two world wars and four fundamentally different political systems, including the Nazi regime (1933–45), meant that German firms were exposed in an extreme fashion to the impact of politics and governments on business. The resulting strategies, especially during the Nazi era, have been examined in detail in studies of several major firms, which have revealed that they devised elaborate organizational structures for their international businesses, designed to circumvent real and potential hostile governmental interventions.[4] They were not alone. Even Swiss companies, despite their neutral and politically stable home country, chose to place their international businesses in separate affiliates located variously in Panama, Lichtenstein, and the United States, often for taxation reasons, but also because of concerns about political risk.[5]

A number of historians have termed the German corporate strategies "cloaking," which has been defined as "the art of concealing the true ownership of a company from authorities."[6] Some researchers have seen such cloaking as one element of businesses' cooperation with the Nazis. They have argued that firms camouflaged their foreign assets in an attempt to improve Germany's economic position and ultimately to help the Nazis pursue their political goals.[7] This strategy was seen as supported by the Nazi government, and so forming one element of the Nazi government's economic preparations for war.[8]

This interpretation has, in turn, been contested by other researchers who have identified commercial reasons behind such cloaking activities.[9] They have argued that German firms used cloaking as a technique to reorganize their business,[10] to avoid taxation, to facilitate the circulation of capital and material between countries, and to protect assets from interference by foreign governments.[11] Attempts by German companies to hide their assets abroad from their own government, in particular during the Nazi regime, have received limited attention so far.[12] While the intentions of cloaking have been widely debated, there remains little evidence on the question whether, and if so how, organizational designs worked in the challenging business environment of wars, foreign exchange controls and expropriations. Kobrak and Wuestenhagen stressed the importance of Swiss holding companies that were placed in the hands of trustees who pledged to return the shares.[13] The success or failure of these cloaking strategies after World War II has however received even less attention.[14]

This chapter explores these issues using new evidence on Beiersdorf, a leading pharmaceutical and skin care company that found itself especially exposed to political risk for two major reasons. First, its Jewish ownership and management meant that it faced considerable threats both abroad, as a German company, and at home during the Nazi era, as a Jewish company. Second, the firm's main competitive advantage lay in its brands and trademarks. The transfer of such intangible assets to other companies posed a major challenge which was potentially even more serious than the loss of physical properties through expropriation. The next section explores how the firm's loss of assets during World War I shaped its future strategies towards risk management. This is followed by an examination of how the firm sought to respond to political risk in both its home and host economies during the interwar years. The firm's reliance on trust as a managerial tool was particularly striking. The following section explores the outcomes of the firm's cloaking strategies during the post-war decades.

THE EARLY YEARS OF THE RING: LEARNING ABOUT CLOAKING (1918–38)

German utility companies had established holding companies in Belgium and Switzerland during the two decades before 1914, primarily for capital-raising and fiscal reasons, and sometimes with the explicit wish to make their ventures look, for example, "Swiss."[15] In the aftermath of wartime expropriations, many other German companies began exploring the opportunities of such "cloak-ing."[16] Beiersdorf, founded in Hamburg in 1882, was no exception. The company was built on the invention of a new type of sticking plaster by the pharmacist Paul Beiersdorf and the physician Paul Unna. In 1882, they received a patent for their innovative band-aids using gutta-percha, a form of natural latex produced from tropical trees, which made the band-aid resistant to the skin's moisture. In 1890 Paul Beiersdorf sold the small manufacturing business for family reasons to Oscar Troplowitz, a young Silesian pharmacist who was financially supported by his uncle and father-in-law-to-be Gustav Mankiewicz. In 1906 Oscar's brother-in-law Otto Hanns Mankiewicz became a partner in the firm.

Oscar Troplowitz expanded the business and its range of products. He was savvy in marketing and distribution, and had a talent for brand-building.[17] In 1905 he developed one of the world's first commercial toothpastes and branded it Pebeco. The toothpaste developed quickly into Beiersdorf's best-selling brand. This laid the foundation for Beiersdorf's wider business in beauty products, and triggered a shift in the product portfolio from purely ther-apeutical to prophylactic products.

In 1911, Beiersdorf launched its iconic skin cream, using the brand name Nivea, which was already employed for the firm's bar soap.[18] The launch was accompanied by an innovative marketing campaign based on print advertise-ments and posters. Troplowitz addressed the self-image of women in Nivea advertisements and employed a well-known poster artist to design an elegant "Nivea woman." He thereby suggested to female consumers that Nivea would make them feel more beautiful.

The successful building of brands such as Pebeco and Nivea was responsi-ble for Beiersdorf's rapid growth. While the company had growing research capabilities derived from its heritage in pharmaceuticals, it was by brand-building that it persuaded customers to pay a premium for its products rather than those of competitors. This brand-building was accompanied by heavy investment in distribution using an in-house sales force as well as wholesalers, wholly-owned distribution companies, and exclusive distributors.

The company manifested international ambitions early. In 1893 Beiersdorf entered the US market and signed an exclusive contract with Lehn & Fink. This US company, founded in New York City in 1874, had already success-fully introducing Lysol, a branded disinfectant, to the United States by import-ing it from Germany. Otto Hanns Mankiewicz had worked for Lehn & Fink before becoming a partner in Beiersdorf. The agreement between Beiersdorf and Lehn & Fink stipulated that the German firm delivered exclusively to the American partner, which in return restrained from selling similar or identical products by competitors.[19] In 1903, Lehn & Fink received a license to manu-facture Beiersdorf Dentifrice, which was renamed Pebeco in 1909.[20] After 1909, Canada was included in the licensing agreement.

At the turn of the century, Beiersdorf extended its initiatives to Britain and Austria, where affiliates were founded in 1906 and 1914 respectively.[21] Beiersdorf's products were also manufactured under license by local firms in Buenos Aires, Copenhagen, Mexico, Moscow, Paris, and Sydney.[22] On the verge of World War I, exports made up 42 percent of Beiersdorf's total sales.[23] The best-selling product was the toothpaste Pebeco, which was successful in many countries and became the market leader in the US. The planned introduction of Nivea cream to foreign markets, by contrast, was frustrated by the outbreak of World War I.

The war put an abrupt end to Beiersdorf's international activities. German businesses lost most of their foreign investments, which were either sold or seized for reparations. In the US, the Trading with the Enemy Act of October 1917 called for the sequestration of all enemy-owned property. Similarly, in Britain, German-owned assets of approximately $8 million were seized.[24] Between 1914 and 1922, German total FDI fell from $2.6 billion to $0.4 billion.[25] By the end of the war, Beiersdorf's business abroad had ceased to exist.

The United States and other Allied nations expropriated the intellectual property of enemy firms, as well as physical assets. As a result, Beiersdorf lost the trademarks it had registered internationally. In the US, the trademark for the successful toothpaste Pebeco was seized in 1919 and sold to the former partner Lehn & Fink.[26] The license fee due by Lehn & Fink was transferred to a custodian account, and Beiersdorf was caught up in lengthy disputes. The situation was only partially retrieved by the fortuitous deaths of Oscar Troplowitz and Otto Hanns Mankiewicz in the previous year. Mankiewicz's heirs were born in Posen, which became Polish territory by the Treaty of Versailles. Poland was not treated as an enemy state by the United States, and an amendment to the Trading with the Enemy Act, adopted in 1920, stipulated that proceeds of sales of seized property should be returned to persons who had become citizens of new states carved out of the former German empire. After a decade of litigation, American courts refunded Beiersdorf's $1 million for the lost assets.[27] By the early 1920s, Lehn & Fink had resumed selling Pebeco, but the brand never regained its strong market position, perhaps because of its German associations, as well as a medicinal taste which handicapped the brand as toothpastes became increasingly cosmetic.[28] Beiersdorf's relationship with Lehn & Fink never recovered. Beiersdorf founded its own US affiliate, P. Beiersdorf & Co. Inc., in 1921. The New York-based company was held by an American trustee, Herman A. Metz. His company, the Metz Laboratories, was designated to cooperate with Beiersdorf in the US.[29]

The loss of tangible assets and brands was particularly damaging for Beiersdorf and other German companies. The confiscations crippled industries where brands and patents were the most valuable assets, like the pharmaceutical industry.[30] The pharmaceutical company Schering, for example, lost its trademarks in the US, and like Beiersdorf was caught up in legal struggles to recover them.[31] Bayer, which before the war had been a major manufacturer of drugs and chemicals in New York state, was stripped of its famous trademark for Aspirin, which was sold to a competitor. Bayer only recovered the rights to the brand in the United States in 1986.[32] The expropriation of approximately 6000 German patents in the US gave rise to a domestically owned industry which substituted for prewar German products.[33] Beiersdorf, like other German firms, found its trademarks transferred into the hands of strong competitors, which in turn proved a formidable obstacle for reentering some of the most important foreign markets. Moreover, the company was faced with the use of its successful brands by their new owners. International brand identities like Pebeco were endangered by the many different and uncoordinated utilizations of the brand.

The simultaneous loss of foreign markets and the deaths of the founders seemed for a time to be the end of the company. However the ownership was stabilized when the Warburg Bank, long linked to the founding family, took an equity stake. Willy Jacobsohn, a pharmacist and successful manager of Beiersdorf since 1914, was appointed as chief executive in 1921. It was an inspired choice. The marketing director Juan Gregorio Clausen relaunched the Nivea brand in 1925 with what became its classic blue tin and the white Nivea logo, and developed a new sporty marketing image featuring "Nivea girls" and "Nivea boys" in the open air and sun. The emphasis on athletic bodies helped the brand appeal to men as well as women, helping it to strengthen its hold on the domestic German skin cream market.[34]

Jacobsohn also set to work devising strategies to protect the firm from future political risks.[35] Beiersdorf founded new companies in Switzerland and the Netherlands, two countries which had stayed neutral during World War I and would, it was speculated, assume the same position in the event of a future conflict. The choice of these countries was justified by the argument that "on economic-political grounds they were considered the most preferable."[36] In Switzerland, the Chemische Fabrik Pilot AG (hereafter Pilot) was founded in October 1919.[37] It was financed by the German parent company, but the shares were held entirely by the Swiss president Richard Doetsch as trustee.[38]

Pilot was never meant to be a manufacturing affiliate, as Beiersdorf started simultaneously to cooperate with the Swiss company Doetsch, Grether & Cie owned by the same Richard Doetsch. Instead, Pilot was founded with the aim to retrieve, hold and protect property rights abroad. It owned Beiersdorf's trademarks in Switzerland and in some other countries where a Swiss owner seemed politically preferable to a German one. According to the same principle, Beiersdorf founded another affiliate in the Netherlands in 1921, which was jointly owned by the German parent and the Swiss Pilot AG. It was

Table 7.1   Beiersdorf's international expansion, 1929–31

Year of foundation	Country	Firm and location	Prior distribution affiliate
1929	Poland	Pebeco Polskie Wytwory Beiersdorfa SA, Posen	1924
1929	Yugoslavia	Jugoslavische Beiersdorf DSOJ, Maribor	None
1930	Czechoslovakia	Ludwig Merckle, Aussig	None
1930	Latvia	Pilot-Riga Rupn, AS, Riga	None
1931	Britain	Beiersdorf Ltd, Manufacturing Chemists, Welwyn Garden City	1906
1931	France	Beiersdorf SA, Champigny	None
1931	Italy	Beiersdorf SAJ Prodotti Chemici, Milan	1922
1931	Hungary	Beiersdorf Vegyeszeti Gyar RT, Budapest	1925
1931	Romania	Beiersdorf SAR, Kronstadt	n.aa

Source: BA Ausland Allgemein, Umsaetze der Beiersdorf-Gesellschaften, 1935–37 (undated). Ibid., Aufstellungen, Uebersichten, 1908–89 – Tochterfirmen, Vertreter, Lizenzpartner, 25.5.1934.

initially intended to retrieve lost trademarks in Britain, which a Germany-based company would not have been allowed to repurchase.

In a remarkable *tour de force*, Beiersdorf rebuilt its international business during the 1920s. In 1924, it was again making 24 percent of its sales abroad. Between 1929 and 1931, as the Great Depression took hold, the company founded nine new affiliates (see Table 7.1).[39] In contrast to Schroeter's argument that German companies switched to risk-adverse, alternative strategies to FDI, such as licensing and long-term contracts, Beiersdorf also invested directly in the foreign markets.[40]

During the early 1930s new threats to international business emerged with the imposition of exchange controls.[41] During the banking crisis of the summer of 1931, two years before the Nazis came to power, Germany established tight foreign exchange controls, which were continuously widened to embrace the whole of Germany's trading activities.[42] The need for foreign capital led Beiersdorf to establish a system of mutual lending between the foreign affiliates, which was independent of German currency regulations. It was initiated and supervised by Jacobsohn and reinforced closer cooperation between the different affiliates.[43] From 1932, the Dutch affiliate figured as the headquarters for all foreign firms to organize these activities. The system of money circulation and cooperation was the basis of what was eventually to become Beiersdorf's cloaking system, the so-called "ring structure." Beiersdorf was joined by many other German companies which organized their international business after World War I via the Netherlands.[44]

The Nazis' consolidation of power in 1933 confronted Beiersdorf with new, very concrete political challenges. The company's heritage, current ownership and management was mainly Jewish. Beiersdorf's shares were primarily held by the heirs of the Mankiewicz family and the equally Jewish banking house Warburg. The owners were represented with two Jewish members at the supervisory board, Carl Melchior of Warburg and Leo Alport of the Mankiewicz family. More publicly visible were the three high-ranking managers of Jewish faith, Willy Jacobsohn, Hans Gradenwitz, and Eugen Unna.

Within two months after the Nazis' rise to power, several competitors launched a campaign against Beiersdorf trying to trigger a boycott of its products. The "Society for the Interests of German Brands" mobilized the anti-Semitic press and widely circulated a polemic article published on 4 May 1933.[45] Even though the campaign ultimately had little success, the incident made it obvious that neither the Jewish managers nor the management of the foreign business could remain in Germany for much longer. In an act of "voluntary aryanization," the shares held by Warburg were converted into common stock, and all Jewish managers resigned from their posts. Beiersdorf used its foreign affiliates and transferred its Jewish employees to the subsidiary in Amsterdam.[46] This practice of placing Jews outside of Germany was a strategy used by several firms at the time.[47]

Fighting against the accusation of being a Jewish company, Beiersdorf made sure that its marketing was more carefully aligned with the beauty ideals of the regime. Indeed, the firm may have made an even stronger effort to comply with the assumed wishes of the regime. Nivea advertisements featured almost exclusively blond sportive models with no visible make-up. They referred to the working women that the Nazi ideology supported, and used body images that were aligned with Nazi ideals, even if they built on the heritage of the brand with its emphasis on health and athleticism.[48] In its print advertisements, Beiersdorf also used gothic font, which was promoted by the Nazis, although the company avoided the use of Nazi symbols, uniforms or military insignia. Beiersdorf was praised by the Nazi press for its Nivea marketing. The campaign unlike many competitors in the industry allegedly depicted the ideal German woman who, according to the regime's preferences, was "Aryan," athletic and natural. Given that the marketing strategy for foreign markets was completely different, it seems safe to assume that Beiersdorf partly aligned itself with the political propaganda to not raise any doubts about its compliance.[49]

While Beiersdorf's efforts on the domestic market focused on dealing with the regime and the anti-Semitic public opinion, the company simultaneously worked on a new strategy for its international business. Willy Jacobsohn, now based in Amsterdam, continued to work as general manager of Beiersdorf's foreign affiliates. He first tried to organize the 13 foreign companies within a holding company to be based in Britain. This plan failed however because the German authorities refused to give the necessary permission. At the same time the strict Nazi regulations on foreign exchange control required Beiersdorf to pay 8 percent taxes on the annual dividends of each affiliate, independent of the actual payments made to Beiersdorf, which were often fragmentary.[50] In this situation, it seemed economically rational and even unavoidable to separate the foreign affiliates from the parent company to free them from the destructive influence of the German state.

In October 1934, Jacobsohn established what Beiersdorf's management termed the "ring structure." It placed Amsterdam in the middle of a ring of foreign affiliates. The core company in Amsterdam was responsible for purchasing the most important raw materials and ensuring quality control, for jointly organized research, advertising and general administration.[51] This central organization was financed by an annual fee to be paid by the other ring firms. In most countries, such as Switzerland, France, and the US, Beiersdorf's affiliates held only the trademarks and sometimes plants and equipment, whereas the actual business was done by independent partner companies. The profit was divided evenly between the Beiersdorf affiliate and the partner firm. The parent company in Germany received a license fee based on turnover. The contact with Beiersdorf Germany was limited to the fee and the purchase of those raw materials and products that could not be manufactured abroad. Beiersdorf was henceforth composed of two legally separated pillars, the German business and the foreign business.

The German parent company sought to retain its managerial influence by establishing an administrative committee composed of Jacobsohn, the managers Hans E.B. Kruse, Carl Claussen, and Christoph Behrens, and the supervisory board member Rudolf Brinckmann.[52] The parent company also funded the advertising campaigns of the ring firms, and sought to drive strategic planning through regular meetings of the committee with the ring firm directors.[53]

The initial motives for the ring structure, then, were a diverse mixture of political and commercial considerations, partly shaped by past experience, and partly by perceived future threats. The ring's foundations lay in an attempt to revitalize the lost foreign business, secure tax advantages, and in particular enable capital transfers in an environment of rising foreign exchange controls. This was reinforced by Nazi regulations concerning German-owned foreign companies that after 1936 were required to remit to the Reichsbank all funds not essential to ongoing operations as well as all future "surplus" funds, with the Reichsbank determining what constituted a surplus.[54] At the same time, the foreign affiliates especially in the Netherlands, Switzerland, and the US were meant to retrieve lost trademarks, which Germans were not allowed to repurchase. By giving greater autonomy to the affiliates, Beiersdorf also localized management.[55] As the political environment became increasingly hostile, the ring firms were used increasingly to legally separate the foreign businesses from Beiersdorf Hamburg, which was supposed to free them from German authorities that were an immediate political threat. The fear of war and expropriation by enemy countries was a possible but, at the time of the founding of the ring, still hypothetical menace. Faced with the anti-Semitic campaigns in Germany, the ring had yet another benefit. Beiersdorf placed its Jewish employees in the foreign businesses, mostly in the neutral Netherlands.

THE INNER CIRCLE OF TRUST: CLOAKING DURING WAR

A turning point in the evolving structure of Beiersdorf's ring came in 1938. The Nazi annexation of Austria in March of that year signaled that a new war was increasingly likely. In May, Willy Jacobsohn decided to flee to the United States. He went into early retirement at the age of 54 and moved to Los Angeles. He received a pension paid by the ring firms until his death in 1963.[56] The search for a successor led to Richard Doetsch in Basel, with whom Jacobsohn had cooperated to a large extent in the ring. Despite a lot of uncertainty concerning future developments, most German managers at the time believed that Swiss neutrality was the safest to rely on during a potential war and many respectable Swiss managers were willing to act as trustees.[57] Most German firms chose their partners based on economic expertise and more importantly trust and prior relations. Therefore, large companies and firms that internationalized early, like Beiersdorf, had an advantage.

The German-born Swiss national Doetsch had been a member of the supervisory board of Beiersdorf's Swiss affiliate, Pilot AG, since 1923 and held friendly relations with Beiersdorf's managers. It seemed natural therefore to transfer the organizational center of the ring to Pilot AG in Switzerland. Doetsch's appointment as general manager of the foreign affiliates inevitably led to a principal–agent problem as he was president of Pilot and owner-manager of the Swiss partner company Doetsch, Grether & Cie. In this powerful position the relationship between Doetsch, Grether & Cie and the ring depended solely on his decisions, which might have been one reason for him to agree to the arrangement. Pilot held shares of the American, Dutch, French, Italian, and Yugoslavian affiliates, and was therefore also indirectly invested in the, British, Finnish, and Swedish affiliates which they owned. Finally the Hamburg business itself owned the main businesses in Eastern Europe and Argentina.[58]

With the German invasion of Poland on 1 September 1939, World War II started. Over the following two years, Richard Doetsch felt his position as trustee for Beiersdorf Hamburg and the ring firms become increasingly dangerous. He feared that whoever won the war would expropriate Beiersdorf's assets. He was especially concerned about the international trademarks, which his own company's business and those of the foreign affiliates depended on. Beiersdorf was in no position to lose Doetsch as its main trustee. In February 1940 it therefore agreed to sell the Pilot shares for the nominal value of CHF30 000 to Doetsch personally. Doetsch and Beiersdorf signed a gentlemen's agreement stipulating that Doetsch would manage all foreign assets and rights as trustee for Beiersdorf.[59] His newly acquired property rights were supposed to be temporary. The gentlemen's agreement spelled out that Beiersdorf kept the right to repurchase its property at any time at the exact same price that Doetsch had paid. Richard Doetsch continued his work for the ring but, as the contract stipulated, could not be held liable for any losses that might occur in the future.[60]

Several German companies had agreements of this kind in the late 1930s and early 1940s. The Robert Bosch GmbH in Stuttgart entrusted assets to the German–Dutch banker Fritz Mannheimer from 1937, the chemical company IG Farben had a Dutch holding responsible for its business in India, the Berlin-based pharmaceutical company Schering used a Swiss holding to protect its British and American assets.[61] In most cases, the contracts included a secret repurchasing clause. Given that these secret agreements were however difficult to enforce, the structures relied heavily on trust, which can be defined as "the intention to accept vulnerability based upon positive expectations of the intentions or behavior of another."[62] Trust was mainly based on social relations and ethnicity. Beiersdorf chose trustees among its business partners and friends, many of whom were German-born, like Richard Doetsch.

As a consequence of the agreement, Doetsch legally took over ownership of several Beiersdorf affiliates, thereby separating them from the German Beiersdorf. In France, he became the president of the Beiersdorf SA, which cooperated with the Laboratoire Peloille owned by French national Jacques Peloille. The relationship between Beiersdorf France and Peloille was supervised by the manager Henri Gruenstein, who had been sent from Hamburg in 1931.[63]

In Italy, Beiersdorf SpA managed the business itself and did not rely on a local partner firm. The company, founded in 1931, belonged first to three Italian and Swiss founders who waived their rights in favor of Beiersdorf Hamburg. In 1934, the ownership was transferred to the Pilot AG as trustee for

Hamburg. Rises in capital in 1939 and 1942 were financed in the way that Hamburg granted Richard Doetsch an allowance, which he invested in the company. While the shares belonged legally to Doetsch, he confirmed in writing that he would act as trustee for Hamburg.[64]

The Netherlands were under the occupation of Nazi Germany from the spring of 1940. Therefore, Pilot's role in the development was limited. The Beiersdorf NV was under the control of the company's lawyer and Dr D.A. Delprat, the former president of the Amsterdam chamber of commerce. Both disguised the company as a Dutch-owned firm. Already in 1934, the Dutch Beiersdorf had founded a further affiliate in Sweden, which belonged to five Swedish nationals. They, however, waived all their rights in favor of the Dutch Beiersdorf.[65]

In the US, P. Beiersdorf & Co. Inc. was founded in 1921, when the relationship with the former partner Lehn & Fink ended in a legal dispute. The capital of $10 000 was split between Beiersdorf and an American trustee, Herman Metz. In the mid-1920s Metz also took over most of Beiersdorf's shares but agreed to hold them as trustee for Beiersdorf. Metz, who legally owned 96 percent of the shares, died in 1934. His shares were transferred to his former employee Carl Herzog, who became Beiersdorf's new trustee in the US. His company, Duke Laboratories, was the new partner company and responsible for the business in the US, while the American Beiersdorf held the trademarks and owned some plants and equipment.

Legally the company belonged to Herzog (96 percent), Richard Doetsch (1 percent) and a New York-based individual (1 percent), who held the shares as trustees for Beiersdorf. Only 2 percent belonged to Pilot AG and was therefore Swiss property. However, Herzog told the American and British authorities during the war that the beneficiary was the Swiss company Pilot, a fact that was never contested after this official statement had been made.[66]

In 1940, Richard Doetsch personally took over the shares of Pilot and therefore became the sole owner of the US Beiersdorf – as far as the US authorities were concerned. Doetsch, who was less familiar with the organization and business of the ring created by his predecessor Jacobsohn, did not feel up to the task of managing the American affiliate from a distance. He decided to give full power of attorney to Carl Herzog. The agreement with Herzog gave rise to the same principal–agent problem that existed in Switzerland. Herzog, like Doetsch, controlled de facto both the American Beiersdorf and the partner company.

In Britain, Beiersdorf Ltd was originally set up by the American affiliate of Beiersdorf. At the beginning of the war, the German manager of the company was imprisoned.[67] The British authorities, however, were unable to prove the German ownership of the company, which was formally under American control. In 1940, the management renamed the company Herts

Pharmaceuticals in order to conceal its relation to Beiersdorf. The British Beiersdorf had itself launched a further affiliate in Finland in 1933. In 1939, two shares of the Finnish company were sold to a Mr and Mrs Schleutker, who granted a first right of refusal to the British affiliate of Beiersdorf.[68]

It is striking that most of Beiersdorf's cloaking activities occurred independently of the Nazi regulation on cloaking, which itself was ambiguous and faltering.[69] In September 1938, the German minister of economics gave limited permission for cloaking by German firms under the condition of prior state approval. Henceforth, licenses could be issued but were by law restricted to "reliable German firms." Even though reliability was not defined, Beiersdorf, having earlier been attacked as Jewish, could not hope to fall into this category. The attempts by Jacobsohn to receive permission for a holding based in Britain failed. But in any case Nazi support for cloaking was short-lived. With a decree of 12 October 1938, all cloaking permission was revoked unless companies proved that they were not diminishing the flow of foreign currencies into Germany. Furthermore, all companies, even if they did not have prior permission, were requested to uncloak their assets abroad at this point. Depending on an increase in foreign exchange, the Nazis even granted exemption from punishment for companies revealing their cloaked foreign assets to the government. Beiersdorf, however, did not respond to the plea, but continued reorganizing its ring firms and disguising their ownership.

With the outbreak of the war, the Ministry of Economics changed its position once again. On 9 September 1939, the ministry called for the rescue of German assets abroad by concealing German ownership. It bluntly suggested legally separating foreign businesses from German companies but guaranteeing the influence by carefully selecting the individuals that managed those firms.[70] Several companies applied for the necessary authorization.[71] Beiersdorf sold its Pilot shares to Doetsch in February 1940 with the approval of the German authorities. The price of CHF30 000, which had been deposited in Basel for the time being, was transferred to the Reichsbank in March 1942.[72] However, Nazi support for cloaking was once again short-lived. In 1940–41, the Ministry revoked its support in all industries not necessary for military goals. Many companies opposed this decision, arguing that foreign currencies were still crucial for the financing of the war and that sudden uncloaking would put their trustees abroad at risk. A case-by-case evaluation was the outcome, but in 1943 the Nazis finally decided to turn down all cloaking applications.

A review of the Nazi policy shows that it was limited, restricted to "reliable companies," and, most importantly, undependable. Assuming that German MNEs were particularly risk-adverse after the experience of World War I, as several scholars point out, the ambiguous and unpredictable Nazi policy could not have had a strong impact.[73] Beiersdorf as a Jewish firm knew early on that it could not build on governmental support. It therefore looked for alternative strategies to protect itself against political risks, relying more and more on one-to-one relationships rather than legally enforceable contracts. Theoretically speaking, the company lost faith in systemic trust, such as abstract principles and the rule of the law, and instead relied on personal trust.[74]

The ring strategy had some success, then, at least in the short term. In addition to Jacobsohn, the other Jewish managers and members of the board were put out of harm's way. Hans Gradenwitz and Leo Alport died of natural causes, in 1933 and 1935 respectively. Eugen Unna continued to work for Beiersdorf as a chemist and returned to the German parent company in 1945. He remained a member of the management until his retirement in 1947. The ring organization also enabled the company to overcome some of the problems caused by German exchange controls, and the system of mutual financial support and cooperation worked out well. In 1938 the 13 ring firms realized a profit of RM900 000, and paid one-third of it to the parent company.[75]

REBUILDING TRUST AND BRANDS AFTER 1945

The ring structure proved ineffective in preventing the expropriation of foreign assets after the end of World War II. The affiliates in central and eastern European countries were taken over by the new Communist regimes. Elsewhere, the companies in the US, Britain, Austria, and the Netherlands, along with their affiliates in Sweden and Finland, were expropriated by the Allies. International trademarks, especially the leading brand of Nivea, were lost in all of these countries as well as in Denmark, Norway, Mexico, Brazil, Argentina, the British Commonwealth, the French colonies, and many more. The companies in France, Italy, and Switzerland remained in the hands of Richard Doetsch. In Switzerland, the Swiss government came to an accord with the Allies in 1946 to liquidate all German assets and transfer 50 percent to a fund for reparations.[76] Doetsch swore to the Allies under penalty of perjury that Pilot was his property. Despite the gentlemen's agreement between him and Beiersdorf, Doetsch refused to give the property back, arguing, not entirely unreasonably, that in doing so he would put himself at risk.[77]

As Germany began to recover, Beiersdorf sought to regain the lost assets. The relationship with Richard Doetsch was crucial. He continued to act as trustee for the Italian and French companies, and held the shares of the Swiss Pilot AG and the international trademarks. After the war, Allied investigators informed Beiersdorf that Doetsch had been declared to be the sole owner of Pilot and by consequence of P. Beiersdorf & Co. Inc., USA. In 1947, they offered assistance in fighting this statement, which they considered yet another attempt of a "neutral citizen taking advantage of the economically helpless state of Germany."[78] Beiersdorf reacted in calling Doetsch's statement "understandable" and seeing him as someone "who has already taken possession of an article promised to him, but who has still to reach a settlement with his contracting partner regarding payment of the purchase price."[79]

Despite Doetsch's refusal to transfer the assets back to their former owner, Beiersdorf's senior management accepted the postwar status quo.[80] They also continued to claim that a written version of the gentlemen's agreement with Doetsch had been lost during the war.[81] Beiersdorf neither criticized Doetsch's behavior concerning the Swiss company nor the decisions he made as trustee concerning other companies, but instead prioritized restoring good personal relations with him. Doetsch claimed that he agreed to the trustee relationship because of "pure friendship with the old acquaintances," but that his considerable amount of work was little appreciated by the postwar managers.[82] On one occasion, he wrote to the former manager Jacobsohn that Beiersdorf was "the nails to his coffin."[83]

Beiersdorf's managers Hans E.B. Kruse and Carl Claussen devoted a considerable amount of time to the damaged relationship, and visited Doetsch regularly in Basel.[84] Their efforts were rewarded with an agreement in 1953. Doetsch granted Beiersdorf the option to repurchase the Pilot shares at the time of his death for CHF600 000 rather than the CHF30 000 as agreed upon in the gentlemen's agreement. When Doetsch died in 1958, Beiersdorf repurchased the shares at this price. Beiersdorf also continued the long-term relationship with the Swiss partner company Doetsch, Grether & Cie, active in pharmaceuticals and cosmetics, which was to become one of the most profitable partnerships in the 1960s.[85]

Relatively soon after the war, Beiersdorf also managed to regain its property in the formerly occupied countries of Austria and the Netherlands. In Austria, the Beiersdorf GmbH was under the control of the "Administration for Soviet Property in Austria," which operated as a de facto state corporation until the withdrawal of Soviet troops in 1955. When Austria was reestablished as a sovereign state in 1955, the assets were sold to the Austrian government, and Beiersdorf was able to repurchase the firm and valuable trademarks for DM800 000.[86] In the Netherlands, the trustee of the Beiersdorf NV sold his shares in 1952 to Beiersdorf Hamburg (49 percent) and the two Dutch managers (51 percent). The managers in return sold their share to Beiersdorf in 1954 under the condition that the directors of the board remained Dutch until both of them retired.[87] The price was G800 000.

The shares of the Italian Beiersdorf firm had been transferred to Pilot during the war. After the death of Richard Doetsch, his Italian partner Willy Zimmermann became the sole owner of the former Italian affiliate. Thanks to the successful cloaking, there was little struggle over the Italian company after the war, which was owned by a Swiss and an Italian.[88] Zimmermann had good personal relations with Doetsch and Beiersdorf's senior managers. Kruse visited Zimmermann regularly during vacations in Italy. On one of these trips, Zimmermann confided to Kruse that he considered himself "an honest thief."[89] He agreed to transfer the shares to a newly founded Swiss holding company owned by Beiersdorf Hamburg. In return, Beiersdorf offered his son Paul Zimmermann a 5-year contract as chief executive of the Italian company.[90] This concession allowed Zimmerman to continue pursuing a "dynastic motive" for the company that he had managed for several decades.[91] In 1963, the Italian firm belonged once again to Beiersdorf. Willy Zimmermann, the only trustee who gave the assets back without any financial compensation, remained on the board until 1976.

In Denmark, the German firm's trademarks were expropriated and sold to competitors in 1950. An employee of Beiersdorf's former partner firm bought the Nivea trademark for DM270 000. Despite a licensing contract with Beiersdorf, the new owners refused to follow a joint advertising strategy and presented Nivea as an exotic, oriental body care system. Beiersdorf reentered the Danish market in 1962 using the Tesa brand of adhesive tapes. In 1965, the Danish owner E.O. Bruun died unexpectedly, and one year later Beiersdorf repurchased the Danish trademarks for DM2 million, and began re-assembling the Beiersdorf business in one company.[92]

In 1967, Beiersdorf again achieved international sales worth DM200 million, composed of approximately DM20 million in exports, DM36 million in license fees, and DM144 million of sales by the 15 affiliates abroad. The most successful were the ones in Italy and the Netherlands with sales of DM27 and 26 million respectively. Over four-fifths of the international sales were in Western Europe.[93] Given the loss of the Nivea trademark, most of the international business was generated by sales of newer brands. These included Tesa, the deodorant soap 8 x 4, and the hand lotion Atrix. Tesa had been first launched in 1935, and then taken international after World War II. 8 x 4 was launched in 1951 and Atrix in 1955.[94]

The recovery of the Nivea brand in the large markets of France, Britain and the United States proved tortuous. The situation in France was especially complicated. Beiersdorf had only acquired the French Nivea trademark shortly before the war, as Guerlain had already trademarked the name Nivea in 1875. The French company sold these older rights to Beiersdorf in 1930, and Beiersdorf paid in annual installments until 1940. While Beiersdorf SA, then owned by Richard Doetsch, held the trademark, the actual business was operated by the partner firm of Laboratoires Peloille.

The owner of Laboratoires Peloille, Jacques Peloille, and Richard Doetsch signed a new contract in 1946 stipulating the amount that Peloille had to pay to Pilot (annually F300 000, after 1948 F450 000). Regarding the trademark for Nivea, the former Beiersdorf manager Henri Gruenstein, who had changed his name to Gustin during the war, became the most active player. Gustin pointed out to Doetsch that the French Beiersdorf company had debts in US dollars, which were increasing in value owing to the weak French currency. He argued that if the French Beiersdorf started earning a considerable amount of money, it would raise the risk that the French authorities would investigate the ownership structure more closely and discover the connection to Beiersdorf. Gustin, therefore, suggested to Doetsch to sell the trademarks to Peloille, among them Nivea. Doetsch agreed, and sold the trademarks for DM220 000, without first consulting with Beiersdorf in Hamburg.[95] In 1952, Peloille gave his company, now named Nivea SA and including the Nivea trademark, to Henri Gustin, and kept only the rights for adhesive tape brands. The reasons for this step remain unclear; Peloille wrote to the retired Jacobsohn that he was desperately trying to split up the partnership with Gustin, "under whose character he had suffered for 20 years."[96]

In 1957, Nivea SA went public. Unable to repurchase either the company or the brands, Beiersdorf first sought collaboration with the French company, which Gustin declined. In 1964, there were more negotiations, but Gustin demanded too high a price. Instead, Beiersdorf introduced new brands such as Atrix and 8 x 4 to France employing a licensing contract with a new company called Sofrac. In 1968, the aged Gustin finally agreed to sell his Swiss holding company, which held 24 percent of the Nivea SA, to Beiersdorf. In 1974, Beiersdorf raised its ownership to 98.2 percent for a cost of DM25.5 million.

The recovery of the Nivea brand took even longer in the US, where Beiersdorf's assets were expropriated by the government. The partner company Duke Laboratories and its owner Carl Herzog bought the trademarks from the Office of Alien Property. Herzog financed the deal with money that his company did not pay to Germany for license fees. Carl Herzog and Jacobsohn had been good friends previously, but Jacobsohn was outraged by Herzog's betrayal. He informed the Office of Alien Property about Herzog's maneuver. As a consequence, Herzog was forced to pay $600 000 for the trademarks instead of the original price of $75 000.[97]

Despite this open conflict with the retired Jacobsohn, Beiersdorf's managers tried to restore a relationship with Herzog. As in Switzerland, regular visits by and correspondence with high-ranking managers were parts of the strategy.[98] The business situation, however, presented itself very differently. Herzog, who was already 75 years old in 1960, opted for a strategy of no risks and small profits. Competitors launched new products in the space Nivea would have occupied.[99] Beiersdorf opted to wait it out. Managers sought to maintain a dialogue with Herzog and, more importantly, with his lawyer and executor of his will. In order to remain present on the US market, Beiersdorf founded a Tesa corporation in New Jersey in 1971. In 1973, the 88-year-old

Herzog decided to retire. Beiersdorf was finally able to repurchase the brands Nivea, Eucerin, and other trademarks for $4 million.

In Britain, while during the war the affiliate had been successfully cloaked as an American company, in 1947 the authorities became aware that Beiersdorf Germany was the ultimate owner of Herts Pharmaceuticals. The company was sequestrated and came under the control of the Custodian of Enemy Property. It was offered for sale and Smith & Nephew (S&N), a health care company which had shortly before staged an unsuccessful entry into toiletries, purchased it and the Nivea brand in 1951. Beiersdorf had cooperated with S&N in the band-aid market since 1931.[100] In 1959, this cooperation was extended through a license agreement for Atrix (renamed Atrixo in Britain). Beiersdorf consulted S&N in the Nivea business and was paid a commission.[101] By the early 1960s S&N's Nivea accounted for 40 percent of all general-purpose skin creams sold in Britain.[102] S&N resisted Beiersdorf's attempts to build closer relationships, although the German company was able to slowly recover from S&N the rights to the brand in countries which had formerly belonged to the British Empire. It brought the rights for African countries during the 1960s, and in 1977 it acquired the rights for some Asian markets, including Bangladesh, Hong Kong, Malaysia, Singapore, Sri Lanka, and Thailand, as well as Cyprus, Gibraltar, Malta, and some Caribbean countries.[103]

It was not until 1992 that Beiersdorf was able to buy the Nivea brand in Britain and Ireland, as well as in Australia, Canada, India, Israel, New Zealand, Pakistan, and South Africa. The sale price was £46.5 million.[104] The British firm, however, requested to keep the distribution in its hands and it was not until 2000 that Beiersdorf also regained sales and distribution rights.

Given the idiosyncratic situation in each country, then, Beiersdorf had to use multiple strategies in order to reenter international markets and regain lost assets. One of the biggest problems for the skin care company was the loss of control over trademarks, particularly Nivea, as it threatened the coherence of an international brand as new owners, as in Denmark, reinvented the marketing image. As a consequence, Beiersdorf faced a dangerously fragmented brand identity for its most important product line even as it sought to refresh and grow the brand in Germany.[105]

Beiersdorf pursued two strategies to rebuild its international business. First, new brands were used to reenter markets. The Tesa brand in particular was used as a first step back into foreign markets as diverse as Denmark, France, Mexico, Spain, and Sweden. Second, the firm slowly reacquired its expropriated brands, of which Nivea was the most important. Whereas reacquiring assets in Austria (1956), Switzerland (1958), Italy (1963), and Finland (1966) proved comparably cheap, at less than $300 000 each, it was the most difficult and expensive to come to an agreement with the new owners in Denmark

(1966), Sweden (1961/8), France (1968), US (1973) and Britain. The repurchases cost $500 000, $3 million, $6.3 million, $4 million, and $82.3 million respectively.[106]

There appear to be at least four factors influencing the variations in time and cost of the repurchasing strategy. First, the size of the different markets broadly reflected the purchase price. Second, it was important if the trademarks had been sold to Beiersdorf's competitors or to former partners. In Britain, and to some extent France, the competitors who acquired the brand were less inclined to support Beiersdorf's desire to reenter their market. Third, Beiersdorf's strategies were more successful when the company could build a personal relationship with one decision-maker than when assets were held by a publicly owned corporation, as was the case in Britain. In the case of the US and France, shares and rights were held by the former partners, Carl Herzog and Henry Gustin, but the relations were unstable owing to conflicts about the property. The relationship with trustees in Italy, the Netherlands, and Switzerland, by contrast, survived relatively intact. Finally, time mattered. As the Nivea brand was rebuilt in Germany, so its value rose, and the longer the company took to reacquire it the higher became the price. Still, as Beiersdorf slowly reacquired the rights to the brand, it was able to invest in developing its role as a global brand. By the mid-1980s Beiersdorf had a formal marketing strategy to promote Nivea as a global product rather than permitting multiple different national brand identities.[107]

CONCLUSION

This chapter has argued that after the outbreak of World War I the management of political risk became a central concern for firms, especially those operating internationally. These risks were on many levels, from expropriation to exchange controls and other economic policies. German firms, which had flourished during the second industrial revolution of the late nineteenth century, and enthusiastically expanded internationally, found themselves especially exposed to such risks. Moreover, at home, first the policy response to the Great Depression and then the advent of the Nazi regime resulted in a new set of major challenges for businesses. Beiersdorf faced the worst of all worlds. Although far from being one of Germany's giant business enterprises before 1914, it was a determined MNE investor, and so suffered the loss of its businesses in the United States and elsewhere as a result of World War I. As a consumer products manufacturer whose brands and trademarks lay at the heart of its competitive advantages in international markets, the loss of these intangible assets was especially damaging. Finally, as a so-called Jewish business, the arrival of the Nazis put the firm in harm's way in its home market.

The scale of external challenges appears to be so great that Beiersdorf's survival into the second half of the last century seems at least surprising, and perhaps miraculous. There were certainly elements of a miracle in the story – noticeably the owning family's origins in what would become part of Poland. But this chapter has argued that Beiersdorf's survival was due primarily to heavy investment in corporate structures, as well as some ethically questionable flexibility in its home market during the 1930s.

In the wake of World War I, Jacobsohn developed the "ring" organizational structure as a way for affiliates to disguise ownership, circumvent national regulations, or even adopt a different nationality. The firm was not alone among German – and even Swiss – firms in splitting its foreign business from its domestic business in response to perceived risks. Beiersdorf was, however, unusual in its dependence on trust to support this organizational structure. The firm built a network of trustworthy individuals and business partners that enabled it, eventually, to separate the German parent company from its international affiliates. In circumstances when the rule of law was breaking down, the company switched from relying on formal contracts to relying on reliable local partners and friends. Where possible, Beiersdorf relied upon trustees that were linked to the company by prior social and business relations as well as ethnicity. Most of them were German-born business partners or former employees. This strategy allowed Beiersdorf to localize the management of its affiliates, delivering advantages both in the marketplace and in controlling political risks.

The historical path dependency of the company's political risk management reveals such "cloaking" as something other than a mechanism for facilitating cooperation between the Nazi government and German businesses. Beiersdorf's strategy developed slowly over time and combined political motives with urgent economic needs. The ring originally facilitated the flow of goods and capital between countries in the context of severe policy restrictions, acted as an organizational framework to regain assets that were lost during World War I, and reduced the firm's exposure from adverse government interventions both abroad and at home. With the changing political situation, it developed increasingly into a cloaking device designed for the purpose of concealing assets from different political authorities and providing a safe haven for individuals that were politically threatened in Germany. The Nazi government's overall support for cloaking by German firms, itself transient and ambiguous, played no part in Beiersdorf's schemes.

Beiersdorf's strategies were quite successful in the short term. At home it was able to circumvent attacks on its "Jewish" identity from competitors, while getting senior Jewish managers out of the country. The firm was able to rebuild its international business, and to retain it as a profitable business during the 1930s, despite a welter of exchange controls and other restrictions which handicapped German and other firms. The establishment of the ring turned out to encourage stronger cooperation between the different foreign affiliates, most notably between the companies based in Switzerland and the Netherlands, which provided a base on which the company could rebuild its export business after the war.

In the longer term, the ring strategy failed to protect most of the firm's foreign assets from expropriation. Factories and key trademarks were lost in most markets. As the rule of law was reestablished in the international economy, deals done on the basis of trust unraveled. Good friends, such as Carl Herzog, betrayed the trust that had been placed in them, shutting the firm out of the American market for almost three decades. The relationship with Richard Doetsch and Swiss-based Pilot worked somewhat better. In every instance, Beiersdorf was forced to invest much time and energy in rebuilding relationships. The firm's commitment to the Nivea brand reflected a deeply embedded attachment to its value, despite the ability to create new brands such as Atrix and Tesa, which were pragmatically used to reenter markets.

It was a striking testament to the damage caused to German-based MNEs by World War II that Beiersdorf, which had so carefully invested in organizational structures to counter political risk, only recovered ownership of the Nivea brand in the United States and Britain in 1973 and 1992 respectively. Neither contracts nor trust could protect German firms from the consequences of the traumatic political events of these years. Yet Beiersdorf's history shows that there was some room for managerial discretion. Faced by the worse of all worlds, the firm survived and was able, at great cost, to rebuild its business.

NOTES

1. This chapter was originally published as Geoffrey Jones and Christina Lubinski, "Managing political risk in global business: Beiersdorf 1914–1990," *Enterprise & Society*, **13** (1) (2012). I would like to thank Beiersdorf AG, Unilever NV, and J. Walter Thompson for permission to consult their archives, Thorsten Finke for his comments on an earlier draft, and Oona Ceder for her invaluable research assistance.
2. Frans-Paul van der Putten, *Corporate Behaviour and Political Risk: Dutch Companies in China, 1903–1941*, Leiden, Netherlands: Leiden University, 2001; Stephanie Decker, "Advertising and corporate legitimacy. British multinationals and the rhetoric of development from the 1950s to the 1970s," *Business History Review*, **81** (1) (2007), pp. 59–86; idem, "Building up goodwill: British business, development and economic nationalism in Ghana and Nigeria, 1945–1977," *Enterprise & Society*, **9** (4) (2008), pp. 602–13; Nicholas White, *British Business in Post-Colonial Malaysia, 1957–70: 'Neo-Colonialism' or 'Disengagement'?*, London: Routledge, 2004; idem, "Surviving Sukarno: British business in post-colonial Indonesia, 1950–67," *Modern Asian Studies*, **46** (5) (2012), pp. 1277–315; James H. Bamberg, *The History of the British Petroleum Company, vol. 2: The Anglo-Iranian Years, 1928–1954*, Cambridge: Cambridge University Press, 1994; Jones, *Multinationals*, pp. 219–20.
3. For business reactions to political risk in Germany and the effects of dictatorship on busi-

ness, see Christopher Kobrak, Per H. Hansen and Christopher Kopper, "Business, political risk, and historians in the twentieth century," and Mira Wilkins, "Multinationals and dictatorship: Europe in the 1930s and early 1940s," in Christopher Kobrak and Per H. Hansen (eds), *European Business, Dictatorship, and Political Risk, 1920–1945*, New York: Berghahn Books, 2004, pp. 3–21 and 22–38.

4. For Schering, see Christopher Kobrak, *National Cultures and International Competition: The Experience of Schering AG, 1851–1950*, Cambridge: Cambridge University Press, 2002. For IG Farben, see Mario Koenig, *Interhandel: Die SchweizerischeHolding der IG Farben und ihre Metamorphosen - eine Affäre um Eigentum und Interessen, 1910–1999*, Zürich: Chronos, 2001. For Bosch, see Gerald Aalders and Cees Wiebes, *The Art of Cloaking Ownership: The Secret Collaboration and Protection of the German War Industry by the Neutrals: The Case of Sweden*, Amsterdam, Netherlands: Amsterdam University Press, 1996, pp. 37–53. For Deutsche Bank, see Christopher Simpson and Office of Military Government, *War Crimes of the Deutsche Bank and the Dresdner Bank: Office of Military Government (US) Reports*, New York: Holmes & Meier, 2002, and Dieter Ziegler, "German private banks and German industry, 1830–1938," in Youssef Cassis and Philip Cottrell (eds), *The World of Private Banking*, Farnham: Ashgate, 2009, pp. 159–76.

5. See Takafumi Kurosawa, "The Second World War, divided world markets, and Swiss multinational enterprise: Roche, Nestlé, and political risks," paper presented at Business History Conference, St. Louis, 31 March–2 April 2011.

6. Aalders and Wiebes, *Art*, p. 9. For the term "tarnen" (roughly translated as cloaking), see Cornelia Schmitz-Berning, *Vokabular des Nationalsozialismus*, Berlin: de Gruyter, 1998, pp. 603–10, and Christiane Uhlig, Petra Barthelmess, Mario Koenig, Peter Pfaffenroth, and Bettina Zeugin. *Tarnung, Transfer, Transit. Die Schweiz als Drehscheibe verdeckter deutscher Operationen (1938–1952): Herausgegeben von der Unabhängigen Expertenkommission Schweiz-Zweiter Weltkrieg*, Zürich: Chronos, 2001, pp. 53–5.

7. Joseph Borkin, *The Crime and Punishment of IG Farben*, New York: Free Press, 1978; Aalders and Wiebes, *Art*.

8. Uhlig et al., *Tarnung*, p. 54.

9. Koenig, *Interhandel*; Christopher Kobrak and Jana Wuestenhagen. "International investment and Nazi politics: the cloaking of German assets abroad: 1936–1945," *Business History*, **48** (3) (2006) pp. 399–427.

10. Koenig, *Interhandel*.

11. Kobrak and Wuestenhagen, "International". For cloaking activities in MNEs based in Germany, see also Wilkins, "Multinationals," p. 27.

12. For a discussion of home country risks, see Espen Storli, "Out of Norway falls aluminium: the Norwegian aluminium industry in the international economy, 1908–1940," unpublished PhD thesis, Norwegian University of Science and Technology, 2010; Jones, *Multinationals*, pp. 220–3; Kobrak and Hansen, *European Business*.

13. Kobrak and Wuestenhagen, "International," p. 407.

14. For debates on recovering expropriated property on the political level see Aalders and Wiebes, *Art*, pp. 105–52, and Christopher Kobrak and Jana Wuestenhagen. "The politics of globalization: Deutsche Bank, German property and political risk in the United States after World War II," *Entreprises et Histoire*, **49** (2007), pp. 53–77. Little has been published on actual firm strategies, but there are hints that the recovery of assets was a huge problem. For Schering, Kobrak mentions that the company bought its subsidiary in Italy back in 1969 in Kobrak and Wuestenhagen, "International," pp. 424, n. 39. On Schering in Argentina, see Jana Wuestenhagen, "German pharmaceutical companies in South America: the case of Schering AG in Argentina," in Kobrak and Hansen, *European Business*, pp. 81–102.

15. William J. Hausman, Peter Hertner and Mira Wilkins (eds), *Global Electrification: Multinational Enterprise and International Finance in the History of Light and Power 1878–2007*, Cambridge: Cambridge University Press, 2008, pp. 95–104.

16. For other German companies see Kobrak, *National Cultures*, pp. 143–84; Koenig, *Interhandel*, pp. 54–6.

17. Rainer Gries, *Produktkommunikation: Geschichte und Theorie*, Vienna: Facultas, 2008, pp. 455.

18. Beiersdorf AG, *100 Jahre Beiersdorf, 1882–1982*, Hamburg: Beiersdorf AG, 1982, pp. 9–24; Geoffrey Jones, *Beauty Imagined*, Oxford: Oxford University Press, pp. 54–8, 80; Hans Gradenwitz, *Die Entwicklung der Firma Beiersdorf & Co. Hamburg, bis zum 1. Oktober 1915*, Hamburg, Germany: Beiersdorf, 1915; Claudia Hansen and Beiersdorf AG, *Nivea: Evolution of a World-Famous Brand*, Hamburg, Germany: Beiersdorf AG, 2001, pp. 26–7; Rainer Gries, *Produkte als Medien: Kulturgeschichte der Produktkommunikation in der Bundesrepublik und der DDR*, Leipzig, Germany: Leipziger Univ.-Verl., 2003, pp. 453–9.

19. Beiersdorf Corporate Archives (hereafter BA), Entwicklung 1919–1945, Lehn & Fink-Komplex, Vertraege 1893–1924, "Agreement re: Guttapercha-Plastermulls, Salvemulls, etc. of March 25th, 1893 with amendment dated September 15th, 1906". For a general overview see also Beiersdorf AG, *100 Jahre*, pp. 24–5.

20. BA, Entwicklung 1919–1945, Lehn & Fink-Komplex, Vertraege 1893–1924, "Vertrag betreffend: 'Pebeco'; translation of the agreement of 4th/16th Dec. 1903 re: Pebeco".

21. Antje Hagen, *Deutsche Direktinvestitionen in Grossbritannien, 1871–1918, Beiträge zur Unternehmensgeschichte 97*, Stuttgart, Germany: Steiner, 1997, pp. 81, 97.

22. Beiersdorf AG, *100 Jahre*, p. 26.

23. Ibid., p. 46; Jones, *Beauty*, pp. 55; Beiersdorf UK, *Ninety-Seven . . . and Counting: The Story of Beiersdorf in the UK*, unknown, 2003. p. 9.

24. Geoffrey Jones, *Multinationals and Global Capitalism*, Oxford: Oxford University Presss, 2005, p. 203.

25. Harm G. Schröter, "Continuity and change: German multinationals since 1850," in Geoffrey Jones and Harm G. Schröter (eds), *The Rise of Multinationals in Continental Europe*, Aldershot, UK and Brookfield, VT, USA: Edward Elgar, 1993, pp. 28–48.

26. The Nivea line had been sold in the US since 1914, but had not yet grown its sales to the point at which the government deemed it important enough for appropriation.

27. Hellmut Kruse, *Wagen und Winnen: Ein hanseatisches Kaufmannsleben im 20. Jahrhundert*, Hamburg, Germany: Die Hanse/EVA, 2006, pp. 86–93; "$1,000,000 refunded to former enemies: government pays the heirs of 'Pebeco' manufacturers – they are now Polish," *New York Times*, 24 July 1923, p. 6.

28. JWT, account histories, Lehn & Fink, 28 January 1926, JWT account files, Lehn & Fink, 1926, 1967, box 12.

29. BA, Entwicklung 1919–1945, Lehn & Fink-Komplex, Vertraege 1893–1924, "Auseinandersetzung mit Lehn & Fink," undated (1921).

30. Alfred D. Chandler, *Shaping the Industrial Century: The Remarkable Story of the Modern Chemical and Pharmaceutical Industries*, Cambridge, MA: Harvard University Press, 2005; Kobrak, *National Cultures*; Jones, *Multinationals*; Mira Wilkins, *The History of Foreign Investment in the United States, 1914–1945*, Cambridge, MA: Harvard University Press, 2004.

31. Kobrak, *National Cultures*, pp. 76–8.

32. Jones, *Multinationals*, p. 203.

33. Wilkins, *History*, pp. 122.

34. Uta G. Poiger, "Beauty, business and German international relations," *WerkstattGeschichte*, **45** (2007), pp. 56–7.

35. Schröter, "Risk".

36. BA, Ausland Allgemein, Deutsche Waren-Treuhand-Aktiengesellschaft, "Zusammenfassende Darstellung ueber die formellen und materiellen Rechtsverhaeltnisse der sechzehn zum Ausland-Ring gehoerigen Beiersdorf-Gesellschaften nach dem Stande vom 31 Dezember 1938," Hamburg, 31 January 1939, 2 (hereafter Waren-Treuhand Report 1939).

37. The name Pilot is based on the umbrella trademark used since 1905. Ekkehard Kaum, *Oscar Troplowitz: Forscher, Unternehmer, Bürger. Eine Monographie*, Hamburg, Germany: Wesche, 1982, pp. 49–51. Katrin Cura, "Leukoplast und Nivea. 125 Jahre Beiersdorf. Forschung, Marketing und Produktion in der Anfangszeit," in Gudrun

Wolfschmidt (ed.), *Hamburgs Geschichte einmal anders: Entwicklung der Naturwissenschaften, Medizin und Technik, Teil 2*, Norderstedt, Germany: Books on Demand, 2009, p. 114.

38. BA, Ausland Allgemein, Waren-Treuhand Report 1939, p. 8.
39. Beiersdorf AG, *100 Jahre*, p. 48.
40. Schröter, "Risk".
41. Jones, *Multinationals*, pp. 203–4.
42. See Wilkins, "Multinationals," pp. 26–30. For the monetary system of the interwar period, see Barry Eichengreen, *Globalizing Capital: A History of the International Monetary System*, 2nd edn, Princeton, NJ: Princeton University Press, 2008, pp. 43–90.
43. Beiersdorf AG, *100 Jahre*, p. 64.
44. Gerald D. Feldman, *Iron and Steel in the German Inflation, 1916–1923* (Princeton, NJ: Princeton University Press, 1977, p. 265; Marc Frey, *Der Erste Weltkrieg und die Niederlande: Ein neutrales Land im politischen und wirtschaftlichen Kalkül der Kriegsgegner*, Berlin: Akademie Verlag, 1998, pp. 352–70.
45. Frank Bajohr, *"Aryanisation" in Hamburg: The Economic Exclusion of Jews and the Confiscation of their Property in Nazi Germany*, New York: Berghahn Books, 2002, pp. 22–6.
46. For the term "aryanization," see Ingo Köhler, *Die "Arisierung" der Privatbanken im Dritten Reich: Verdrängung, Ausschaltung und die Frage der Wiedergutmachung*, 2nd edn, *Schriftenreihe zur Zeitschrift für Unternehmensgeschichte*, 14, Munich, Germany: Beck, 2008, pp. 38–42.
47. Kobrak and Wuestenhagen, "International," p. 411; Kobrak, *National Cultures*, pp. 267–71; Borkin, *Crime*.
48. Poiger, "Beauty"; Gries, *Produktkommunikation*, 195–215; Hansen and Beiersdorf AG, *Nivea*; Uta G. Poiger, "Fantasies of universality? Neue Frauen, race, and nation in Weimar and Nazi Germany," in Alys Eve Weinbaum, Lynn M. Thomas, Priti Ramamurthy, Uta G. Poiger, Madeleine Yue Dong and Tani E. Barlow (eds), *The Modern Girl Around the World: Consumption, Modernity, and Globalization*, Durham, NC, and London: Duke University Press, 2008, pp. 336–9.
49. Jones, *Beauty*, pp. 124–5; Poiger, "Fantasies," pp. 337–8; Harm G. Schröter, "Erfolgsfaktor Marketing. Der Strukturwandel von der Reklame zur Unternehmenssteuerung," in Wilfried Feldenkirchen, Frauke Schönert-Röhlk and Günther Schulz (eds), *Wirtschaft, Gesellschaft, Unternehmen, Bd. 2*, Stuttgart: Steiner, 1995, p. 1104.
50. Kruse, *Wagen*.
51. BA, Ausland Allgemein, Waren-Treuhand Report 1939.
52. Rudolf Brinckmann was an employee of the Warburg bank after 1920 and took over supervisory board mandates from members of the Jewish Warburg family. Eventually he became senior partner of the bank, which he managed for the Warburgs during the Nazi period. For a detailed account see Ron Chernow, *The Warburgs: The Twentieth-Century Odyssey of a Remarkable Jewish Family*, New York: Random House, 1993, pp. 565–71.
53. BA, Vertriebe, Umsaetze 1901–1970, Monatsberichte.
54. Kobrak and Wuestenhagen, "International," p. 410; Wuestenhagen, "German," p. 85.
55. BA Ringfirmen. Nachkriegskorrespondenz von grosser Wichtigkeit, vor allem Briefwechsel Dr Jacobsohn-Doetsch 1950–55, letter by Doetsch to Jacobsohn dated 27 March 1950 and letter by Jacobsohn to Doetsch dated 30 March 1950.
56. Kruse, *Wagen*, p. 97.
57. Uhlig et al., *Tarnung*, pp. 68–9.
58. BA Ausland Allgemein, Waren-Treuhand Report 1939.
59. BA, Ausland Allgemein, Deutsche Waren-Treuhand-Aktiengesellschaft, "Zusammenfassung der formellen und materiellen Rechtsverhaeltnisse der Beiersdorf Auslandsgesellschaften nach dem Stande vom 31. Maerz 1942," Hamburg, 6 June 1942, 3 (hereafter Waren-Treuhand Report 1942).
60. Beiersdorf claimed that the contract with Doetsch was lost during the war. Information about it comes from the postwar negotiations with Doetsch. There was, however, little

dispute about the content of the contract. Cf. BA Ausland Ringfirmen, Nachkriegs-Korrespondenz Untersuchungen der USA und Großbritanniens 1946–1948.

61. Aalders and Wiebes, *Art*, pp. 38–45; Uhlig et al., *Tarnung*, pp. 56–7.
62. Denise M. Rousseau, Sim B. Sitkin, Ronald S. Burt, and Colin Camerer, "Not so different after all: a cross-discipline view of trust," *Academy of Management Review*, **23** (3) (1998), p. 395.
63. Kruse, *Wagen*, pp. 28–32.
64. Waren-Treuhand Report 1942.
65. Ibid.
66. Ibid.
67. Beiersdorf UK, Ninety-Seven, p. 21.
68. Ibid.
69. Kobrak and Wuestenhagen, "International," pp. 412–18. Uhlig et al., *Tarnung*, pp. 57–61.
70. Uhlig et al., *Tarnung*, pp. 59–60.
71. Uhlig et al. estimate the total number of approvals at over 500 but less than 1000. Ibid., p. 61.
72. Waren-Treuhand Report 1942.
73. Harm G. Schröter, "Risk and control in multinational enterprise: German businesses in Scandinavia, 1918–1939," *Business History Review*, **62** (3) (1988), pp. 420–43. Paz Estrella Tolentino, *Multinational Corporations: Emergence and Evolution*, London: Routledge, 2000, pp. 159–78.
74. For the theoretical distinction of systemic and personal trust, see Niklas Luhmann, *Vertrauen: Ein Mechanismus der Reduktion sozialer Komplexität*, 3rd edn, Stuttgart, Germany: Enke, 1989.
75. Kruse, *Wagen*, p. 120.
76. Uhlig et al., *Tarnung*, pp. 305.
77. BA Ausland Allgemein, written statement by Richard Doetsch for Dr Brinckmann, dated 28 February 1952. See also BA Ringfirmen, Nachkriegskorrespondenz von grosser Wichtigkeit, vor allem Briefwechsel Dr Jacobsohn-Doetsch 1950–55, letter dated 4 May 1953, Kruse to Jacobsohn.
78. BA Ausland Ringfirmen, Nachkriegs-Korrespondenz Untersuchungen der USA und Großbritanniens 1946–1948, letter dated 6 October 1947.
79. BA Ausland Ringfirmen, Nachkriegs-Korrespondenz Untersuchungen der USA und Großbritanniens 1946–1948, letter dated 15 October 1947.
80. BA Ausland Allgemein, written statement by Richard Doetsch for Dr Brinckmann, dated 28 February 1952.
81. BA Ausland Ringfirmen, Nachkriegs-Korrespondenz Untersuchungen der USA und Großbritanniens 1946–1948, letter dated 30 April 1946, Beiersdorf to Sen. Com. Cillwood, Finance Dept, Reichsbank.
82. BA Ausland Allgemein, written statement by Richard Doetsch for Dr Brinckmann, dated 28 February 1952.
83. BA Ringfirmen, Nachkriegskorrespondenz von grosser Wichtigkeit, vor allem Briefwechsel Dr Jacobsohn-Doetsch 1950–55, letter dated 22 October 1952, Doetsch to Jacobsohn.
84. About the visits cf. for example BA Ringfirmen, Nachkriegskorrespondenz von grosser Wichtigkeit, vor allem Briefwechsel Dr Jacobsohn-Doetsch 1950–55, letter dated 30 September 1952, Doetsch to Jacobsohn, and letter dated 4 May 1953 Kruse to Jacobsohn. BA Ausland Allgemein, written statement by Richard Doetsch for Dr Brinckmann, dated 28 February 1952.
85. Kruse, *Wagen*, p. 116; BA, Ausland Allgemein, Umsaetze 1959–62, Betrachtung ueber die Entwicklung der Umsaetze und Lizenzertraege in der Auslandsfabrikation, Vergleich 1958-1959, 7.
86. Kruse, *Wagen*, p. 117. Beiersdorf AG, *100 Jahre*, p. 84.
87. BA Ausland allgemein, Aufstellungen Uebersichten 1908–1989 Tochterfirmen, Vertreter, Lizenzpartner, Uebersicht ueber Auslandsgesellschaften, undated, approximately 1967
88. BA Ringfirmen, Nachkriegskorrespondenz von grosser Wichtigkeit, vor allem

Briefwechsel Dr Jacobsohn-Doetsch 1950–55, letter by Doetsch to Jacobsohn, dated 4 May 1950.
89.   Kruse, *Wagen*, p. 124.
90.   Ibid.
91.   For the dynastic motive of family firms see Mark Casson, "The economics of the family firm," *Scandinavian Economic History Review*, **47** (1) (1999), pp. 10–23.
92.   Jones, *Beauty*, pp. 223–4.
93.   BA Ausland Allgemein, Unser Auslandsgeschaeft 1967.
94.   Beiersdorf AG, *100 Jahre*, p. 76.
95.   BA Ausland Allgemein, written statement by Richard Doetsch for Dr Brinckmann, dated 28 February 1952. BA Ringfirmen, Nachkriegskorrespondenz von grosser Wichtigkeit, vor allem Briefwechsel Dr Jacobsohn-Doetsch 1950–55, letter dated 22 October 1952, Doetsch to Jacobsohn.
96.   BA Ringfirmen, Nachkriegskorrespondenz von grosser Wichtigkeit, vor allem Briefwechsel Dr Jacobsohn-Doetsch 1950–55, letter dated 26 September 1952, Peloille to Jacobsohn. Compare also letter dated 14 October 1952, Gustin to Jacobsohn and letter dated 20 October 1952, Jacobsohn to Gustin.
97.   Kruse, *Wagen*, p. 139·
98.   Ibid., pp. 139–40.
99.   Jones, *Beauty*, p. 223; James Foreman-Peck, *Smith & Nephew in the Health Care Industry*, Aldershot, UK and Brookfield, VT, USA: Edward Elgar, 1995, p. 63.
100. Beiersdorf UK, *Ninety-Seven*, p. 14.
101. BA, Ausland Allgemein, Umsaetze; see also Harm G. Schröter, "Marketing als ange-wandte Sozialtechnik und Veränderungen im Konsumverhalten. Nivea als internationale Dachmarke 1960–1994," in Helmuth Kaelble, Jürgen Kocka and Hannes Siegrist (eds), *Europäische Konsumgeschichte: Zur Gesellschafts- und Kulturgeschichte des Konsums (18. bis 20. Jahrhundert)*, Frankfurt, Germany and New York: Campus, 1997, pp. 639–40.
102. Foreman-Peck, *Smith*, p. 132.
103. Ibid., p. 137.
104. Beiersdorf UK, *Ninety-Seven*, p. 63.
105. Schröter, "Marketing," pp. 639–41. A new marketing concept for Nivea was developed in 1967, and the brand was relaunched in Germany in 1970; see Schröter, "Erfolgsfaktor," pp. 1109–11.
106. More financial details are given in table 2 of the original article.
107. Schröter, "Marketing," pp. 639–41. See also the "Nivea Brand Philosophy," reprinted with an introduction in Harm G. Schröter, "Nivea and the globalization of the German econ-omy," *Entreprises et Histoire*, **16** (1997), pp. 113–15.

8. Learning to live with governments: Unilever in India and Turkey, 1950–80[1]

OVERVIEW

The geographical clustering of FDI is a prominent feature of the second global economy. In 2011 two-thirds of the stock of world inward FDI was located in developed countries, but it was far from evenly spread. For example, the small island nation of Ireland had about the same stock of inward FDI as Japan. The unevenness was even greater in the case of the FDI located in developing countries. In 2011, Brazil, China, Hong Kong, Mexico, and Singapore accounted for four-fifths of world inward FDI stock outside the developed world.

Among the larger emerging economies with much less inward FDI were India and Turkey. In 1990 inward FDI as a share of GDP had been low by international standards in both countries; the ratio in India had been 0.5 percent and in Turkey 5.5 percent. By 2011 the inward FDI stocks of India and Turkey were $20 billion and $14 billion respectively, which represented only 1.6 percent of world FDI, but the ratio to GDP had risen to 10.4 percent and 18 percent respectively. By comparison, the world average was 30 percent, and in some fast-growing emerging economies like Malaysia and Thailand it was around 40 percent.[2]

The subdued level of FDI in contemporary India and Turkey was puzzling, given that both countries greatly liberalized their regulations on inward FDI from the 1980s.[3] Historical research has emphasized the contingency of this phenomenon. India, whose stock of FDI was small in 1980, had been among the world's largest host economies in 1914 and 1929.[4] The former Ottoman Empire was much less important than British India as a host for FDI, but had certainly received a fair amount.[5]

Within this context, the experience of Unilever, the Anglo-Dutch consumer goods corporation formed by merger in 1929, is noteworthy. During the post-war decades Unilever owned large businesses in both India and Turkey. In both countries it remains today among the largest private-sector companies.[6] These countries formed part of an extensive business empire throughout the

165

developing world, spanning Latin America and Africa as well as Asia.[7] Unilever retained and expanded its business in developing countries after World War II, just as other Western corporations were focusing their investments on the politically safer Western world.

Unilever's historical importance in developing countries is especially striking for two reasons. First, although the firm's businesses spanned the oligopolistic detergents and toothpaste markets, its presence in so many developing countries was not matched by international competitors. Among its major US competitors, Procter & Gamble ventured beyond developed countries only in special cases before the 1980s, although Colgate-Palmolive was widely represented in toothpaste markets in developing countries.[8] German-based Henkel's only ventures beyond Europe, to Brazil, and South Africa, were sold in the mid-1980s, in the former case to Unilever. Unilever also sold foods products, especially margarine, tea, and frozen products including ice cream. Among competitor companies, both General Foods and CPC had large foods businesses in Latin America, but not elsewhere, although Swiss-based Nestlé was more similar to Unilever in being widely spread over developing countries.

Second, Unilever's business was also quite profitable. Unilever grouped most of its developing-country business in manufacturing in a management group known as the Overseas Committee. (It also operated a large trading and manufacturing business in Africa which was managed by a separate management group, the United Africa Company, or UAC.)[9] The Overseas Committee also included Unilever's business in Australia and New Zealand, and a small loss-making business in Japan. As Table 8.1 below shows, the Overseas countries were important components of the overall Unilever business.

The Overseas countries were always more important than the United States as a source of profits for Unilever between 1960 and 1990. (This reflected especially the poor performance of Unilever's Lever Brothers affiliate.)[10] In

Table 8.1   Overseas Committee revenues and pre-tax profits as a percentage of total Unilever revenues and pre-tax profits at benchmark dates 1969–81 (percent)

Date	Revenues	Profits
1969	13	5
1974	10	17
1979	11	21
1981	14	41

Source: Unilever Archives London (hereafter UAL)

Table 8.2   *Overseas Committee yield and average Unilever yield 1969–81*
           (percent)

Date	Overseas	Unilever average
1969	7.6	7.5
1974	13.4	8.1
1979	13.8	6.8
1981	15.7	7.0

Source: UAL.

1981 they even briefly surpassed Europe to become Unilever's largest source of profits. The greater profitability of Unilever's business in Overseas countries is confirmed by Unilever's internal calculation of what the firm called yield, defined as pre-tax profits divided by gross capital employed. This is shown in Table 8.2.

The yield earned by the Overseas Committee was consistently above that of the Unilever average and, from the 1960s, in excess of that earned either in Europe or North America. Indeed, only the UAC at the height of its profitability in the mid-1970s earned higher yields within Unilever.[11] After the first oil crisis in 1973, Unilever's margins in the Overseas countries were virtually double those in Europe for the remainder of that decade.[12]

This chapter begins with a brief survey of the nature of Unilever's business as a whole in developing countries before turning to the specific cases of India and Turkey.

UNILEVER IN DEVELOPING COUNTRIES

Unilever and its predecessors were early to invest in developing countries. By the 1930s the scale of Unilever's businesses in India, Indonesia, South Africa, and a number of other countries was already substantial. It was often the first manufacturing facility. In China, where Lever Brothers established the China Soap Company in Shanghai in 1923, soap sales constituted around 2 percent of Unilever's worldwide total by the mid-1930s, when it was the only Western firm manufacturing soap. Unilever also sold margarine, and by the end of the 1930s had plans to enter ice cream and meat processing in China.[13]

World War II and its aftermath were a major disruption. Unilever's initial focus was on rebuilding a European business devastated by war. Subsequent decolonization and the spread of anti-Western sentiments made investment prospects look less than attractive. The Unilever business in China was devastated first by the Pacific War, and then by the Revolution in 1949. However during the 1940s and 1950s there was a flurry of investments in new countries, usually in politically safe British colonies. In Africa, where Unilever had manufactured in Nigeria since 1923, soap manufacture was begun in Southern Rhodesia (Zimbabwe) in 1943, and other factories followed over the next decade in Northern Rhodesia (Zambia) and Nyasaland (Malawi). In 1953 an edible-oils factory was also opened in Kenya.[14] In 1952 a soap factory was opened in Malaya, despite the growing political instability in that still British-ruled country.

From the late 1950s the Overseas Committee began a program of new expansion based on a clearly articulated view of both risks and opportunities of the period. As Andrew Knox, the executive heading the Overseas Committee, later wrote in his autobiography,

> The calm certainties of currency and political stability on which I was brought up disappeared. The protection of the sterling area faded away as red gradually receded from the map of the world – at least as printed in Britain – and instability followed in the wake of a widespread but untutored rush for political independence . . . The certainties had gone, but so had the stagnation. Vast numbers of the peoples of the world were not only finding it possible but were being encouraged and taught to aspire to something more than the simple wants of a primitive and constricted existence. We would have lacked the essential element of our calling – enterprise – if we had not gone out to meet this surge of demand for the everyday products which Unilever sells.[15]

Unilever launched itself, then, on an entrepreneurial mission designed to supply "everyday products" to new swathes of consumers in developing countries as their incomes rose. The company sometimes entered new countries just as Procter & Gamble fled. This was the case in Chile in 1963, when it bought the former factory of Procter & Gamble, which had decided to divest fearing a left-wing victory in that country's next elections. Unilever seldom divested from a country.

During the 1960s the political risks began rising. A number of countries nationalized Unilever businesses. Foreign firms were subject to multiple controls on prices, imports, production, dividends, borrowings, remittances, expatriate employment, and salaries. Governments restricted the payment of dividends and service fees. There was a surge of demands for local equity participation. Such requests were anathema to many large US firms, such as IBM and Coca Cola, who both left India as a result during the 1970s. Unilever also disliked them, fearing knowledge leakage, loss of trademarks, and moral hazard issues.[16] However, Unilever became a master at delaying tactics, using its extensive contacts and goodwill in many countries to modify regulations, and generally bargaining with governments.

Whatever the severity of government pressures, Unilever was careful to strictly limit its involvement in politics to the kind of lobbying and engagement seen in all business systems. There was never any question of involvement in regime changes on the lines pursued in Central and South America by the more infamous US corporations such as United Fruit or ITT. Nor did Unilever fund political parties, either in government or opposition, in any country. The company also did not bribe politicians and officials. The spread of government regulations in many developing countries provided opportunities for corruption, but although in some countries small facilitating payments were sometimes made to make things happen, Unilever had a strict policy to avoid corrupt payments on a grander scale. In 1968 a proposal by one Unilever company "to make a substantial payment to a public official to encourage him to give suitable attention to an outstanding matter of company business" led to a ruling that Unilever companies "should not, as a matter of general policy, enter into any transaction of this kind".[17]

In some of Unilever's most important markets corruption was endemic in corporate and public life, but Unilever's size facilitated its policy to stay clean. There were, however, costs. "You need to have established strength and, if everybody knows you don't pay, they stop asking", a vice-chairman of the Indian affiliate Hindustan Lever in the late 1960s later explained.

> It means that you have to employ a lot of minions running around from government office to government office persuading the right clerk to put the file on the top of the pile instead of at the bottom. You don't in any way pay for the decision but you take a lot of trouble to get the thing dealt with properly.[18]

The major problem faced by Unilever was to make sure local managements followed corporate rules in this respect. There were occasional unwelcome discoveries of irregular payments being made by local companies, often but not always recently acquired ones. Here Italy rather than developing countries was the main problem.[19] During 1978 the Argentine company was also discovered to have deposited "black cash" in a bank in Uruguay to be used as a special fund in case of kidnapping, while in Turkey it was discovered that funds had been used for payments to expatriates to circumvent government regulations.[20] In some cases the problem lay in differing definitions of what constituted a "bribe." It was often, it was noted, "extremely hard to draw the line between what was acceptable and what was not."[21]

Unilever had appointed the first local nationals to managerial positions in developing countries – India and Ghana – in the 1930s. More followed during and after World War II. During the mid-1950s the head of the Overseas Committee identified the issue "as one of overriding urgency" both in response to the aspirations of rising nationalism and also in Unilever's best interests. He argued that Unilever companies would benefit from being managed by nationals who truly know the country and the business as a whole would have a broader base or original thought, a wider field from which to recruit senior management and a much more truly international aspect.

In 1955 Unilever had over 800 managers in overseas companies in developing countries of whom 32 percent were expatriates. By 1966 it had 2965 managers of whom only 8 percent were expatriates.[22] This localization of management was aligned with Unilever's postwar culture which emphasized local autonomy of its affiliates, and the importance of local knowledge and responsiveness to local markets.[23]

Unilever continued to employ European expatriates. This was considered important in supplying expertise to local companies, in maintaining personal relationships within Unilever's large businesses, and in providing postings for managers identified as "rising stars." However, nationals from developing countries were increasingly also used as expatriates in third-party countries. By the 1970s the Overseas Committee had a policy of internationalization;

[B]y that we didn't just mean putting Europeans into developing countries, we meant having about 15 percent of the management team in any country non-nationals; so we might have Dutchmen or Englishmen or Indians or Nigerians or Brazilians or Australians working in countries other than their own; what we didn't want was a situation where it was the Europeans going out and showing them.[24]

The "everyday products" Unilever sold were primarily home and personal care. In many developing countries, Unilever products were often one of the first things people purchased when they had discretionary income. They often made their first purchase of hard soap to wash their clothes, or sometimes fat to make their food more palatable. As incomes rose, the demand rose for more expensive products. While hard soaps were the standard for washing clothes, over time Unilever could begin selling detergent paste, and then powders, and ultimately liquid detergents and fabric conditioners. Unilever primarily cascaded products and brands sold in developed markets. The only fundamental research in developing countries was conducted in India. However there was constant product adaptation in formulations and brand images. In Thailand, where Unilever held in the early 1980s nearly 50 percent of the total toilet soap market with Lux, the local company formulated its toilet soap with no tallow, using palm oil.[25]

In many developing countries, Unilever was a "first mover" in soaps, and occupied a commanding market position. In Unilever's market share position in soap and detergents included 58 percent in South Africa, 40 percent in Turkey, 37 percent in Brazil, and 23 percent in India.[26] Hard soap and fabric products were usually the mainstays in lower-income markets. The absence of major international, though not local, competitors, meant that Unilever could avoid heavy spending on marketing and innovation, so margins were often good in many countries.

Unilever also sold personal care products. It was successful selling shampoos. In lower-income markets hair cleansing was typically an extension of personal washing, and either no separate product was employed or else oil was used to provide manageability. In these markets Unilever introduced its Sunsilk brand targeted at the rich elites who had begun to use hairdressers, and a large socially aspirant group of women who had enough disposable income to sue a specialist hair product occasionally. Unilever's shampoos achieved impressive shares in a range of countries. Colgate-Palmolive and Johnson & Johnson were the only competitors which came remotely near to Unilever's spread of business, although Revlon, Kao, Procter & Gamble, Beechams, and L'Oréal were active in certain countries. In the early 1980s Unilever was a strong market leader in India and Indonesia – with approaching 40 percent of the overall market – and also in Brazil, although it was dwarfed by Kao in Thailand, Colgate-Palmolive in the Philippines, and Beecham in Malaysia.[27]

Unilever also sold toothpaste in some countries. Close-Up was Unilever's leading brand, though Pepsodent was in a leading position in Indonesia, Venezeula, and Chile, and in English-speaking West Africa, while Signal dominated in francophone Africa. Imaginative ways were developed to expand the market. In 1984 Unilever launched Close-Up in sachet form in Thailand designed to encourage first-time users in rural areas. Unilever faced major competition from Colgate-Palmolive, which pioneered the introduction of toothpaste in many markets. In the mid-1960s Colgate-Palmolive held around 30 percent of the Brazilian toothpaste market, and 50 percent of the Indian and South African market. Unilever had a bare 6 percent of the Indian market. However in other markets, including Turkey and Nigeria, where Unilever held 40 percent of the markets, there was no competition from Colgate-Palmolive.[28]

In contrast, Unilever did not develop a large foods business in developing countries. It was hard to sell its major product, margarine, in countries which did not eat much bread, which ruled out much of Asia. Unilever's large business in convenience and frozen foods, including ice cream, was hard to exploit in developing markets. There was a general problem for frozen products in many developing countries because electricity supplies were not reliable, with consequent problems for distribution and cold storage.[29] Ice cream required a certain level of purchasing power to be viable, and also involved complex logistics from the initial stage of milk acquisition through to delivery of the final product in a good condition to the consumer. There was little demand for convenience products. In most countries there were often plentiful fresh vegetables and fruits – and the cooking skills to make use of them – and so no great demand for convenience foods. In Asian countries the urban middle class was accustomed to eating on a daily basis in numerous street stalls and restaurants which served delicious food at low prices. It was an uphill struggle to persuade such consumers to buy more expensive packaged products which they needed to cook in their own homes.

There was a contrast between Unilever and Nestlé's much larger foods business which was widely spread in Latin America, Africa, and Asia. While instant coffee and milk products gave them a much better basis for growth than Unilever's "core" food products, Nestlé also leveraged its strong research base in foods by locating development laboratories close to markets. In the mid-1980s the Swiss company opened a research facility in Singapore dedicated to the development of products based on soy and other oil-yielding plants and dehydrated culinary products. It was also more willing than Unilever to use joint ventures to access local markets. The upshot was that Nestlé built a much larger foods businesses in many countries in which Unilever was long established, including in Asia the Philippines, Thailand, and Malaysia.

HINDUSTAN LEVER

Unilever had a long history in India. Lever Brothers had exported soap to India since before the First World War. In 1924 a small factory was opened in Calcutta which manufactured soap. A new modern soap factory was constructed in Mumbai in 1934. In 1932 a factory was opened just outside Mumbai to make vegetable ghee or vanaspati, a product whose use as an additive to natural ghee had grown over the previous decade.[30]

After Indian independence in 1947, the government progressively introduced a planned economy, with licensing of capacity, price controls, and import and exchange controls. Taxation levels rose sharply. However, as elsewhere, the high level of protection sheltered Unilever and other firms such as Colgate-Palmolive who manufactured locally from international competition.[31] By the mid-1950s the Indian government had also begun to encourage Unilever to allow a local shareholding in the business. In 1956 the separate detergents, vanaspati, and personal products businesses were reorganized into Hindustan Lever, with 10 percent of the equity sold to the public. Further government pressure raised the local shareholding by 1965 to 14 percent.

The Indian government also encouraged the appointment of Indian nationals as managers. While in 1940 virtually all of Unilever's 150 managers in India were expatriates, by 1950 the number of expatriates had fallen to 50. In 1949 a management training scheme was started. By 1966 there were only six expatriates out of a total of 360 managers. In 1961 an Indian national, P.L. Tandon, was appointed chairman. Tandon's appointment was the first time that an Indian had become the chairman of a large foreign-owned company. He proved effective at getting the company in India "seen to be Indian," by working with the government and joining the boards of several large public companies. Tandon eventually resigned his chairmanship of Hindustan Lever in 1968 to head a large state trading corporation.[32] Unilever became extremely attractive as an employer. During the 1980s Hindustan Lever regularly received 8000 applicants annually for 30 or 40 places.

Although the recruitment of local talent was enormously important for the firm's future in India, it could not protect it from the vagaries of government policies. During the 1960s profits from the vanaspati business fell away with growing competition and price controls. Government controls over imports of raw materials kept vegetable oil prices artificially high and so reduced the relative cheapness of vanaspati as compared with natural ghee. Official control over imports of capital equipment also effectively blocked technical improvements in methods of manufacture, making it impossible for Unilever to introduce more upscale brands of the product. Unilever's share of vanaspati production declined from almost 30 percent in 1948 to 18 percent in 1965. Soap, which was not subject to government price controls, remained profitable. Unilever held a particularly strong position in branded premium soaps. However the domestic markets for such branded goods was rather small, while government controls over foreign exchange and a lack of local alkalis meant that Unilever was unable to begin manufacture of synthetic detergents.

Unilever also diversified into other product areas. In 1943 a factory was built in Calcutta to manufacture personal products. However while talcum powder and shaving soap grew quite quickly, sales of toothpaste made no progress against Colgate-Palmolive. From the mid-1950s Unilever also began to consider schemes for further diversification, both to use capital released from sale of equity and to convince the government of Unilever's contribution to the economy, which was the key to getting import licenses to import capital equipment and so on. A particular concern was to move into areas not subject to price controls. In 1957 a small research facility was also established in Mumbai, initially to explore the potential for fruit processing.

During the late 1950s and early 1960s a number of new initiatives were launched in processed foods. Tandon was especially enthused with the potential of convenience foods. He believed that there was potential for producing and marketing dehydrated peas and dried milk curd, but it became apparent that this would involve Unilever organizing its own supplies. Both projects were launched in the state of Uttar Pradesh. In 1959 a pilot project for growing peas on contract was started, and pea hydration operations began at its Ghaziabad factory. A larger project involved building a new factory for milk products at Etah which would be surrounded by a large number of milk-collecting stations and milking centers. Hindustan Lever made contracts with local farmers to bring their cattle to the milking centers, and then transferred the milk to collecting centers and on to the central factory for processing. In 1960, and largely at the behest of the Indian government, Hindustan Lever entered cottonseed processing, designed both to expand the supply of vegetable oil and to provide a market for farmers. Unilever's oil-milling business also led to investment in compound cattle feedstuffs.[33]

In the late 1960s Hindustan Lever was a much diversified business in terms both of India and of Unilever. By 1967 its turnover of R932.8 million ranked it in the top five private sector firms in India in terms of sales, with almost 7000 employees and six factories. It had a wide span of businesses, though in terms of share of total sales soaps and detergents (over 50 percent) and edible fats (around 36 percent) dominated. Sunlight, in laundry soap, and Lifebuoy and Lux in toilet soap, had large sales. There were also the Etah dairy products, which included skim milk powder and baby foods, and milk drinks and milk sweets. The latter included a quick-cooking mix for the sticky but delicious Gulab Jamun, a widely consumed sweet which was later to become a standard feature of Indian restaurants in Britain. There were small sales of dehydrated peas and dried soup mix. And Unilever even distributed condoms on behalf of the government family planning program.

Unilever's commitment to research in India expanded in 1967 when a new research centre was formally inaugurated by the deputy prime minister. At the center of much of the Indian laboratory's research was the use of indigenous materials. During the 1970s its research began to contribute significantly to the Indian economy through import substitution. The use of unconventional oils for soapmaking reduced imports of tallow. In chemicals, new processes were developed relying on Indian turpentine, Javanese citronella (grown in the 1970s under contract for Hindustan Lever at a price half that of indigenous oils), and Indian lemon grass oil for perfume. By the end of the 1970s Hindustan Lever had developed four chemicals from lemon grass, five from citronella, and one from turpentine. The R&D program enhanced the company's reputation with the Indian government and the Indian professional classes, the latter facilitating the recruitment of excellent staff.[34]

In terms of profits, the Indian business had become anything but diversified by this period. During the second half of the 1960s virtually all profits originated in soap and detergents, which cross-subsidized the losses everywhere else in the business. By then the effect of price controls on vanaspati had reduced Unilever's gross margins to 4 percent, yet it was generally accepted as impossible for the company to withdraw from making this mass consumption article without incurring the wrath of the government.[35] Nevertheless the fact that substantial profits could be made at least in detergents, and that the business had grown amid difficult political and economic conditions which included a war with Pakistan, droughts, and a major devaluation provided grounds for optimism. Moreover Hindustan Lever was a considerable contributor to Unilever coffers. During 1956 to 1969 it remitted dividends amounting to £7.8 million to its parents.[36]

The strategy to build successful businesses beyond soap and detergents ran into considerable difficulties. Tandon's vision of the importance of convenience foods was ahead of its time, as was shown by the ultimate failure of the dried pea business, which was abandoned in 1970. The dried pea operation required Unilever to expand pea cultivation around the factory at Galziabad just outside Delhi. Unilever had to give the small farmers the seed they wanted them to grow and the fertilizer to grow it under an arrangement whereby the farmer contracted to grow peas in a certain number of acres at an agreed price. By the end of the 1960s Unilever had around 8000 acres of land under pea cultivation with three to four thousand farmers. However the project ran into trouble at the marketing stage. In India's hot and humid climate, peas needed expensive packaging in a laminate of paper, aluminum and plastic. The resulting product was too expensive for middle-class consumers, while the rich had servants who could buy peas from the market and shell them.[37]

The most pressing issue in the late 1960s was the accumulating losses on the Etah project. The initial problems at Etah related to a shortage in the supply of milk resulting in a less than 50 percent utilization of the factory capacity. However there were also technical failings as Hindustan Lever opted for roller driers for drying the milk rather than spraydrying, which dissolved the milk faster, with the result that the product was not as good as competitors'. Then between 1965 and 1967 poor monsoons led to a fall in milk supplies, prices doubled, and production fell below sales requirements. In response, the government imposed controls on baby food prices and began importing cheap skim milk powder. Subsequently Unilever's sales faltered as milk supplies improved and imports of skim milk powder increased. Yet Unilever's management felt locked into the project because of its high-profile image and because of the hope that a profitable foods business might compensate for blocked opportunities elsewhere.[38]

By 1971 Hindustan Lever was firmly committed to selling the Etah dairy plant by 1973 "at any means."[39] In practice trade union pressure provided a major obstacle to any sale. Unilever tried to give it away for nothing to the government of the United Provinces, which declined the offer. Unilever realized that the success of the factory depended on increasing the milk availability in the Etah district, and that this was linked to the overall socio-economic development of the region. In 1976 the then chairman of Hindustan Lever, T. Thomas, reviewed the situation. Thomas sent five supervisors from the factory and assigned them to different villages within the district. The supervisors were all agricultural graduates who had been trained within the company in the milk procurement operation. They were also from the area around Etah and therefore were familiar with the local environment. The supervisors were assigned villages and told to investigate data on a wide range of matters and to work with the villagers in improving agricultural output, without the company having to subsidize the operations financially. After six weeks Thomas met the supervisors who identified a number of problems facing the villagers in lack of finance, lack of professional guidance in agriculture and animal husbandry, lack of reliable sources of supply for essential inputs such as fertilizers, and lack of warehousing and marketing facilities.

The outcome was a development program aimed at improving the prosperity level of the Etah district farmers through their own efforts by providing them with animal husbandry skills. The five supervisors were placed in permanent residence in the villages they had surveyed. Selected farmers were used as role models and helped in deciding on crop rotation, seed selection, fertilizer dosage, irrigation intervals, and weeding. Farmers were helped to get loans. Under the old system, Thomas later explained,

> if you are a farmer and you wanted a loan, you had to go through a bureaucracy. The first stage is the local tax-collecting official for the village. The farmer has to bribe him to get a certificate from him saying that he owned the land. Armed with this, the farmer will go to the Bank in the nearest town. The Bank staff also demanded their cut. So by the time he gets the loan, already a good portion has gone. He takes the loan at a very high cost and defaults. So he never takes another loan.[40]

Hindustan Lever intervened with both the banks and the tax authorities to do away with these abuses. As yields rose, the program was extended beyond the original six villages. A medical scheme was introduced primarily aimed at preventive measures, such as vaccinations, and for spreading hygiene in the villages, and the training of villagers in paramedical activities and mechanical equipment repair was started. In 1979 a program was commenced for the reclamation of uncultivable alkaline and saline land, which represented over 5 percent of the Etah district. Throughout the project Thomas remained personally involved, visiting every month. By 1978 the dairy project had become profitable, but perhaps even more important was the goodwill it generated in India towards Unilever.

During the 1970s Unilever, like other foreign firms, was badly affected as the regulatory and political environment for foreign companies in India deteriorated. Price controls had a serious impact on profitability. By 1971 the vanaspati business had been rendered completely unprofitable, but there was also no prospect of selling it, and, even if they could, no prospect of repatriating any money from such a sale.[41] While some local firms were able to use unorthodox methods to avoid price controls, this option was not open to Unilever, which through the 1960s sought to maintain margins by expanding volume and reducing raw material and processing costs, but by the early 1970s the room for further efficiency improvements was not great. During 1972 the decision was taken to withdraw from vanaspati "as quickly as it is commercially and politically feasible."[42] However Unilever's synthetic detergents business remained not subject to price controls, and was quite profitable.

Between 1972 and 1974 Unilever undertook extensive negotiations with the Indian government for relief from the effects of price control. The eventual deal was that price control was removed on soaps, conditional on the large manufacturers introducing a poor man's toilet soap at a controlled price. A critical part of the arrangement was that Thomas persuaded the government that it could make soap by using non-edible oils like castor oil and rice bran oil instead of imported tallow, permitting the government to use the foreign exchange it had allocated for the import of tallow to import badly needed fertilizers instead. This involved Hindustan Lever rethinking its brand strategies for premium soaps. In 1975 price control was also removed from vanaspati. This led to a reversal of the decision to withdraw from the product and a new policy to reestablish the Dalda brand, as well as to introduce a colored and flavored margarine.[43] Profits soon rose. By the end of the decade Unilever directors were beginning to wax lyrical about the merits of their Indian company. "Talent for innovation shown by the management in India was quite remarkable right through the business," one director returning from India observed. "They were very clever at adapting to circumstances and overcoming shortages."[44]

Unilever, like other foreign companies, was challenged by the enactment of the FERA legislation under which all companies not engaged in "core" or non-technology industries had to bring their shareholding down to 40 percent from 1974. Unilever had no wish for a minority equity stake in its large Indian business. Thomas's strategy was to resist reducing the Unilever shareholding down to 40 percent, and seek instead to retain the 74 percent shareholding permitted for firms in the high-technology or core sectors. After long and complex negotiations, an agreement was negotiated with the government under which a foreign company was permitted to hold 51 percent of the equity, provided that 60 percent of its turnover was in the core or high-technology sectors, and that it exported 10 percent of its production.

Hindustan Lever then set about about satisfying the government that it met these criteria. The company began to expand its exports from India. Large exports of detergents and soaps were made to the Soviet Union. Hindustan Lever began exporting a wide range of products, including a mandatory 10 percent of its total exports from the small-scale sector. Not only company products were exported, but also carpets, shoes, garments, marine goods, and other products processed under company supervision and specification. By the early 1980s Hindustan Lever had become India's second-largest private sector exporter. Thomas also sought to persuade the government that the technologies it had developed for using non-edible oils in soap manufacture represented a sophisticated technology, though this claim was ultimately rejected. In 1977 the Congress Party lost power for the first time since Independence. The fractious, left-wing Janata Party took power, and adopted new measures to restrict foreign multinationals. An order was issued requiring Unilever to go down to a 40 percent shareholding by 1979.

Thomas adopted delaying tactics. He argued that Unilever should be allowed to reduce the shareholding in two stages. The first step to 51 percent was implemented in 1978, but by 1980 the advent of a new government provided an opportunity to delay the second stage. By this date Thomas had expanded the chemicals side of the business with a project begun in 1974 to manufacture sodium tripolyphosphate (STPP). This project had encountered considerable skepticism within Unilever's management group for chemicals, known as Chemicals Co-ordination, because "they felt that Unilever had no know-how in that area and had no confidence that the Indian Co. could manage something as complex as a large chemical plant." However, senior management supported the Indian company, and a plant went into operation at the end of 1979.[45]

The perception of Hindustan Lever as a high-technology company was ultimately facilitated by a transfer of assets between it and another Unilever company in India, Lipton. The Indian company proved the most troublesome affiliate of the British-based Lipton International tea business acquired by Unilever in 1971. Lipton was a one-product company engaged in packing and distribution of tea, competing both against small packers who controlled 90 percent of the Indian domestic tea market and against Brooke Bond (also British-owned) which had twice its size in tea-packing and in tea and coffee plantations. The major part of the business, including the head office and the main factory, was in Calcutta, yet this represented only 13 percent of the Indian market. Worst of all, the poorly managed company was hugely overmanned. Thomas estimated that 1400 of the 1800 salesmen were surplus to requirements if a Hindustan Lever type of distribution was introduced, while around 1000 workers in the Calcutta factory were also surplus to requirements.[46]

The full horror of this situation had not been noticed as the Indian affiliates' accounts had been subsumed into those of Lipton as a whole. However the formation of a separate company, Lipton India Ltd, with a 60 percent Indian shareholding – there was no possibility of a tea company escaping the FERA legislation – revealed the scale of the problems. An attempt to improve the situation led to a 5-month strike in 1979, the loss of all its financial reserves, and a fall in market share down to less than 20 percent. The virtual bankruptcy of Lipton prompted consideration of divestment.[47] However Unilever's top management rejected this advice, stressing the moral commitment to the outside Indian shareholders.[48] During the following 2 years Unilever transferred management staff from Hindustan Lever and made an attempt to turn the business around. By 1982 it made a small profit, though no radical changes could be made because of the complexities of getting the agreement of the Indian shareholders to any plans for structural change or refinancing.[49] In 1984 Hindustan Lever's business in vanaspati was transferred to Lipton.

Meanwhile the 1970s had seen Unilever's fortunes in India at low ebb. While senior management attention was focused on government negotiations, Hindustan Lever faced unexpectedly serious competitive pressure from Karsanbhai Patel's Nirma Industries, which challenged during the long-established hold on the Indian market by Unilever by introducing a game-changing low-priced detergent.[50] It was only after a significant delay that Hindustan Lever was able to respond with low-cost but quality products. The growth of Hindustan Lever's revenues and profits were slower than in other major markets such as Brazil and South Africa. While overall revenues (in constant prices) of the Overseas Committee grew at 4.1 percent per annum between 1965 and 1980, Indian revenues grew only by 0.8 percent. Over the same period, while total Overseas pre-tax profits grew at 4.5 percent, the growth of pre-tax profits per annum in India was negative at –0.04 percent. Remittances from the Indian business became very small during the second half of the 1970s. They were dwarfed by those of South Africa, and more or less on a par with far smaller businesses such as Thailand. There were multiple reasons for this, including that Hindustan Lever was only a 51-percent-owned company, that no service fees were received because the Indian government prevented such payments, that corporate taxation was high, and that a high proportion of funds – about one-third of distributable profits – had to be retained in the business given the high rates of tax.[51]

In January 1980 the Janata Party lost the election, and the Congress Party returned to power. Prime Minister Indira Gandhi, chastened by the previous loss of power to the Janata Party as well as India's slow economic growth and mounting macroeconomic difficulties, no longer pursued a socialist agenda, and began to slowly relax government planning controls.[52] Thomas's delaying strategy had worked. In 1981 the government finally permitted Unilever to retain a majority shareholding in Hindustan Lever. Unilever became one of a relatively small number of foreign companies which successfully bargained with the Indian state to maintain its majority shareholding.[53] Given the wide dispersal of ownership of the shares held by the public – in 1980 almost 90 000 Indians held Hindustan stock – this left Unilever in more-or-less full control of the company.

A number of factors were important in Unilever's survival and growth in India. In addition to its long-established presence in the country, the early commitment to localization of senior staff provided a series of outstanding chairmen able to negotiate within the Indian political system. They were permitted to pursue the rural development and heavy chemicals projects which enhanced the company's image and standing within India. The business grew with a strong local management cadre, and indeed India became an exporter of management talent within Unilever. Unilever itself pursued a flexible business strategy, including the acceptance of low levels of remittances for decades, which saw its operations through complex political circumstances and enabled it to develop.

TURKEY: WAITING FOR BETTER DAYS

The entry of Unilever into Turkey became a corporate legend. It was widely believed that – either in 1939 or 1949 – the Dutch director Sydney van den Bergh had arrived in Istanbul by accident when his plane developed technical problems, and then noticed how much bread was eaten in the country and thought it would be a good market for margarine.[54] Although there is no evidence to support this account, Van den Bergh was certainly the prime mover behind the decision to invest in the country in the late 1940s. At a time of tight exchange controls in Europe which made the transfer of funds difficult, and in the context of the wishes of the Turkish government for Turkish shareholders in the proposed Unilever company, Unilever sought local partners. Vehbi Koç, whose business group expanded rapidly after World War II, declined an invitation on the grounds that there was no future and profit in margarine – a decision he later told Unilever executives he very much regretted.[55] However the government-owned Iş Bank did become Unilever's sole partners, holding 20 percent of the equity of the new Unilever-Iş.

The decision to invest in Turkey in 1950 was a pioneering one, as it was not until the 1960s that the country began to industrialize on a large scale. Unilever's first product was a vegetable ghee known as Vita, which was much cheaper than the natural ghee previously used in Turkey. Unilever transferred a production manager from its Indian business to develop the manufacture of the ghee, which was sold in tins which were subsequently used for many purposes including roofing houses. Subsequently Sana margarine was developed manufactured from sunflower oil and soybean oil imported cheaply from the United States under an aid program put at the disposal of the margarine industry to help keep the cost of living down. The cheap prices of the products and a fast rate of population growth contributed to a formidable increase in sales.[56]

Unilever-Iş had no competitors, but it was also successful in creating a market for margarine by consistent advertising and efficient distribution. Products manufactured in Istanbul were distributed through depots to wholesalers in the main towns quickly and cheaply. Product consistency was a novel feature in the market and an attractive one.[57] By the mid-1960s – by which time the Turkish economy was growing quickly at over 7 percent per annum – Unilever-İş supplied about one-third of all fat consumed in Turkey, including butter and olive oil. Butter remained the preferred choice of Turks to margarine, both for its taste and for its nutritional value, but the market for margarine was dominated by Unilever. At the end of the 1960s, Sana was estimated to hold around 90 percent of the margarine market and Vita around two thirds of the vegetable ghee market.[58]

Unilever-İş also invested in a number of agricultural projects. In 1962, when Turkey's sunflower crop was ruined by infestation with the vegetable parasite broomrape (*Orobanche cumana* Wallr.), it supplied farmers with a resistant strain of sunflower seed with a higher oil yield which was obtained from Russia via France. By 1973 the local sunflower seed crop had increased from an oil equivalent of about 25 000 tons to at least 80 000 tons, making Turkey self-sufficient in vegetable oils in a good crop year.[49] In 1965 Unilever began a project to develop a jasmine plantation in the Antalya region designed to supply jasmine perfume to a French firm. There was a rationale beyond Unilever's penchant for diversification in this era, for it was hoped that the generation of exports from Turkey would protect the profit remittances from the edibles business.[60]

The upshot was a national institution largely run by Turks. By the late 1950s there were only 10 expatriates out of over 500 employees. Unilever was a model employer providing a range of health and social benefits, including cooperative housing schemes. The company was embedded in the lifestyles of the population. As a future Unilever chairman who had worked in Turkey during the 1950s, Van den Hoven later recalled, "You couldn't meet the government minister or the prime minister, or anybody in the country, who didn't know the name of our product, 'Vita.' And who would not say that his life depended on it."[61]

It was a successful business. Unilever's Turkish operations delivered hard-currency dividends, amounting to some $23 million between 1953 and 1978.[62] During the 1950s and first half of the 1960s, returns to capital invested were among the highest of any Unilever subsidiary worldwide. It was the only firm which made margarine and vegetable ghee with vegetable oil and water without using animal fats. Without competitors, advertising expenditure was minimal. The company spent no more than 2 percent of sales on advertising, compared with upwards of 14 percent in South Africa. The oils imported under the PL 480 program were also quite cheap.[63]

The major problem, which got worse over time, was the government. The first signs of difficulty occurred in detergents. Before the 1950s Unilever products such as Lux toilet soap and Vim scourers had been sold in Turkey through the agency of the Couteaux family, who were of Belgian origin but resident in

Turkey. In 1954 the government granted Unilever a license to make toilet soap and soap powder, and it began manufacturing with Couteaux as Lever Brothers (Turkey). By the late 1950s Unilever wanted to expand its detergents manufacture on a larger scale, and to expand into laundry soaps and synthetic detergents. A license was granted in 1960, but a change of government – a military coup overthrew the government of the Democratic Party in that year – was followed by intense lobbying by local soap makers. Eventually the government ruled that it could only proceed with its plans if the entire production was exported.[64]

Unilever also encountered problems remitting profits from the detergents business, for only Unilever-İş had the right under law to remit funds abroad. A solution was found by appointing the merchant firm of G. and A. Baker – long owned by Unilever's UAC and at one time the owner of Turkey's largest department store in Istanbul – as the agent for both companies, for having been established for more than 100 years it had rights to export profits. Unilever ended up with a complicated business structure with three companies doing different things under different laws. Unilever-İş was licensed to trade only in margarine and vegetable ghee; Lever was licensed to deal only in soap products; G. and A. Baker was licensed to trade in any commodity, but had no borrowing rights and had to declare and remit 100 percent of post-tax profits.

Unilever's business became progressively restricted by government controls and restrictions. Its managers responded by trying to seek growth in areas that the government might approve. Government pressure on foreign firms remitting profits to develop compensating export facilities led to an investment in a tomato paste processing venture as a minority partner with Turkish interests.[65] Dosan, which had a 25 percent Unilever shareholding, was launched in 1971, with a tomato puree production plant located in a large tomato- and onion-growing area. Dosan was committed to export 60 percent of its output as a condition of the government agreeing to Unilever participation. By 1976 Dosan had become the second-largest tomato paste producer in Turkey.[66]

A search began for ingenious schemes to build a detergents business despite government restrictions. During the early 1970s Unilever launched a new company called Desas, wholly owned by its partners Couteaux, to pack its Omo detergent powder. Desas delivered to Baker and extended credits to Baker, giving that firm a source of funds. This was a risky arrangement as Unilever ultimately had no control over the business.[67] A more permanent solution was sought through an alliance with the Koç group.[68] An agreement was negotiated in 1973 under which Unilever's existing detergents operations would be placed under a new company in which Unilever held a 37 percent shareholding along with Koç.[69] Unilever senior management approved the new proposal, even though considering it "far from ideal,"[70] but the government rejected it.[71]

Eventually a new set of arrangements were put in place. Baker ceased manufacturing itself, and instead marketed products made by two third-party Turkish companies, Temsa and Marmora Kozmetik. Temsa, which made toilet soap and detergents, was owned 49 percent by Desas and 50 percent by the Iş Bank Pension Fund, but its general manager and some staff were seconded from Unilever-Iş or Baker. Marmora Kozmetik, which began operations in 1978, was owned in part by the Couteaux family and made shampoo and other hair products, deodorants, and skin cream. Baker worked for those companies on commission. These arrangements finally enabled Unilever to build a strong market share for its detergents, but the business remained fragile as Baker's control over Temsa rested entirely from putting key personnel in the company.

During the second half of the 1970s government controls were pushing even Unilever-Iş's edibles business into loss. There were tight controls over the prices both of oil to the factory and of margarine and ghee to consumers. While the other large manufacturers were government-owned and so were less concerned about losses, Unilever was squeezed. The Turkish government also implemented a so-called "fixed assets" ruling which specified that the extent to which the value of a firm's assets exceeded its capital caused profits to be frozen proportionately and deposited in a bank, usable with special permission only for beneficent works and a few other purposes within Turkey. If Unilever produced less to cut costs, the government would be furious, while if it produced more by putting in labor- and cost-saving machinery, resulting prof-its would be blocked.

Unilever's resolution to stay in business in Turkey in spite of horrendously complex controls reflected its outlook on the prospects of emerging economies. The country's population of over 40 million offered a tantalizingly large market, while Unilever had also developed a highly respected cadre of managers some of whom were already sent as expatriates elsewhere. The result was a resolutely long-term view of the need to stay in Turkey. One report written at the height of Unilever's difficulties in 1978 reflected:

> [W]e will take a long-term view on the assumption of [sic] Turkey's entry into the EEC in 2 decades will result then or before in a liberalization of investment and the removal of these many constraints . ... By the time Turkey enters the community it will be a country of some 70 to 80 million people. If it does liberalize, competitive investment in consumer goods will soon arrive. Better we should already be estab-lished than have to reenter, hence it should be worthwhile hanging on now even if the effective freezing of remittance levels does not adequately justify the effort in the short-term.[72]

The late 1970s were the testing point for this philosophy. Unilever had no wish to withdraw from the country, but nor was it willing to devote resources to try and expand the business.[73] The country appeared to be disintegrating. Badly affected by rising oil prices, Turkey ran chronic current account deficits, which were financed primarily by external borrowing. By 1980 the country's external debt was $16 billion, or one-quarter of the GDP, and debt servicing costs were 33 percent of exports. Inflation reached triple digits. The stock of inward FDI had only been $300 million in 1971, and during the 1970s the average annual inflow was only $90 million. As a result, Turkey had by far the lowest amount of FDI of any comparable economy.[74] As the economy went into free fall, terrorism and political unrest spread.

In the autumn of 1977 the cessation of remittances by the Central Bank prompted the first thoughts of divestment at Unilever. It was eventually resolved to stay, but senior management became progressively more skeptical that things would improve.

> They felt that the Turks were incapable of running the country properly and it would always be lurching from one crisis to another. They did however stick to the laws and as long as we could continue to get some money out we might as well stay there.[75]

During the second half of the 1970s remittances fell to low levels. In 1977 there were no remittances at all. The business shrank in terms of constant money. The overall revenues (in constant prices) of the Turkish business shrank by –3.8 percent per annum, while pre-tax profits shrank by –1.65 percent per annum. The business was loss-making in four years between 1974 and 1979.

Despite the bleakest of environments, the executive transferred in 1978 from Unilever's German affiliate Langnese-Iglo to Unilever-İş was able to make some progress. His brief on transfer was simply to keep the business alive until better days came, but even this brief required thinking out of the box. The company responded to the chronic unreliability of electricity supplies by laying down their own electricity lines from the power station to the factory. Unilever persuaded the government to allow it to export margarine to Iran, and to use the proceeds to buy raw materials for margarine manufacture and to make dividend payments. This in turn made the Overseas Committee more willing to accept the increasingly urgent need to build a new factory at Corlu because water supplies at its old factory at Bakirköy were becoming difficult, and the site was surrounded by residential buildings whose inhabitants disliked a factory in their midst.[76]

In 1980 there was another military coup. The army, which had watched the growing violence and instability with alarm, dissolved the National Assembly, and banned political parties and trade unions. The coup marked the beginning of a change in the environment faced by Unilever. Although political liberties were severely curbed, the coup began a transition to more stable economic policies with tighter monetary control and depreciating exchange rates, which helped double Turkish exports within two years. Turkish policies began shift from a protectionist import substitution growth strategy to export promotion. In the new environment, Unilever's edibles business was rescued as the availability of raw materials improved and price controls were lifted. The free supply of oil from 1980 onwards enabled Unilever to expand production, and permission was also given to build its new factory at Corlu.

The major problem remained Unilever's detergents business in Turkey. In terms of market share and brand strength this had become successful, but the business was grossly undercapitalized, which put Unilever at a considerable cost disadvantage against its main – local – competitor. The asset base in Baker also meant that Unilever could not remit dividends at a level proportionate to the management involvement. Although Unilever effectively managed the business, it received only 35 percent of the net profits. Additional challenges emerged as the new liberal policy regime began to attract the entry into Turkey of other firms.

During the 1980s, and beyond, Turkey was to remain one of the non-Communist countries with the lowest amount of inward FDI. Despite policy liberalization, a poor institutional environment for business persisted, including political interference with business, a weak justice system, and widespread corruption. Most MNEs preferred to conduct their business through Turkish agents. The situation only began to change significantly after the EU opened membership negotiations with Turkey in 2004, and even after then FDI flows remained low given the size of the economy.[77]

Within this context, Unilever's achievement in building and sustaining a large Turkish business, which was operated fully within the norms of Unilever's worldwide ethical standards, was striking. Sana was Unilever's largest single margarine brand in the world in 1980. As in the case of India, a long-term strategy and a willingness to accept little or no returns over long periods was combined with strategic flexibility and the recruitment of an excellent local management. As in India also, the legacy of government controls meant that Unilever's business was fragmented into several different entities, but a potentially highly successful and deeply rooted business was in place.

CONCLUSIONS

Unilever's ability to retain a large business in countries as India and Turkey during the period discussed was remarkable. Certainly it was much less exposed than mining, petroleum, agricultural, and utility companies to anti-foreign hostility. It did not operate on the basis of concessions, nor (before the acquisition of Brooke Bond in 1984) did it employ thousands of plantation workers, and its products were not in a "strategic industry." Nevertheless the plethora of controls and regulations were quite sufficient to deter or drive away other consumer products companies, including Procter & Gamble. There were at least five factors which explain Unilever's ability and willingness to persist in countries such as India and Turkey.

First, it held first-mover advantage in many countries. As import substitution regimes were adopted, it was well situated in protected domestic markets, even though it had to contend with price and capacity controls, dividend limitations, and other government regulations. Unilever was able to transfer brands, technologies, and marketing methods from its businesses in developed countries, and exploit them behind tariff walls.

Second, Unilever took a long-term investment horizon based on the view that sooner or later as incomes rose people would want to consume the company's products. The company was prepared to accept low dividend remittances for years, or decades, both to build up businesses, and to wait for better times. It made large investments in plant and equipment – often at the expense of short-term remittances for dividends to its shareholders – in order to build sustainable businesses. Its size and financial strength enabled it to wait for future income flows. As Unilever was more willing to accept the risks of developing countries than many large Western competitors, it was rewarded by limited competition from international rivals, notably Procter & Gamble.

Third, Unilever pursued flexible business strategies. The company made margarine from sunflower oil, and toilet soap from palm oil. It invested in tomato puree, jasmine plantations, and chemicals. It exported shoes. It engaged in rural development and built its own power plants to run factories. Unilever's decentralized management structure permitted flexibility in adjusting to the different environments of developing countries.

Fourth, Unilever's high standards of corporate ethics were a significant factor in its business success. Its refusal to tolerate corruption in highly corrupt environments was noteworthy, as was its refusal to make political payments. The policy of staying outside of party politics meant that the company had few enemies. Indeed, in India, Turkey, and elsewhere it made products which many poorer people bought, or aspired to buy, and politicians had no motivation whatever to be seen denying access to such products by crippling Unilever.

Finally, and most importantly, Unilever became embedded in local business and political systems. The early localization of senior management was critical in providing voice, contacts, and legitimacy in countries such as India and Turkey. In many countries Unilever identified, and promoted to the most senior positions, some of the best business leaders of their generation. This meant not only that Unilever's businesses were managed by extremely good people, but also that Unilever was able to function as a quasi-insider within governmental and business networks in many countries.

The reasons for Unilever's survival and growth in countries such as India and Turkey also explain why the company was an outlier, and why the level of FDI shrank to low levels in those countries, and has remained low. Few other companies had either the deep pockets to sustain businesses with low remittances over long periods or the willingness and desire to diversify into exporting shoes or making tomato puree. Nor did they have the organizational culture which would have permitted them to localize their management. Meanwhile the formidable complexities and downsides of trying to doing business in countries such as Turkey and India during the 1960s and 1970s seemed to have stayed in collective corporate memories long after the more restrictive policies began to be relaxed. It took the IT boom from the 1990s onwards, and the more radical liberalization measures of that decade, to change corporate perceptions of investing in India, while Turkey's image change has taken much longer.

NOTES

1. This chapter is a revised version of an article published in *Entreprises et Histoire*, **49** (December) (2007), 79–101. I would like to thank Unilever PLC and Unilever NV for permission to cite their archives.
2. United Nations, *World Investment Report 2012*, Geneva: UNCTAD, 2012.
3. For Turkey, see H. Loewendahl and E. Ertugal-Loewendahl, "Turkey's performance in attracting foreign direct investment," ENEPRI working paper no. 8, 2001.
4. Mira Wilkins, "Comparative hosts," *Business History*, **6** (1) (1994), pp. 18–50.
5. Sevket Pamuk, *The Ottoman Empire and European Capitalism, 1820–1913: Trade, Investment, and Production*, Cambridge: Cambridge University Press, 1987; Philip L Cottrell, Monika Pohle Fraser and Iain L. Fraser (eds), *East Meets West: Banking, Commerce and Investment in the Ottoman Empire*, Aldershot: Ashgate, 2008.
6. In India, it is the 25th-largest business in terms of revenues, and the 11th if finance and resources are excluded. In Turkey, it is the 25th-largest, excluding finance and resources.
7. There is an extensive literature on the history of Unilever. Charles Wilson, *The History of Unilever*, 2 vols, London: Cassell, 1954, and *Unilever 1945–1965*, London: Cassell, 1968, discusses the formation and history of Unilever. Geoffrey Jones, *Renewing Unilever: Transformation and Tradition*, Oxford: Oxford University Press, 2005, takes the story forward from 1965.
8. Unilever Archives Rotterdam (hereafter UAR), Economics Department; Procter and Gamble's Strategy Overseas, 1984; E&S Department, Colgate-Palmolive; "A competitor study," July, 1975, ES 75235; E&S Department, Henkel, for its detergents business, July, 1974.
9. David Fieldhouse, *Merchant Capital and Economic Decolonization*, Oxford: Oxford University Press, 1994; Jones, *Renewing*, pp. 191–7.
10. Geoffrey Jones, "Control, performance, and knowledge transfers in large multinationals: Unilever in the United States 1945–1980," *Business History Review*, **76** (3) (2002), pp. 435–478.
11. UAC profits soared in oil-producing Nigeria after the oil price rises in 1973.
12. Unilever Archives London (hereafter UAL), "OSC profitability – a review," Economics Department, July 1982.

13. Wilson, *Unilever*, vol. 2, pp. 364–5; F. van der Putten, *Corporate Behaviour and Political Risk: Dutch Companies in China 1903–1941*, Leiden, Netherlands: Research School of Asian, African and Amerindian Studies at Leiden University, 2001.
14. David Fieldhouse, *Unilever Overseas*, London: Croom Helm, 1978, pp. 387–405.
15. Andrew Knox, *Coming Clean*, London: Heinemann, 1976, p. 213.
16. UAL, Minutes of OSC meeting, 5 and 6, 1978.
17. UAL, N.A. Smith to S.L. Agarwal, 25 November 1968, Special Committee supporting papers 22–56 AA.
18. UAL, interview by Charles Wilson with R.W. Archer, 7 February, 1989.
19. UAL, minutes of conference of directors, 9 September, 1977.
20. UAL, private note of discussion, 20 March 1978.
21. UAL, private note of discussion, 20 October 1976.
22. Knox, *Coming Clean*, pp. 161–71.
23. Jones, *Renewing*, ch. 9.
24. UAL, interview by W.J. Reader with Fraser Sedcole, 29 November 1988.
25. UAL, board meeting, 13 January 1983.
26. UAR, CSAC 1 background paper: detergents, 17 June 1983, ES831738.
27. UAR, Economics Department, "Shampoo overseas," March 1983, ES 83111.
28. UAR, "Toothpaste strategy: an economics contribution," May 1987, ES 87017; Economics Department, "Colgate-Palmolive report, appendices," January 1988.
29. UAL, Conference on Innovation Overseas, 15 March 1984; interview with Hans Eggerstedt, 8 May 2000.
30. Fieldhouse, *Unilever Overseas*, pp. 148–81. The following section draws on the Fieldhouse study and Jones, *Renewing*, pp. 169–74.
31. Dennis J. Encarnation, *Dislodging Multinationals: India's Strategy in Comparative Perspective*, Ithaca, NY: Cornell University Press, 1989, ch. 2.
32. UAL, interview with T. Thomas, 21 December 1989.
33. Fieldhouse, *Unilever Overseas*, pp. 148–244.
34. Jack N. Behrman and William A. Fischer, *Overseas R&D Activities of Transnational Companies*, Cambridge, MA: Oelgeschlager, Gunn & Hain, 1980, pp. 231–7; Jones, *Renewing*, p. 280.
35. UAL, minutes of meeting of the Special Committee with the OSC, 26 July 1967.
36. UAL, OSC memorandum to Special Committee on India-corporate strategy, 7 January 1971, Overseas Committee supporting document no 4945.
37. UAL, interview with T. Thomas, 21 December 1988.
38. UAL, The Etah Project, 6 January 1970, Overseas Committee supporting document no. 4567.
39. UAL, annual estimate 1972. Overseas summary.
40. UAL, interview with T. Thomas, 21 December 1988.
41. UAL, meeting of Special Committee with Overseas Committee, 13 April 1971.
42. UAR, annual estimate 1973. Overseas summary.
43. UAR, annual estimate 1976. Overseas summary.
44. UAL, minutes of conference of directors on 24 January 1980, EXCO: LACA, India, 1980–87.
45. UAL, interview with T. Thomas, 21 December 1988.
46. UAL, minutes of OSC meeting, 30 January 1980. Central filing: OSC 1980.
47. UAL, memorandum to the Special Committee, 16 December 1980, EXCO: LACA, India 80–1987.
48. UAL, private note of discussions held on 17 December 1980.
49. UAL, Overseas Committee annual estimate, 13 December 1982.
50. C. K. Prahalad, *The Fortune at the Bottom of the Pyramid: Eradicating Poverty Through Profits*, Upper Saddle River, NJ: Wharton School Publishing, 2010, pp. 78–82.
51. UAL, OSC memorandum to the Special Committee on Hindustan Lever Limited, 29 June 1985. The original article provides annual data on dividend and service fee remittances between 1965 and 1979.
52. Arvind Panagariya, *India: The Emerging Giant*, Oxford: Oxford University Press, 2008, ch. 4.

53. Encarnation, *Dislodging Multinationals*, pp. 111–12, 182.
54. Interview with H. F. van den Hoven by P. W. Klein, 29 May 1989, UAR. Fieldhouse, *Unilever Overseas*, pp. 419–47, provides background on Unilever's business in Turkey before 1965.
55. UAR, J. P. Erbé to H.A. Kinghorn, 19 September 1977, AHK2123/928. On the Koç group, see Asli M. Colpan and Geoffrey Jones, "Vehbi Koç and the making of Turkey's largest business group," Harvard Business School case no. 811081, revised 2 November 2012.
56. Fieldhouse, *Unilever Overseas*, pp. 428–35.
57. UAR, J.P. Eerie to H.A. Kinghorn, 19 September 1977, AHK 2123/928.
58. UAR, Economics and Statistics Department, Turkey-foods 1 study, April 1971.
59. UAR, note attached to J.P. Eerie to de Munich, 15 June 1973.
60. UAR, memorandum by OSC to the Special Committee, 14 July 1971, OSC supporting paper no. 3388.
61. UAR, interview by P.W. Klein with H.F. van den Hoven, 29 May 1989.
62. UAR, proposals for dealing with the current situation of our business in Turkey, 23 July 1980, EXCO: LACA Turkey 1965–1986.
63. Fieldhouse, *Unilever Overseas*, p. 444.
64. Ibid., pp. 436–8.
65. UAL, minutes of meeting of OSC with Special Committee, 13 May 1969.
66. UAR, report on visit to Turkey, 26–29 January 1976, sundry foods and drinks co-ordination, 3 February 1976, AHK 2004.
67. UAL, OSC memorandum to the Special Committee, 28 July 1972. OSC supporting paper no. 5546.
68. UAL, meeting of the OSC with the Special Committee, 5 June 1972.
69. UAL, minutes of Special Committee, July 28, 1972; minutes of Special Committee with Overseas Committee, 5 April 1973, EXCO: Turkey 1965–86.
70. UAL, minutes of Special Committee, 12 June 1974.
71. AL, memorandum to the Special Committee on Turkey by OSC, 5 September 1975.
72. UAR, visit report to Unilever-Iş by F. Martin, 30 January–3 February 1978, AHK 2242.
73. UAL, minutes of the Special Committee, 28 July 1977, EXCO: LACA, Turkey, 1965–86.
74. Vudayagi N. Balasubramanyam, "Foreign direct investment in Turkey," in Sübidey Togran and Vudayagi N. Balasubramanyam (eds), *The Economy of Turkey since Liberalization*, New York: Palgrave Macmillan, 1996.
75. UAL, minutes of the Special Committee, 25 July 1978.
76. UAR, interview with Hans Eggerstedt, 8 May 2000.
77. Maria Giovanna Bosco, "FDI in Turkey: an out-of-sample analysis of unexploited potential," *Review of Middle East Economics and Finance*, **7** (3) (2012), pp. 1–21.

9. The end of nationality? Global firms and borderless worlds[1]

OVERVIEW

The view that global firms were becoming divorced from the nation state began to be widely expressed as the pace of globalization accelerated from the 1980s. The consequences of the growing global integration of international production, the international dispersion of key functions such as technological innovation within MNE systems, and the fact that some MNEs employ far greater numbers of people and sell far more products and services outside their home economy than within have all encouraged the hypothesis of a "borderless world," in the words of Kenichi Ohmae, in 1990.[2]

The limitations of the "borderless world" hypothesis have since been much discussed. It has been shown that the importance of geography has not disappeared, and that trade and investment flows continue to display patterns which suggest that the world is more regionalized than globalized. Rugman has described the "regionalization" of production, while Ghemawat has talked of "semi-globalization."[3] However the scale and scope of a handful of global corporations continued to prompt descriptions of how they dwarfed national states. Chandler and Mazlish described them as the new Leviathans.[4]

The political science literature has long had a strong inclination to characterize MNEs as a threat to the sovereignty of the nation state.[5] A forceful exponent of an "end of nationality" hypothesis, for example, was Robert Reich. In *The Work of Nations*, written two decades ago, he put the case for "the coming irrelevance of corporate nationality." Reich noted that many of the best-known names in US corporate history – CBS Records, Columbia Pictures, American Can, Pillsbury – had become foreign-owned, and went on to suggest that those who expressed fears of this foreign takeover were guilty of "outmoded thinking." The reason was that while in the past there were recognizable US corporations whose interests could be identified with those of the United States, contemporary MNEs bore only a superficial resemblance to their mid-twentieth-century counterparts.[6]

In the mid-twentieth century, Reich hypothesized, the nationality of a MNE had been easy to identify. US – and other – MNEs were large, integrated corporations with clearly defined boundaries, in which ownership and control lay indisputably in the home economy. Contemporary MNEs, Reich postulated, were different. They were organized more as a web than as a bureaucracy. Core corporations no longer planned and implemented the production of a large volume of goods and services. Rather they resembled a facade, behind which teemed an array of decentralized groups and subgroups continuously contracting with similarly diffuse working units all over the world. The value of such corporations lay in their problem-solving skills. The new organization consisted of webs of high-value enterprise joined by computers, fax machines, and satellites reaching across the globe, their "nationality" more and more irrelevant.

Reich's thesis had a political agenda within the United States. The point he sought to make was that a "foreign" corporation manufacturing in the United States contributed more to the American economy than an "American" company which manufactured most of its products abroad, and as a result it was inappropriate for the US government to pursue policies towards foreign-owned firms based on a "them" and "us" mentality. However there was also an explicit historical hypothesis in the Reich argument. This was that in the past firms had a clear nationality, but that in recent years fundamental changes in the organization of work had made the nationality of MNEs irrelevant. They had become stateless "global webs."

This chapter will provide an assessment of the historical evidence on the nationality of firms to examine whether there is anything truly "new" in the second global economy. It begins with some definitional issues, including the ways the economics and legal literatures have dealt with the issue of corporate nationality. It will then consider the evidence on different chronological periods since the nineteenth century.

CONCEPTUALIZING THE NATIONALITY OF MNES

As the economic theory of MNEs developed in the 1960s, it took the nation state as its starting point, and firmly linked the explanation of MNEs to their national origins. The title of Stephen Hymer's pioneering dissertation presented at the Massachusetts Institute of Technology in 1960 was "The International Operation of National Firms." He argued that MNEs came from one country, and that they needed an "advantage" of some sort to operate and compete in unfamiliar foreign environments. Foreign countries were seen as difficult and risky locations to which firms would prefer to export if only there were not obstacles such as tariff barriers, and in which they had little chance to survive unless they held a big advantage over the locals.[7] This perspective led to the strong view in the international business literature that a foreign firm required what was termed ownership advantages over local rivals, typically resting in management, technology, marketing skills, or finance. In the eclectic paradigm developed by Dunning, a firm could possess both firm-specific and/or nation-specific advantages, the latter resting on its country of origin.[8] Thus the international strength of German MNEs in chemicals and pharmaceuticals was ascribed to Germany's national system of scientific and technical education.

The significance of nationality was stressed in other economic theories of the MNE. The product cycle model, first put forward by Vernon in the mid-1960s, argued that firms based in the United States had a greater propensity to develop new products because of high per capita incomes and high unit labor costs in their home economy. Vernon suggested that when a new product was developed in the US, a firm normally chose a domestic production location because of the need for close contact with customers and suppliers. As a product matured, long-run production with established technology became possible. When it became economic to invest abroad, Western Europe was the preferred location since demand patterns were close to the US while labor costs were lower. When the product entered its standardized phase, low costs became critical, and production would be transferred to developing countries.[9] These authors assumed that the definition of nationality was a straightforward matter of identifying where the ownership and control of a firm resided. In practice, this has never been entirely straightforward. For example, the symbol of "British" banking in Asia, the Hong Kong and Shanghai Banking Corporation, was founded in 1865 by a cosmopolitan mixture of British, American, German, and Indian shareholders, while the first manager was a French national.[10] The place of registration and head office of the bank remained in Hong Kong until 1991, when domicile was shifted to Britain, but all the senior management of the bank were British nationals born in Britain and much of the shareholding was held there. This chapter will provide many other examples of ambiguous nationality in the history of MNEs.

Lawyers have been required to seek more precise definitions of the nationality of MNEs. There remains no single legal test of corporate nationality, however, and a variety of different criteria have been employed. In national legal systems derived from Anglo-American common law, the state of incorporation is the main test of nationality. However in most civil law systems in Continental Europe and other countries influenced by them, the test is that of the company's "seat" (*siège social*) defined as the place where the central administration and direction is located. The two tests lead to similar results in many cases, but where the place of incorporation does not coincide with the place where the direction is actually exercised, the latter is normally taken in many Continental legal systems.

However there are also other legal tests of nationality. Lawyers have sometimes used the nationality of the shareholders who "control" the operation as a test. This criterion is especially employed in wars and other politically tense situations. The nationality of the senior management or the country where most of the business is done is other possible legal tests. The former would redefine the Hong Kong and Shanghai Banking Corporation as "British" between 1865 and 1991. In international law, the rules governing the nationality of corporations remain far from settled, for it has developed the concept of nationality almost exclusively in the context of individual persons, and there remain no rules of international law governing the nationality of goods other than airplanes, ships, and historical cultural artifacts.[11]

NATIONALITY IN THE FIRST GLOBAL ECONOMY

As MNE business grew rapidly during the first global economy, country of origin mattered in explaining the source and direction of FDI. In 1914 Britain alone accounted for 45 percent of total world FDI. Subsequently the United States replaced Britain as the world's largest outward investor, but these two countries plus the Netherlands were disproportionately important as home for MNEs for much of the twentieth century. Between 1914 and 1980 these three countries accounted for between two-thirds and three-quarters of world FDI. Apart from the Dutch, the Swiss and the Swedes also became persistently large outward MNE investors. In contrast, other small European economies – including Norway, Denmark, Austria, and Portugal – displayed much weaker propensities to engage in direct investment.[12]

There were equally strong nationality influences on the location of FDI. US firms invested disproportionately in the neighboring countries of Mexico and Canada, just as when Japanese companies began to make direct investments they were skewed towards Asia. Within Europe, the firms of most countries had strong historical preferences for investing in neighboring countries. There is little doubt that the physical location of the country in which a firm is based has exercised systematic influence on location and decisions. The reason for this influence is also straightforward: firms seek to reduce risk by investing in geographically (or in some cases culturally) close environments.[13]

If the influence of nationality on international business appears strong when the sources and location of FDI is examined, at the level of the firm ambiguities begin to be apparent. In the nineteenth century a great deal of international business activity turns out to be hard to categorize in national terms.

Many ambiguities arose from the fact that in an era of high migration, people as well as capital moved across borders. The founders of numerous iconic American businesses were emigrants, including William Colgate, William Procter, and James Gamble – the founders of present-day consumer goods giants Colgate-Palmolive and Procter & Gamble – and the steel magnate Andrew Carnegie. While their firms merged into the emergent American business culture, elsewhere their equivalents retained a more hybrid feel. This was the case with the Nobel oil business in pre-Revolutionary Russia. Members of Sweden's Nobel family settled in Russia in the 1870s and transformed the Russian oil industry by introducing modern technology. The resulting company was managed by family members, but its headquarters and decision-making were located in Russia and there was no control from a parent company located in Sweden. Its equity was held in various Western European countries, as well as in Russia, and German banks were the single most important international shareholder category.[14]

Ambiguous nationality was almost the norm rather than the exception in the extensive international business in services outside Western Europe and North America. In Latin America and some Asian ports much merchant and financial activity lay in the hands of what one author has termed a "cosmopolitan bourgeoisie."[15] This was composed of highly ethnically mixed people with links back to their home countries as well as in the host country. They were often described as, for example, "Anglo-Argentines" or "German-Argentines." It is often difficult to classify the nationality of their ventures. It is evident that, for example, a substantial percentage of the so-called FDI in late nineteenth-century Argentina was made by Europeans who finally never returned to their home countries.

The nationality of many international businesses built by entrepreneurs who originated beyond Western Europe or North America was frequently ambiguous. During the nineteenth century ethnic Greek merchant houses created extensive businesses stretching from Russia through the Mediterranean to Western Europe. Few if any of these businesses were managed from the newly created and impoverished Greek state. This highly cosmopolitan tradition persisted in Greek shipping companies, which frequently used London – and for a time after World War II New York – as operational centers, even while retaining strong Greek ethnic identities and drawing their seamen from closely defined ethnic and kinship networks.[16] In nineteenth-century Southeast Asia, ethnic Chinese created large businesses which spanned British, Dutch, and French colonial boundaries and independent states such as Thailand. They sometimes sent remittances back to and retained familial links with China, but were not controlled from that country.[17]

The ambiguous nationality of ethnic Chinese business was not atypical in Asia before 1914. It was quite common for entrepreneurs of particular ethnic or religious origins to build business which took advantage of the legal and other infrastructures created by European colonial regimes, but which spanned such borders rather than reflecting them in terms of the location of ownership and control. Consider the case of the Sassoons, a prominent Baghdad Jewish merchant family who moved to Bombay in British India in 1832 to escape persecution from the Ottoman Empire. They established a mercantile business which stretched over large parts of Asia, but located their operations in the British-controlled parts in South and Southeast Asia. They formed close relations with the British imperial structures, but the Sassoon firms were managed almost exclusively by Jews of "Baghdadi" extraction. The Sassoons were extremely successful selling opium to China, rapidly gaining market share from the British merchant houses which had formerly dominated the business. In time the family moved their base to London, with one member receiving a British knighthood in 1872. By the 1880s the Sassoon companies began to record commercial translations in English rather than Judaeo-Arabic, and to adopt British accounting practices in preference to their traditional methods, but they continued to function on grounds of shared kinship ties and personal trust with Baghdadi co-religionists. They could legitimately over the space of five decades have been described as Iraqi, Indian, or British businesses.[18]

In the environment before World War I where exchange controls were non-existent, firms were free to seek funds worldwide, and this often led to discrepancies between the respective nationalities of a firm's ownership and control. Foreign firms regularly sought funds in London, the world's largest equity market. An example was a group of Canadian companies which made large investments in Latin America utilities from the 1890s. The largest of these companies was Brazilian Traction, which established a large electricity-generating, water, gas, and eventually telephone business in Southeast Brazil which – by the late 1940s – employed 50 000 Brazilians and controlled 60 percent of the country's electricity and 75 percent of its telephones. The driving force behind this venture was an American engineer, and the key purchasing functions were in New York. However the headquarters were in Toronto. And most of the stock was issued on the London market.[19] This large business could, according to different criteria, be identified as a Canadian, British, or American venture before 1914.

There are many cases of this phenomenon which, taken together, cast doubts over existing FDI estimates – and the strong national patterns they suggest. The case of Britain – apparently the source of up to 45 percent of world FDI in 1914 – is instructive. A considerable amount of British FDI in Latin America, Asia, and Africa was undertaken by trading companies which, over time, diversified from trade into resource exploitation, infrastructure and processing. These diversification strategies were achieved by establishing new "free-standing" companies, in which the parent trading company often held only a small share of the equity. However this equity relationship between the new company and the parent trader formed only one of several connections which included flows of loans and deposits, cross-directorships, and management contracts.[20]

The result was a network form of enterprise whose "nationality" depends on the kind of criteria used. The trading companies established both British and locally registered companies. The latter, which would typically have a mix of shareholding by expatriates, "locals" and others, are excluded from estimates of British FDI, but the place of registration criteria provides no indication of the nationality of ultimate control, which was exercised from Britain by linkages other than equity. After 1914 these ultimately British controlled but locally registered companies became a vehicle for local business groups to capture control, because if they could buy enough shares and concentrate their shareholdings they could ultimately remove the British managers. This phenomenon was evident in interwar India when Marwari business groups brought into "British" companies in Calcutta; in Malaysia in the 1960s and the 1970s when control of "British" firms such as Sime Darby was acquired by local interests; and in Hong Kong in the 1970s and 1980s when "British" firms like Hutchinson Whampoa and Wheelock Marden were acquired by local Chinese. In these cases, companies retained the same place of registration, but the ultimate nationality of control shifted.

There were also plenty of ambiguities concerning the nationality of enterprises even in Western Europe before 1914. The predecessor to Alusuisse, Aluminium Industrie AG, was ostensibly Swiss, but had a strong German influence before and after 1914.[21] The role of European "mixed" banks in international business provides an example. During the nineteenth century, French, Belgian, and other European banks took strategic equity holdings in numerous foreign industrial enterprises, typically with partners, often with partners from other countries, with the result that the "nationality" of the consequent enterprise is unclear. The managerial and financial influence of Paribas in the early development of Norway's Norsk Hydro renders it, by most modern definitions, a case of French FDI in Norway, although there was also a Swedish dimension through Wallenberg investment, as well as Norwegian control over some areas of the company's business.[22]

The Norsk Hydro story was not exceptional. In the late nineteenth century the German electrical companies Siemens and AEG invested in public utilities in southern Europe and Latin America using financial holding companies. The German big banks were investors, but Belgian, French, Italian, and Swiss links also took equity, and they often had their legal seat in Belgium or Switzerland. These substantial and capital-intensive ventures might well be best regarded as mixed-nationality ventures rather than belonging to a single country.[23]

A final level of complexity relates to the use of the nation state as a unit of analysis. FDI is defined as capital flows across national borders, but this is not as straightforward as it seems. As noted earlier, MNEs have always tended to invest in neighboring countries in order to reduce risk. Wilkins and Schröter have termed this "nearby" investment. In nineteenth-century Europe a large number of French, German, Swiss, and other investments were literally "nearby" in the sense that they were just over the border. An extreme example was provided by the Swiss dyestuffs companies in Basle which established plants within walking distance over the German border in Grenzach. Rather similarly, Ford's first foreign factory was in Canada just across the Detroit River from its US base. A case could be made for regarding regions, rather than nations, as the valid unit of analysis, although even highly geographically proximate investments involved firms crossing national judicial, fiscal, and other borders.[24]

The ambiguity in the nationality of many MNEs before 1914 was striking. As recent research in political science has suggested, while there was a long academic tradition which argued that the concept of sovereign states emerged and grew ever stronger after the Treaty of Westphalia in 1648, in reality overlapping sovereignties and non-state actors persisted well into the twentieth century.[25] Global business formed part of this fluid world before 1914.

CERTAINTIES IN THE ERA OF WAR AND NATIONALISM 1914–45

The complexities of the "cosmopolitan capitalism" during the first global economy gave way to much sharper definitions of nationality as the twentieth century progressed. World War I was important in this respect. The warring countries investigated who really "owned" the companies registered in their countries, and who really "controlled" companies whose names sounded respectably local. The firms ultimately discovered to be owned by "enemies" were sequestrated on both sides and transferred into local hands. The phenomenon of sequestration on the basis of ultimate "control" was new.

The new importance of nationality in international corporate life, however, provided incentives for firms to shift their nationality for political or tax reasons, or else disguise it. An example of the former was Italy's Pirelli, which in 1920 placed all its foreign operations into a new financial company – Compagnie Internationale Pirelli – registered in Belgium. However the Belgian company was ultimately controlled by the Pirelli family. In 1937 Pirelli Holdings was founded as a Swiss company with its seat in Brazil, and by 1940 all Pirelli's overseas operations were controlled by it. The Pirelli family held less than 30 percent in the Swiss company, but nonetheless exercised managerial control over it. This arrangement proved most convenient during World War II, when the Allies accepted that it was a Swiss company and it escaped sequestration.[26]

A number of firms became "migrating" MNEs, or firms which shifted their nationalities in terms of place of incorporation, seat, or nationality of shareholders. These shifts were real, and not cosmetic as in the case of Pirelli or the "cloaking" discussed above. A nineteenth-century example was W.R. Grace, a merchant firm established by Peruvians of Irish descent which relocated its head office to New York City in 1865.[27] The twentieth century saw migrations of several large firms. An early example was the case of British American Tobacco (BAT), which moved from US to British ownership.[28]

The nationalism seen in the interwar years intensified debates on the nationality of both firms and their products. Regarding the latter, France was exceptional in interwar Europe in requiring all imported goods to specify their national origins. In Germany, the courts were left to decide the nationality of goods following a law passed in 1909, but they struggled to decide whether the criterion was goods made by German-owned companies or goods made in Germany. By the late 1920s they had largely moved to the latter: Singer sewing machines manufactured in Germany were classified as national. After 1933 the Nazi regime banned foreign firms calling themselves German in their names, but their locally made products were classified as German.[29]

Most foreign companies in Nazi Germany were quite successful in making changes to their employment and other practices to be regarded by the regime as national firms. Claiming to be authentically German became a source of competitive advantage. Opel, acquired by General Motors in 1929, placed great emphasis on its German identity.[30] Ford, whose American parent operated a highly centralized organization, was slower to assert its national claims, although from the late 1930s its German business became closely aligned with Nazi plans.[31] All foreign-owned firms in Nazi Germany found themselves in ambiguous situations as they sought to survive in a hostile political and moral climate, and in some cases (such as IBM) had pro-Nazi local chief executives. Survival depended on stressing their German identities: the degree to which firms collaborated fully with Nazi political goals varied.[32] Nonetheless there was often a gap between rhetoric and reality. Despite some Nazi rhetoric which was anti-cosmetics, the prominent US cosmetics firm Elizabeth Arden was able to use the same advertising in Germany as in the United States, albeit but with subtle modifications. Arden continued to highlight its American connections until the outbreak of the war, when its location in fashionable foreign cities was removed from advertising.[33]

If the nationalism of the interwar years pushed the affiliates of foreign firms to become more "national," it is worth noting that there were noteworthy exceptions to this trend. Unilever was created by an Anglo-Dutch merger in 1929. This was only the second attempt, after the British and Dutch merger which created Shell in 1907, to create a bi-national corporation. Both companies survived the Great Depression and World War II. A third bi-national endeavor was created by a merger of Dutch and German rayon companies to create the Algemeene Kunstzijde Unie in 1929.[34]

The numerous international cartels in the interwar years also raised new complexities concerning nationality. International cartels became extremely important in many primary commodities and in manufacturing industries characterized by a small number of producers and relatively slow-growing markets, such as chemicals, engineering and iron and steel. In these industries, cartels were used as an alternative to FDI, or when FDI was impossible, and exercised a decisive influence on prices and output.[35]

In some cases international cartels can be identified with a nationality in that the firm of one country had sufficient influence to control decisions. Although General Electric of the US never formally joined the interwar electric lamp cartel, it was able to exercise a decisive influence on its policies owing to its strong patent position and equity shareholding in companies which were members.[36] The international dyestuffs cartel was similarly more or less controlled by Germany's IG Farben.[37] But in most cases the "control" of international cartels lay in the hands of several parties from several countries. Sometimes the cartels had a "seat" in countries with discrete or liberal regulations, such as Belgium and Switzerland, but this gave no indication where control actually rested. The Electric Lamp Cartel, for example, was administered by a Swiss company – Phoebus SA – but in no sense can its "control" be said to have rested in Switzerland.

NATIONALITY IN THE ERA OF POSTWAR ECONOMIC MIRACLES 1945–80

The decades between the end of World War II and the 1970s were the "classic era" of the MNE when large, integrated US corporations appeared to be the dominant organizational form in international business. There was, Reich plausibly asserts, little doubt that firms such as Ford, General Motors, and IBM were American. Coincidently, this was also the era in international politics when concepts of the importance of national sovereignty became firmly rooted in the new international institutions of the era including the United Nations, the World Bank and the International Monetary Fund.[38]

However, the interwar legacy of autonomous affiliates remained strong. Local affiliates of foreign firms retained distinct local identities. The subsidiaries of large US manufacturing corporations in Europe largely stood alone from their US parent or other subsidiaries. The level of intra-firm manufacturing imports and exports remained low, and subsidiaries often manufactured distinctive national products. European companies were even more extreme in this regard. Unilever had originally pursued a policy of centralization after its formation, but was forcibly decentralized during World War II – when the British and Continental elements were on opposite sides – and emerged as a highly decentralized corporation in which national affiliates had strong autonomy. This became an article of faith within the company during the postwar decades.[39]

During the 1960s and 1970s many Western European governments resisted foreign ownership in key strategic sectors, favoring or promoting national champions, usually with little success. This encouraged some foreign subsidiaries to further enhance their local credentials, although again there was a diversity of practice. For example, in postwar Norway the two largest companies in the telecommunications industry were owned by ITT (US) and Ericsson (Sweden) respectively. However, the managers of the two affiliates pursued divergent strategies in the postwar decades. The Ericsson affiliate increasingly emphasized its Norwegian identity, seeking to develop Norwegian products and contribute to the industrial development of Norway; the ITT affiliate emphasized to the government the benefits of its position within the ITT network.[40]

As foreign-owned affiliates evolved within their host economies, they often grew as large businesses with distinctive characteristics in their own right. Over time they often assumed many higher-order activities, including technology and human resources. They were in effect hybrid organizations reflecting a mixture of the characteristics of their parent and their host economy. This was certainly evident in the US subsidiaries in postwar Europe. There can be no doubt that in their organization, technology, and culture an American influence was evident. The best indication of this is that in almost every European host economy the productivity performance of US manufacturing affiliates was superior to that of indigenous competitors. However the strong national identities of these subsidiaries, alongside the fact that the transfer of US practices was hardly ever complete, meant that they were hybrids in their organizational structures and practices, rather than replicas of their American parents. The same observation has been made about Japanese-owned affiliates in the United States in the 1990s.[41]

The autonomy of national subsidiaries began to slowly lessen in the 1960s when a few US corporations began to integrate their North American and European operations. A key development was IBM's System 360 computers, launched in 1964, and designed to be manufactured and sold worldwide, which necessitated a much greater degree of international coordination than seen previously. During the 1950s IBM's foreign subsidiaries were hardly coordinated at all. Twenty years later the firm had two regional production networks, in Europe and North America. In the mid-1960s Ford decided to integrate its manufacturing on a regional basis. Beginning with the integration of the US and Canada in 1965, in 1967 Ford of Europe was created which began to integrate previously autonomous national affiliates. Previously

Ford's major European subsidiaries in Britain and Germany had operated virtually independently, and produced unrelated passenger car models. The first Europe-wide model – the Capri – was launched in 1969. European-owned MNEs were often much slower at regional integration. Unilever's struggle with the close integration of its European affiliates continued until well into the 1990s.[42] While US corporations created European corporate entities, many European managers – like their politicians – remained preoccupied with the differences between European countries rather than the similarities of their markets.

The continuing exchange controls and other restrictions of this era continued to prompt the occasional MNE to "migrate." In 1976 ANZ Bank, one of the largest domestic banks in Australia, shifted domicile from Britain to Australia. The bank was a legacy of the British overseas banks established in the nineteenth century to operate in British colonies. ANZ had its board of directors, its head office and a substantial international banking business based in London, but no domestic British commercial banking business, while some 95 percent of the shareholders were residents of Britain. However British exchange controls during the 1970s prevented the bank from raising funds or spending sterling outside the sterling area, thus blocking the management's ambition to extend operations to Asia and the United States. In 1976 ANZ resolved to emigrate to Australia. The old London board of directors was dissolved and a new one established in Melbourne. By 1981, 70 percent of the shares were listed on the Australian share register, and the bank had become thoroughly Australian by any measure.[43] There was no one-way flow of firms into Australia, however. In 2004 the giant media company News Corporation shifted domicile from Australia to the United States.

NATIONALITY IN THE SECOND GLOBAL ECONOMY

Paradoxically, the global integration strategies which were pursued by more MNEs as a new wave of globalization intensified from the 1980s may have reduced ambiguity surrounding the nationality of MNEs by ending the autonomy of affiliates. The new, globally integrated corporations increasingly located functions wherever they could best fulfill the firm's overall strategy. This allocation was still made at the higher reaches of corporations which remained the preserve of nationals of the home country except in a number of atypical situations. In these circumstances, it is possible to reach a conclusion the opposite of that of Reich, that the ultimate "nationality" of MNEs has become clearer and more important as a result of recent trends.

There were certainly high-profile exceptions which symbolized a new fluidity in capital and other markets. Arcelor Mittal, the world's largest steelmaker in 2013, was established in 1976 by the Indian entrepreneur Lakshmi N. Mittal. It took its present form after a merger in 2002 with the European steel companies Arbed (Luxembourg), Aceralia (Spain) and Usinor (France). The holding company was registered in Luxembourg, and over 40 percent of the shares were owned by the Mittal family. Mittal himself held an Indian passport but lived in Britain. MNEs continued to migrate. In particular, there were examples of firms based in countries experiencing economic turbulence which chose to domicile some, or all, of their business in more stable locations with lower capital raising costs. In 2012, for example, Coca-Cola Hellenic Bottling Company, Greece's largest quoted company, responded to the financial and economic turbulence that that country had experienced for several years in favor of a Swiss domicile and a listing on the London Stock Exchange.[44]

At the very least, however, it can be asserted that the idea that contemporary MNEs are stateless "global webs" is implausible. The national influence on MNE corporations remains strong. Boards of directors have remained heavily biased toward home country nationals even if the globalization of capital markets has led to the ownership of the equity of large corporations being widely dispersed between countries. The speed of internationalization of boards and chief executives was more glacial than dramatic. There were striking exceptions: French-owned L'Oréal had a British chief executive, Lindsay Owen-Jones, between 1984 and 2006; the iconic Japanese electronics company Sony had a British-born US national, Sir Howard Stringer, as chief executive between 2005 and 2012; and the Brazilian Carlos Ghosn served as chief executive of France's Renault and Japan's Nissan. These cases remained exceptional however, rather than the norm. In some cases the pressures for transparency in corporate governance led to the clarification of ambiguities concerning nationality. For example, the Shell Group finally abolished its dual-nationality holding company structure in 2005, creating a single British parent company, albeit one with a head office in the Netherlands.

The globalization of key functions such as R&D also remained limited. In the 1990s almost 90 percent of the R&D expenditure by US MNEs conducted on their own behalf was still incurred within the United States. To some extent, the international dispersion of R&D by MNEs which has occurred has mainly resulted in an upgrading of the R&D conducted at home. By locating some less sophisticated R&D activities abroad, resources are freed at home for employment in more sophisticated activities.

However, although the influence of nationality in the strategic direction of firms and decisions about overall resource allocation was strong, the increasing ability and willingness to locate different parts of the value chain in different locations certainly made the nationality of individual products highly ambiguous. Integrated production systems, outsourcing, and the use of contract manufacturing made labels such as "Made in America" increasingly meaningless, because such products and services may have been assembled from components from a dozen or more countries. For example, over the last decade leading cosmetics firms such as L'Oréal and US-owned Estée Lauder have contracted the manufacturing of color cosmetics and other products to contract manufacturers such as the Milan-based Intercos.[45] In these cases, it is primarily the origin of a brand name which brings a French or American identity to their products.

During the second global economy it became increasingly common for firms to buy and sell brands which embodied strong national identities. In branded consumer products such as alcoholic beverages, this was a major driver of mergers and acquisitions.[46] In the personal care industry, where brands often embodied strong national images, the nationality of the ownership of firms and the brands they sold became divorced. During the 1980s Unilever, for example, acquired American brands such as Pond's Cream, Elizabeth Arden, and Calvin Klein Cosmetics and marketed them worldwide, and though the latter two were sold between 2001 and 2005. While Arden reverted to American ownership, Calvin Klein Cosmetics was acquired by Coty, a New York-based affiliate of the German family-owned firm of Johann A. Benckiser.[47]

In financial services, the creation of the Euromarkets in the 1960s began a process whereby a great deal of financial intermediation was divorced from the nation states and their regulators in which they are located. This was true of the City of London, where most financial transactions were handled by non-British institutions and did not involve the domestic economy. Even more extreme examples were provided by small islands which functioned as offshore financial centers, such as the Cayman Islands in banking or Bermuda in insurance. This played havoc with official FDI figures. For example, official figures reported Hong Kong's outward FDI stock as $370 billion in 2002 – or larger than that of the Netherlands, but a breakdown of this amount showed one-half was invested in the British Virgin Islands, a small British territory in the Caribbean which served as an offshore financial center.[48]

The above example was part of a wider problem of the interpretation of national-based definitions of FDI. For example, during the 1990s there were huge flows of FDI between Hong Kong and China. Hong Kong was a British colony before July 1997, and so technically this investment was FDI. In practice, almost all of the investment went to the southern Chinese provinces with which Hong Kong's economy was progressively integrated. The incorporation of Hong Kong into China, albeit under the "one country, two systems" rubric, made the national classification of this investment even more problematic, especially as most studies suggested that much FDI ostensibly from Hong Kong originated in China, but was "round-tripped" for fiscal reasons.[49]

During the first decade of the twenty-first century terrorist incidents such as the September 2001 al-Qaeda attack on the United States, the 2008 financial crisis, and geopolitical tensions between the United States and China, resulted in issues related to corporate nationality rising up government agendas. Developments in the United States, including the peremptory expulsion of foreign firms from the S&P 500 in 2002, the public outcry four years later when a Dubai company acquired a British company which operated ports in the United States, and political opposition to Huawei and other Chinese firms as security risks, certainly pointed in this direction.[50]

CONCLUSION

This chapter has argued that the view that in the past the nationality of MNEs was clear, while for contemporary MNEs corporate nationality is both unclear and irrelevant, is not supported by historical evidence. There have always been a range of ambiguities and complexities involved in the issue of the relationship between MNEs and nationality, even if the nature of complexity and ambiguity has shifted over time.

Historically, the influence of nationality on international business is strongest if attention is focused on FDI estimates. These show, for example, that firms of some countries are disproportionally more likely to invest abroad than the firms of other nationalities. It is also evident that the direction of FDI flows was heavily influenced by nation-specific factors. However, once disaggregation occurs it is clear that a great deal of international business in the first global economy was cosmopolitan and not easily fitted into national categories.

After 1914 cosmopolitan capitalism was replaced by sharper national identities. It became politically important to be seen as a local firm, and this has largely remained the case until the present day. The era of constrained globalization encouraged national subsidiaries of MNEs to emphasize strong local identities and become mini-replicas of their parents. While from a US perspective Ford and IBM may have been unequivocally American in appearance in the 1950s and 1960s, from host country perspectives they resembled hybrids with a strong local input.

During the second global economy nationality remained an important influence on the composition of boards and senior management and the location of higher-value-added activities such as R&D. There has been no recreation of the cosmopolitan capitalism seen in the first global economy. This reflected the proliferation of nation states – there were 196 by 2013 – each with its own laws and regulations, as well as the on-going tight restrictions on labor mobility. However, global firms have increasingly traded in the brands and other assets from numerous countries, while technological advances which permitted different parts of the value chain of production and services to be located in different places meant that the nationality of products was thoroughly ambiguous.

NOTES

1. The original version of this chapter was published as Geoffrey Jones, "The end of nationality? Global firms and borderless worlds," *Zeitschrift für Unternehmensgeschichte*, **51** (2) (2006) pp. 149–66.
2. Kenichi Ohmae *The Borderless World: Power and Strategy in the Interlinked Economy*, New York: Harper Business, 1990.
3. Alan M. Rugman *The End of Globalization*, London: Random House, 2000; Pankaj Ghemawat "Semi-globalization and international business strategy," *Journal of International Business Studies*, **34** (2) (2003), pp. 138–52.
4. Alfred D. Chandler and Bruce Mazlish (eds), *Leviathans: Multinational Corporations and the New Global History*, Cambridge: Cambridge University Press, 2005.
5. James H. Mittelman, "Globalization: captors and captive," *Third World Quarterly*, **2** (6) (2000), pp. 917–29.
6. Robert Reich, *The Work of Nations: Preparing Ourselves for 21 Century Capitalism*, New York: Vintage Books, 1990.
7. Geoffrey Jones, *Multinationals and Global Capitalism: From the Nineteenth to the Twenty First Century*, Oxford: Oxford University Press, 2005, pp. 7 ff.
8. John H. Dunning and Sarianna M. Lundan, *Multinational Enterprises and the Global Economy*, Cheltenham, UK and Northampton, MA, USA: Edward Elgar, 2008, pp. 95–109.
9. Raymond Vernon, "International investment and international trade in the product cycle," *Quarterly Journal of Economics*, **80** (2) (1966), pp. 190–207.
10. Frank H.H. King, *The Hong Kong Bank in Late Imperial China 1864–1902*, Cambridge: Cambridge University Press, 1984.
11. Seymour J. Rubin and Don Wallace (eds), *Transnational Corporations and National Law*, New York: Routledge, 1994; Arghyrios A. Fatouros (ed.), *Transnational Corporations: The International Legal Framework*, New York: Routledge, 1994.
12. Jones, *Multinationals*, ch. 2.
13. William H. Davidson, "The location of foreign direct investment activity: country characteristics and experience effects," *Journal of International Business Studies*, **11** (2) (1980), 9–22.
14. Aleksandr A. Fursenko, "The oil industries," in Rondo Cameron and Valerij I. Bovykin (eds), *International Banking 1870–1914*, New York: Oxford University Press, 1991.
15. Charles Jones, *International Business in the Nineteenth Century*, Brighton: Wheatsheaf, 1987.
16. Ioanna P. Minoglou and Helen Louri, "Diaspora Entrepreneurial Networks in the Black Sea and Greece, 1870–1917," *Journal of European Economic History*, **26** (1) (1997), pp. 69–104; Gelina Harlfatis, *A History of Greek-Owned Shipping*, London: Routledge, 1993.
17. Rajeswary A. Brown, *Chinese Big Business and the Wealth of Nations*, London: Palgrave, 2000; Jennifer W. Cushman, "The Khaw Group: Chinese business in early twentieth century Penang," *Journal of Southeast Asian Studies*, **17** (1) (1986), pp. 58–79.
18. Chiara Betta, "The trade diaspora of Baghdadi Jews: from India to China's Treaty Ports, 1842–1937," in Ina Baghdiantz McCabe, Gelina Harlaftis and Inonna Pelelasis Minoglou (eds), *Diaspora Entrepreneurial Networks*, Oxford: Berg, 2005.
19. Duncan McDowell, *The Light: Brazilian Traction, Light and Power Company Ltd, 1899–1945*, Toronto, Canada: Toronto University Press, 1988.
20. Stanley Chapman, "British-based investment groups before 1914," *Economic History Review*, **38** (2) (1985), pp. 230–51; Geoffrey Jones, *Multinationals*; Mira Wilkins and Harm

G. Schröter (eds), *The Free-Standing Company in the World Economy, 1830–1996*, Oxford: Oxford University Press, 1998.
21. Donald H. Wallace, *Market Control in the Aluminium Industry*, Cambridge, MA: Harvard University Press, 1937.
22. Eric Bussiere, *Paribas: Europe and the World 1872–1992*, Antwerp, Belgium: Fonds Mercator, 1992, pp. 79–80; Ketil G. Andersen, *Flaggskip i fremmed eie: Hydro 1905–1945*, Oslo: Pax Forlag, 2005.
23. Peter Hertner, "A typical factor of German international market strategy: agreements between the US and German electrotechnical industries up to 1939," in Alice Teichova, Maurice Lévy-Leboyer and Helga Nussbaum (eds), *Multinational Enterprise in Historical Perspective*, Cambridge: Cambridge University Press, 1986.
24. Mira Wilkins, "European and North American multinationals, 1870–1914: comparisons and contrasts," *Business History*, **30** (1) (1988), pp. 8–45; Harm G. Schröter, *Aufstieg der Kleinen*, Berlin: Duncker und Humbolt, 1993.
25. Sebastian Schmidt, "To order the minds of scholars: the discourse of the Peace of Westphalia in international relations literature," *International Studies Quarterly*, **55** (3) (2011), pp. 601–23.
26. Angelo Montenegro, "The development of Pirelli as an Italian multinational 1872–1992," Geoffrey Jones and Harm G. Schröter (eds), *The Rise of Multinationals in Continental Europe*, Aldershot, UK and Brookfield, VT, USA: Edward Elgar, 1993, pp. 184–200.
27. Lawrence A. Clayton, *Grace: W.R. Grace & Company, 1850–1930* (Ottawa, IL: Jameson Books, 1985.
28. See Chapter 4.
29. Victoria de Grazia, *Irresistible Empire: America's Advance through Twentieth Century Europe*, Cambridge, MA: Harvard University Press, 2005, pp. 214–17.
30. Ibid., p. 216.
31. Steven Tolliday, "The origins of Ford of Europe: from multidomestic to transnational corporation, 1903–1976," in Hubert Bonin, Yannick Lung and Steven Tolliday (eds), *Ford: The European History 1903–2003*, Paris: Plage, 2003, vol. 1, pp. 166ff.
32. Henry A. Turner, *General Motors and the Nazis*, New Haven, CT: Yale University Press, 2005); Simon Reich, "Corporate social responsibility and the issue of compensation: the case of Ford and Nazi Germany," in F.R. Nicosia and J. Huener (eds), *Business and Industry in Nazi Germany*, New York: Berg, 2004; Lars Heide, "Between parent and 'child': IBM and its German subsidiary, 1910–1945," and Neil Forbes, "Managing risk in the Third Reich: British business with Germany in the 1930s," both in Christopher Kobrak and Per H. Hansen (eds), *European Business, Dictatorship, and Political Risk, 1920–1945*, New York: Berg, 2004.
33. Yvonne B. Houy, "'Of course the German woman should be modern'; the modernization of women's appearances during National Socialism," unpublished PhD thesis, Cornell University, 2002, ch. 4.
34. Ben P.A. Gales and Keetie E. Sluyterman, "Outward bound: the rise of Dutch multinationals," in Jones and Schröter, *Rise*.
35. Harm G. Schröter, "Risk and control in multinational enterprise: German businesses in Scandinavia, 1918–1939," *Business History Review*, **62** (3) (1988), pp. 420–43.
36. Leonard S. Reich, "General Electric and the world cartelisation of electric lamps," in Akira Kudo and Terushi Hara (eds), *International Cartels in Business History*, Tokyo: University of Tokyo Press, 1992.
37. Harm G. Schröter, "Cartels as a form of concentration in industry; the example of the international dyestuffs cartel from 1927 to 1939," *German Yearbook on Business History* (1988), pp. 113–44.
38. Schmidt, "Order".
39. Jones, *Multinationals*; Ben Wubs, *International Business and National War Interests: Unilever Between Reich and Empire, 1939–45*, London: Routledge, 2008; Geoffrey Jones, *Renewing Unilever: Transformation and Tradition*, Oxford: Oxford University Press, 2005.
40. Sverre A. Christensen, "Switching relations: the rise and fall of the Norwegian telecom industry," unpublished PhD thesis, BI Norwegian School of Management, 2006.

41. Tetsuo Abo (ed.), *Hybrid Factory*, Oxford: Oxford University Press, 1994.
42. Jones, *Renewing*.
43. David Merrett, *ANZ Bank*, Sydney: Allen & Unwin, 1985; Geoffrey Jones, *British Multinational Banking 1830–1990*, Oxford: Oxford University Press, 1993.
44. Louise Lucas and Dimitris Kontogiannis, "Coca-Cola Hellenic quits Greece for Swiss stability and a London listing," *Financial Times*, 12 October, 2012.
45. Chris Hendry, Nigel Courtney and Clive Holtham, "Unlocking the hidden wealth of organizations: the development and communication of intangible assets," Cass Business School working paper, 2003.
46. Teresa Lopes, "Brands and the evolution of multinationals in alcoholic beverages," *Business History*, **44** (3) (2002), pp. 1–30.
47. Geoffrey Jones and David Kiron, "Cisco goes to China: routing an emerging economy," Harvard Business School case no. 808133, revised June, 2012.
48. Jones, *Multinationals*, pp. 248f.
49. Yasheng Huang, *Selling China: Foreign Direct Investment during the Reform Era*, Cambridge: Cambridge University Press, 2003, pp. 37–41.
50. Tom Orlik, "No way for Huawei in US," *Wall Street Journal*, 11 October, 2012.

Postscript

This book has explored how entrepreneurs and firms can be included in narratives of the making of the modern world. Today's complex world combines unrelenting globalization, symbolized by the web and other technologies which permit instantaneous sharing of information between locations anywhere on the planet, with growing yearnings for local identity, manifested everywhere from regional independence movements in long-established European nation states like Spain and Britain to the revival of interest in local beauty ideals. As citizens, business leaders, and politicians struggle to comprehend the complexity, understanding how we reached this situation matters, as does what the past can tell us about the likely trajectories of the future.

It has been shown here how business enterprises have been important actors in the making of this world over the last two centuries. They were not black boxes responding to exogenous factors such as government policies, institutions, or resource endowments. Individual entrepreneurs and managers invented new products and shaped consumer demand. The firms they created diffused technologies and products, alongside the values in which they were embedded. They facilitated globalization by creating trade flows, constructing marketing channels, and building infrastructure. When governments attempted to reverse globalization, firms redesigned their international businesses rather than abandon them. MNEs preserved dimensions of globalization even as governments closed down flows of trade and capital across borders.

The incorporation of firms into narratives of the making of the modern world provides greater nuance and complexity in explaining the big issues of modern history such as the drivers of globalization and the Great Divergence. Institutions, human capital, factor endowments, and value systems all help to explain why the Rest struggled to catch up with the West as modern economic growth spread, but these explanations become more compelling when their relationship to levels of entrepreneurship, and especially whether it was productive or redistributive, are examined. It was a two-way relationship. Entrepreneurs and firms had agency. There were different entrepreneurial outcomes in the face of the same national institutions. Firms were shapers and responders, which both changed the world and responded to changes in the world. They were hugely heterogeneous, and this heterogeneity matters when considering outcomes. Parsees and Marwaris responded with considerable entrepreneurial vigor to the institutions put in place in British India, but most of Indian society did not.

The historical evidence presented here confirms Chandler and Mazlish's intuition that MNEs have had "an impact on almost every sphere of modern life." During the first global economy these firms lit up the cities of the world with electricity, turned India into the world's largest tea producer, transferred Western beauty ideals around the world, and much more. Singer's sewing machines had huge societal impact, including on opportunities for women, as the firm globalized. The Imperial Bank took modern banking to Iran. Western MNEs were huge employers of labor in Asia. During the middle of the twentieth century, even if globalization was constrained, US firms transferred advanced technologies and branding skills to European countries like Britain. After World War II, Unilever created the market for margarine in Turkey and Volkswagen created Latin America's largest automobile manufacturing industry in Brazil.

It is less evident, though, that MNEs were Leviathans. Their ability to transfer technology was constrained by the institutional, educational and cultural conditions of host economies. Beauty companies could transfer brands across borders, but they could not fully dictate consumer preferences about skin, color, and smell. The examples of Karsanbhai Patel's Nirma, and Ren Zhengfei's Huawei Technologies showed that, at least from the last decades of the twentieth century, Western MNEs held no divine right of incumbency. After the demise of the first global economy, governments were persistent constraints on the autonomy of firms. The Imperial Bank was driven out of Iran by a disgruntled former manager who became head of the country's central bank. Beiersdorf had its assets and trademarks outside Germany sequestrated in the two world wars, and its Jewish managers had to flee their own country after the advent of the Nazi regime. Unilever might have been a model MNE employer and diffuser of new products to Turkey and India, but it was almost regulated out of existence in both countries during the 1970s.

There remains the issue of the overall impact of business on the social good. The heterogeneity of business enterprise renders this question challenging to answer, and perhaps misleading even to ask. In the broadest sense, the growth of global capitalism has been associated with enormous increases in the wealth, as well as dramatic rises in the longevity, of humanity. It was equally associated, however, with the persistence of the Great Divergence. For the most part, though, alternatives to global capitalism such as Communist and other types of state planning had serious downsides, including low levels of economic efficiency, the fueling of corruption, and often much worse. Capitalism too has had its dark side. Its amoral nature has been evident in the preceding pages, whether in opium trading in nineteenth-century China, Beiersdorf's competitors using its Jewishness to gain competitive advantage in

Nazi Germany, or Cisco Systems selling the equipment to enable the Chinese government to censor the web and identify political opponents. Yet the unique ability of capitalism to create wealth for society, as well as for individual capitalists, through innovation is the feature which most stands out from these chapters. This makes understanding the conditions which encouraged productive entrepreneurship in the past so important for understanding how the blight of global poverty can be alleviated in the future.

Select bibliography

Acemoglu, Daren and James A. Robinson (2012), *Why Nations Fail: The Origins of Power, Prosperity, and Poverty,* New York: Crown.

Amsden, Alice H. (1989), *Asia's Next Giant: South Korea and Late Industrialization*, Oxford: Oxford University Press.

Amsden, Alice H. (2003), *The Rise of "the Rest": Challenges to the West from Late-Industrializing Countries*, Oxford: Oxford University Press.

Bayley, Christopher A. (2004), *The Birth of the Modern World 1780–1914*, Oxford: Blackwell.

Bordo, Michael D., Alan M. Taylor and Jeffrey G. Williamson (eds) (2001), *Globalization in Historical Perspective*, Chicago, IL: University of Chicago Press.

Boyce, Gordon (2001), *Co-operative Structures in Global Business*, London: Routledge.

Brown, Rajeswary A. (1994), *Capital and Entrepreneurship in Southeast Asia*, London: Macmillan.

Brown, Rajeswary A. (2000), *Chinese Big Business and the Wealth of Asian Nations*, London: Palgrave.

Bucheli, Marcelo (2004), *Bananas and Business: The United Fruit Company in Columbia, 1899–2000*, New York: New York University Press.

Casson, Mark (1982), *The Entrepreneur: An Economic Theory*, Oxford: Martin Robertson.

Casson, Mark (1987), *The Firm and the Market*, Oxford: Basil Blackwell.

Casson, Mark (1990), *Enterprise and Competiveness*, Oxford: Clarendon Press.

Casson, Mark (1991), *The Economics of Business Culture*, Oxford: Clarendon Press.

Casson, Mark (2000), *Enterprise and Leadership: Studies on Firms, Markets and Networks*, Cheltenham, UK and Northampton, MA, USA: Edward Elgar.

Chandler, Alfred D. Jr. (1962), *Strategy and Structure*, Cambridge, MA: MIT Press.

Chandler, Alfred D. Jr. (1977), *The Visible Hand*, Cambridge, MA: Harvard University Press.

Chandler, Alfred D. Jr. (1990), *Scale and Scope*, Cambridge, MA: Harvard University Press.

Chandler, Alfred D. Jr. (2001), *Inventing the Electronic Century,* New York: The Free Press.

Chandler, Alfred D. Jr. (2005), *Shaping the Industrial Century: The Remarkable Story of the Modern Chemical and Pharmaceutical Industries,* Cambridge, MA: Harvard University Press.

Chandler, Alfred D. Jr., Franco Amatori and Takashi Hikino (eds) (1997), *Big Business and the Wealth of Nations,* Cambridge: Cambridge University Press.

Chandler, Alfred D. Jr. and Bruce Mazlish (eds) (2005), *Leviathans: Multinational Corporations and the New Global History,* Cambridge: Cambridge University Press.

Clarence-Smith, William G. and Steven Topik (eds) (2003), *The Global Coffee Economy in Africa, Asia, and Latin America, 1500-1989,* Cambridge: Cambridge University Press.

Cochran, Sherman (1980), *Big Business in China,* Cambridge, MA: Harvard University Press.

Cochran, Sherman (2000), *Encountering Chinese Networks,* Berkeley, CA: University of California Press.

De Grazia, Victoria (2005), *Irresistible Empire,* Cambridge, MA: Harvard University Press.

Dunning, John H. and Sarianna M. Lundan (2008), *Multinational Enterprises and the Global Economy,* Cheltenham, UK and Northampton, MA, USA: Edward Elgar.

Eichengreen, Barry J. (2008), *Globalizing Capital: A History of the International Monetary System,* 2nd edn, Princeton, NJ: Princeton University Press.

Engerman, Stanley L. and Kenneth L. Sokoloff (2012), *Economic Development in the Americas since 1500,* New York: Cambridge University Press.

Frieden, Jeffry A. (2006), *Global Capitalism: Its Fall and Rise in the Twentieth Century,* New York: W.W. Norton.

Ghemawat, Pankaj (2007), *Redefining Global Strategy: Crossing Borders in a World Where Differences Still Matter,* Boston, MA: Harvard Business School Press.

Hausman, William J., Peter Hertner and Mira Wilkins (eds) (2008), *Global Electrification: MNE Enterprise and International Finance in the History of Light and Power 1878-2007,* Cambridge: Cambridge University Press.

Hertner, Peter and Geoffrey Jones (eds) (1986), *Multinationals: Theory and History,* Aldershot: Gower.

James, Harold (2001), *The End of Globalization; Lessons from the Great Depression,* Cambridge, MA: Harvard University Press.

Jones, Geoffrey (1986), *Banking and Empire in Iran,* Cambridge: Cambridge University Press.

Jones, Geoffrey (1993), *British Multinational Banking 1830-1990*, Oxford: Clarendon Press.

Jones, Geoffrey (2000), *Merchants to Multinationals*, Oxford: Oxford University Press.

Jones, Geoffrey (2005), *Multinationals and Global Capitalism,* Oxford: Oxford University Press.

Jones, Geoffrey (2005), *Renewing Unilever*, Oxford: Oxford University Press.

Jones, Geoffrey (2010), *Beauty Imagined: A History of the Global Beauty Industry*, Oxford: Oxford University Press.

Jones, Geoffrey and Jonathan Zeitlin (eds) (2008), *The Oxford Handbook of Business History*, Oxford: Oxford University Press.

Kobrak, Christopher and Per H. Hansen (eds) (2004), *European Business, Dictatorship, and Political Risk, 1920–1945*, New York: Berghahn Books.

Landes, David S., Joel Mokyr and William J. Baumol (eds) (2010), *The Invention of Enterprise*, Princeton, NJ: Princeton University Press.

Lipson, Charles (1985), *Standing Guard: Protecting Foreign Capital in the Nineteenth and Twentieth Centuries*, Berkeley, CA: University of California Press.

Magee, Gary B and Andrew S. Thompson (2010), *Empire and Globalization*, Cambridge: Cambridge University Press.

Mathews, John A. (2002), *Dragon Multinational: A New Model for Global Growth*, Oxford: Oxford University Press.

McCabe, Ina Baghdiantz, Gelina Harlaftis and Ioanna Pepelais Minoglou (eds) (2005), *Diaspora Entrepreneurial Networks*, Oxford: Berg.

Miller, Michael B. (2012), *Europe and the Maritime World*, Cambridge: Cambridge University Press.

North, Douglass C. (1990), *Institutions, Institutional Change and Economic Performance*, Cambridge: Cambridge University Press.

North, Douglass C. (2005), *Understanding the Process of Economic Change*, Princeton, NJ: Princeton University Press.

O'Rourke, Kevin H. and Jeffrey G. Williamson (1996), *Globalization and History: The Evolution of a Nineteenth Century Atlantic Economy*, Cambridge, MA: MIT Press.

Spar, Debora L. (1994), *The Co-operative Edge: The Internal Politics of International Cartels*, Ithaca, NY: Cornell University Press.

Teichova, Alice, Maurice Lévy-Leboyer and Helga Nussbaum (eds) (1986), *Multinational Enterprises in Historical Perspective,* Cambridge: Cambridge University Press.

Tignor, Robert L. (1998), *Capitalism and Nationalism at the End of Empire*, Princeton, NJ: Princeton University Press.

Vernon, Raymond (1971), *Sovereignty at Bay: The Multinational Spread of US Enterprises*, New York: Basic Books.

White, Nicholas (2004), *British Business in Post-Colonial Malaysia, 1957–70: 'Neo-Colonialism' or 'Disengagement'?*, London: Routledge.

Wilkins, Mira (1970), *The Emergence of Multinational Enterprise*, Cambridge, MA: Harvard University Press.

Wilkins, Mira (1974), *The Maturing of Multinational Enterprise*, Cambridge, MA: Harvard University Press.

Wilkins, Mira (1989), *The History of Foreign Investment in the United States before 1914*, Cambridge, MA: Harvard University Press.

Wilkins, Mira (2004), *The History of Foreign Investment in the United States 1914–1945*, Cambridge, MA: Harvard University Press.

Wilkins, Mira and Harm G. Schröter (eds) (1998), *The Free Standing Company in the World Economy, 1836–1996*, Oxford: Oxford University Press.

Index

Printed and bound by CPI Group (UK) Ltd, Croydon, CR0 4YY

23/04/2025

14660960-0002